Computer Networking: Principles and Practice

Computer Networking: Principles and Practice

Paxton Byrne

www.willfordpress.com

Published by Willford Press,
118-35 Queens Blvd., Suite 400,
Forest Hills, NY 11375, USA

ISBN: 978-1-64728-021-5

Cataloging-in-Publication Data

Computer networking : principles and practice / Paxton Byrne.
    p. cm.
Includes bibliographical references and index.
ISBN 978-1-64728-021-5
1. Computer networks. 2. Cyberinfrastructure. 3. Network computers.
4. Electronic data processing--Distributed processing. I. Byrne, Paxton.
TK5105.5 .C66 2022
004.6--dc23

For information on all Willford Press publications
visit our website at www.willfordpress.com

Contents

Permissions

Index

Preface

A computer network is a digital telecommunications network. It allows computing devices in sharing data with each other using data links between nodes. Network nodes are the network computer devices which originate, route and terminate data. Hosts such as phones, servers and personal computers, along with networking hardware like switches and routers can act as nodes. Computer networks can be formed by linking devices using a variety of transmission media such as radio waves, optical fiber and electrical cable. Networks are characterized by their organizational purpose as well as their physical capacity. A few examples of different types of networks are nanoscale network, local area network and wide area network. The topics included in this textbook on computer networking are of utmost significance and bound to provide incredible insights to readers. It covers in detail some existent theories and innovative concepts related to this field. Those in search of information to further their knowledge will be greatly assisted by this book.

A short introduction to every chapter is written below to provide an overview of the content of the book:

Chapter 1 - The practice of exchanging and transporting data among nodes over a shared medium within an information system is known as computer networking. The set of computers which are connected to each other in order to share resources is known as a computer network. This is an introductory chapter which will introduce briefly all the significant aspects of computer networks and computer networking.; **Chapter 2** - The formal standards which contain procedures, rules and formats that govern the communication between different devices are known as network protocols. Some of the different standards are X.500 and IEEE 802.4 standard. The topics elaborated in this chapter will help in gaining a better perspective about these protocols, models and standards of networking.; **Chapter 3** - The topological structure of a network is known as network topology. It can be depicted either physically or logically. Some of the different types of network topologies are bus network topology, ring network topology and tree network topology. The topics elaborated in this chapter will help in gaining a better perspective about these branches of network topology. **Chapter 4** - Computer networking devices, also called nodes, are devices which originate, route and terminate the data. A few common devices which function as nodes are hubs, bridges and routers. The chapter closely examines these key types of computer networking devices to provide an extensive understanding of the subject.; **Chapter 5** - The measures which are taken by businesses and organizations for the monitoring and prevention of unauthorized access to data are collectively known as computer network security. Some of the other aspects which fall within this field are cloud computing and security network segmentation. This chapter discusses in detail these theories and methodologies related to computer network security.

I extend my sincere thanks to the publisher for considering me worthy of this task. Finally, I thank my family for being a source of support and help.

Paxton Byrne

Understanding Computer Networking

The practice of exchanging and transporting data among nodes over a shared medium within an information system is known as computer networking. The set of computers which are connected to each other in order to share resources is known as a computer network. This is an introductory chapter which will introduce briefly all the significant aspects of computer networks and computer networking.

Networking, also known as computer networking, is the practice of transporting and exchanging data between nodes over a shared medium in an information system. Networking comprises not only the design, construction and use of a network, but also the management, maintenance and operation of the network infrastructure, software and policies.

Networking is referred as connecting computers electronically for the purpose of sharing information. Resources such as files, applications, printers and software are common information shared in a networking. The advantage of networking can be seen clearly in terms of security, efficiency, manageability and cost effectiveness as it allows collaboration between users in a wide range. Basically, network consists of hardware component such as computer, hubs, switches, routers and other devices which form the network infrastructure. These are the devices that play an important role in data transfer from one place to another using different technology such as radio waves and wires.

Computer networking enables devices and endpoints to be connected to each other on a local area network (LAN) or to a larger network, such as the internet or a private wide area network (WAN). This is an essential function for service providers, businesses and consumers worldwide to share resources, use or offer services, and communicate. Networking facilitates everything from telephone calls to text messaging to streaming video to the internet of things (IoT).

The level of skill required to operate a network directly correlates to the complexity of a given network. For example, a large enterprise may have thousands of nodes and rigorous security requirements, such as end-to-end encryption, requiring specialized network administrators to oversee the network.

At the other end of the spectrum, a layperson may set up and perform basic troubleshooting for a home Wi-Fi network with a short instruction manual. Both examples constitute computer networking.

Types of Networking

There are two primary types of computer networking: wired networking and wireless networking.

1. Wired networking requires the use of a physical medium for transport between nodes. Copper-based Ethernet cabling, popular due to its low cost and durability, is commonly used for digital communications in businesses and homes. Alternatively, optical fiber is used to transport data over greater distances and at faster speeds, but it has several tradeoffs, including higher costs and more fragile components.

2. Wireless networking uses radio waves to transport data over the air, enabling devices to be connected to a network without any cabling. Wireless LANs are the most well-known and widely deployed form of wireless networking. Alternatives include microwave, satellite, cellular and Bluetooth, among others.

As a general rule, wired networking offers greater speed, reliability and security compared to wireless networks; wireless networking tends to provide more flexibility, mobility and scalability.

It should be noted that these types of networking concern the physical layer of the network. Networking can also be classified according to how it's built and designed, encompassing approaches that include software-defined networking (SDN) or overlay networks. Networking can also be categorized by environment and scale, such as LAN, campus, WAN, data center networks or storage area networks.

Components of Networking

Computer networking requires the use of physical network infrastructure -- including switches, routers and wireless access points -- and the underlying firmware that operates such equipment. Other components include the software necessary to monitor, manage and secure the network.

Additionally, networks rely on the use of standard protocols to uniformly perform discrete functions or communicate different types of data, regardless of the underlying hardware.

For example, voice over IP (VoIP) can transport IP telephony traffic to any endpoint that supports the protocol. HTTP provides a common way for browsers to display webpages. The internet protocol suite, also known as TCP/IP, is a family of protocols responsible for transporting data and services over an IP-based network.

Basics of Computer Networking

1. Open system: A system which is connected to the network and is ready for communication.

2. Closed system: A system which is not connected to the network and can't be communicated with.

3. OSI: OSI stands for Open Systems Interconnection. It is a reference model that specifies standards for communications protocols and also the functionalities of each layer.

4. Protocol: A protocol is the set of rules or algorithms which define the way how two entities can communicate across the network and there exists different protocol defined at each layer of the OSI model. Few of such protocols are TCP, IP, UDP, ARP, DHCP, FTP and so on.

Computer Network

Computer networks are built with a combination of hardware and software.

Network Design

Computer networks also differ in their design approach. The two basic forms of network design are called client-server and peer-to-peer. Client-server networks feature centralized server computers that store email, web pages, files, and applications accessed by client computers and other client devices. On a peer-to-peer network, conversely, all devices tend to support the same functions. Client-server networks are common in business and peer-to-peer networks are common in homes.

A network topology defines the network layout or structure from the point of view of data flow. In bus networks, for example, all computers share and communicate across one common conduit, whereas in a star network, data flows through one centralized device. Common types of network topologies include bus, star, ring, and mesh.

Computer Network Hardware and Software

Special purpose communication devices including network routers, access points, and network cables physically glue a network together. Network operating systems and other software applications generate network traffic and enable users to do useful things.

Home Computer Networking

While other types of networks are built and maintained by engineers, home networks belong to homeowners who often have little or no technical background. Various manufacturers produce broadband router hardware designed to simplify home network setup. A home router enables devices in different rooms to efficiently share a broadband internet connection, helps household members share files and printers within the network, and improves overall network security.

Home networks have increased in capability with each generation of new technology.

Years ago, people commonly set up a home network to connect a few PCs, share documents, and perhaps share a printer. Now it's common for households to network game consoles, digital video recorders, and smartphones for streaming sound and video. Home automation systems have also existed for many years, but these have grown in popularity recently with practical systems that control lights, digital thermostats, and appliances.

Business Computer Networks

Small and home office (SOHO) environments use technology that is similar to home networks. Businesses often have additional communication, data storage, and security requirements that require expanding networks in different ways, particularly as the business gets larger.

Whereas a home network generally functions as one LAN, a business network tends to contain multiple LANs. Companies with buildings in multiple locations utilize wide-area networking to connect these branch offices together. Though also available and used by some households, voice over IP communication, network storage, and backup technologies are prevalent in businesses. Larger companies also maintain internal web sites, called intranets, to help with employee business communication.

Networking and the Internet

The popularity of computer networks sharply increased with the creation of the World Wide Web (WWW) in the 1990s. Public web sites, peer-to-peer (P2P) file sharing systems, and various other services run on internet servers across the world.

Wired vs. Wireless Computer Networking

Many of the same protocols such as TCP/IP work in both wired and wireless networks. Networks with Ethernet cables predominated in businesses, schools, and homes for several decades. Wi-Fi has emerged as the preferred option for building new computer networks, in part to support smartphones and the other wireless gadgets that have triggered the rise of mobile networking.

Network Device

Not every computer, handheld gadget, or other piece of equipment is capable of joining a network. A network device possesses special communications hardware to make the necessary physical connections to other devices. Most modern network devices have communication electronics integrated onto their circuit boards.

Some PCs, older Xbox game consoles, and other older devices do not have built-in communications hardware but can be set up as network devices by plugging in separate network adapters in the form of USB peripherals. Very old desktop PCs required physically inserting separate large add-in cards into the system motherboard, originating the term Network Interface Card (NIC).

Newer generations of consumer appliances and gadgets are being built as network devices when older generations were not. For example, traditional home thermostats did not contain any communications hardware, nor could they be joined to a home network via peripherals.

Finally, some kinds of equipment do not support networking at all. Consumer devices that neither have built-in network hardware nor accept peripherals include older Apple iPods, many televisions, and toaster ovens.

Device Roles on Computer Networks

Devices on computer networks function in different roles. The two most common roles are clients and servers. Examples of network clients include PCs, phones and tablets, and network printers. Clients generally make a request and consume data stored in network servers, devices generally designed with large amounts of memory and/or disk storage and high-performance processors to better support clients. Examples of network servers include web servers and game servers. Networks naturally tend to support many more clients than servers. Both clients and servers are sometimes called network nodes.

Network devices may also be capable of functioning as both clients and servers. In a peer to peer networking, for example, pairs of devices share files or other data with each other, one acting as a server hosting some data while simultaneously working as a client to request different data from other peer devices.

Special Purpose Network Devices

Client and server nodes can be added or removed from a network without blocking the communication of other devices that still remain. Certain other types of network hardware, however, exist for the sole purpose of enabling a network to run:

- A network hub enables any node connected to it to directly send data to others.

- Network switches perform the same function as hubs but include additional hardware logic that opens up multiple communication paths allowing multiple connected nodes to send data directly to each other instead of to all others on the network as with hubs.

- Network routers further expand the capabilities of network switches by supporting connections outward from it-self to other networks, joining them together without disrupting the functionality of each one individually.

- A network repeater receives the physical signals sent across a network connection and amplifies their strength (such as electrical or radio power) to enable the signal to travel longer distances.

- A less common type of device nowadays, the network bridge device connects two different kinds of physical network links together that otherwise would be incompatible, such as bridges that enable wireless devices to join a wired network. (Modern bridge technology is often physically integrated into other types of devices.)

Unique Identifiers of Network

Host Name

Each device in the network is associated with a unique device name known as Hostname.

Type "hostname" in the command prompt and press 'Enter', this displays the hostname of your machine.

IP Address (Internet Protocol address)

Also, known as the Logical Address, is the network address of the system across the network.

- To identify each device in the world-wide-web, Internet Assigned Numbers Authority (IANA) assigns IPV4 (Version 4) address as a unique identifier for each device on the Internet.

- Length of the IP address is 32-bits. (Hence we have 232 IP addresses available.)

- Type "ipconfig" in the command prompt and press 'Enter', this gives us the IP address of the device.

MAC Address (Media Access Control address)

Also known as physical address is the unique identifier of each host and is associated with the NIC (Network Interface Card).

- MAC address is assigned to the NIC at the time of manufacturing.

- Length of the MAC address is: 12-nibble/ 6 bytes/ 48 bits.

Type "ipconfig/all" in the command prompt and press 'Enter', this gives us the MAC address.

Port

Port can be referred as a logical channel through which data can be sent/received to an application. Any host may have multiple applications running, and each of this application is identified using the port number on which they are running.

Port number is a 16-bit integer hence we have 2^{16} ports available which are categorized as shown below:

PORT TYPES	RANGE
Well known Ports	0 – 1023
Registered Ports	1024 – 49151
Ephemeral Ports	49152 – 65535

Number of ports: 65,536

Range: 0 – 65535.

Type "netstat -a" in the command prompt and press 'Enter', this lists all the ports being used.

Socket

The unique combination of IP address and Port number together are termed as Socket.

Few more concepts:

DNS Server

- DNS stands for Domain Name system.

- DNS is basically a server which translates web addresses or URL into their corresponding IP addresses. We don't have to remember all the IP addresses of each and every website.

The command 'nslookup' gives you the IP address of the domain you are looking for. This also provides the information of our DNS Server.

ARP

ARP stands for Address Resolution Protocol.

- It is used to convert the IP address to its corresponding Physical Address (i.e. MAC Address).

- ARP is used by the Data Link Layer to identify the MAC address of the Receiver's machine.

RARP

RARP stands for Reverse Address Resolution Protocol.

- As the name suggests, it provides the IP address of the device given a physical address as input. But RARP has become obsolete since the time DHCP has come into the picture.

References

- Introduction-to-networking: researchgate.net, Retrieved 2 March, 2019

- Networking: searchnetworking.techtarget.com, Retrieved 1 May, 2019

- Basics-computer-networking: geeksforgeeks.org, Retrieved 11 January, 2019

- What-is-computer-networking: lifewire.com, Retrieved 12 August, 2019

- How-computer-networks-work: lifewire.com, Retrieved 22 February, 2019

- Basics-computer-networking: geeksforgeeks.org, Retrieved 25 June, 2019

2

Networking: Standards, Protocol and (OSI) Model

The formal standards which contain procedures, rules and formats that govern the communication between different devices are known as network protocols. Some of the different standards are X.500 and IEEE 802.4 standard. The topics elaborated in this chapter will help in gaining a better perspective about these protocols, models and standards of networking.

Networking Standards

Networking standards ensure the interoperability of networking technologies by defining the rules of communication among networked devices. Networking standards exist to help ensure products of different vendors are able to work together in a network without risk of incompatibility.

Types of Standards

X.500

X.500 is a series of computer networking standards used to develop the equivalent of an electronic directory that is very similar to the concept of a physical telephone directory. Its purpose is to centralize an organization's contacts so that anyone within (and sometimes without) the organization who has Internet access can look up other people in the same organization by name or department. Several large institutions and multinational corporations have implemented X.500.

An X.500 directory is organized under a common root directory out of which other branches grow according to the individual organization's structure.

For example, a large multinational company called GlobalCorp that is headquartered in the U.S. with branches in Asia, Europe and South America would have an X.500 directory with the following attributes:

1. The root would be named Globalcorp, and the first-level branches would be the various continents (North America, Asia, South America and Europe).

2. Flowing from each of these branches would be the second-level sub-branches. Therefore, under the North American branch, there would be branches labeled New York, Los Angeles, Chicago, and so on.

3. Under these second-level branches are listed the departments, then the employees in each department. So for Chicago, there may be Accounts, Human Resources, IT and so on.

4. The employees will then be listed depending on which department they work in. For each employee, there may be several attributes, such as email address, phone number, photo and employee grade. Other attributes may be at the departmental level, such as street address, building name and floor number.

Therefore, Ming-Dae Kim who works in the South Korean office will have a directory structure as follows: GlobalCorp => Asia => S.Korea => Seoul => Accounts => Ming-Dae Kim (mingdaekim@globalcorp.co.kw">mingdaekim@globalcorp.co.kw; +850 233 0980435; Senior Accountant).

Branches can be added to any level by the directory administrator. Each organization can have its own X.500 directory structure as long as all branches adhere to some pre-defined basic schema or layout. For example, all employees must belong to a department and must have at least an email address and phone number.

IEEE Standards

The IEEE is best known for developing standards for the computer and electronics industry.

The Institute of Electrical and Electronic Engineers (IEEE) is a global association and organization of professionals working toward the development, implementation and maintenance of technology-centered products and services.

IEEE is a nonprofit organization founded in 1963. It works solely toward innovating, educating and standardizing the electrical and electronic development industry. It is best known for its development of standards such as IEEE 802.11. EEE is pronounced as "Eye- Triple E".

IEEE in computing is widely popular for the development of standards for computer networking and its suite of services. IEEE develops many different standards, such as IEEE 802 and IEEE 802.11 (commonly known as Wi-Fi), and provides ongoing innovation, amendments and maintenance services for these standards. IEEE also maintains thousands of student and professional chapters globally, has numerous focus societies and sponsors regular conferences and seminars. While the organization is US-based, its standards often become internationally accepted.

The Standardization Process

Each year, the IEEE-SA conducts over 200 standards ballots, a process by which proposed standards are voted upon for technical reliability and soundness. In 2017, IEEE had over 1100 active standards, with over 600 standards under development. One of the more notable are the IEEE 802 LAN/MAN group of standards, with the widely used computer networking standards for both wired (ethernet, aka IEEE 802.3) and wireless (IEEE 802.11 and IEEE 802.16) networks.

The IEEE standards development process can be broken down into seven basic steps:

1. Securing Sponsorship: An IEEE-approved organization must sponsor a standard. A sponsoring organization is in charge of coordinating and supervising the standard development from inception to completion. The professional societies within IEEE serve as the natural sponsor for many standards.

2. Requesting Project Authorization: To gain authorization for the standard a Project Authorization Request (PAR) is submitted to the IEEE-SA Standards Board. The New Standards Committee (NesCom) of the IEEE-SA Standards Board reviews the PAR and makes a recommendation to the Standards Board about whether to approve the PAR.

3. Assembling a Working Group: After the PAR is approved, a working group of individuals affected by, or interested in, the standard is organized to develop the standard. IEEE-SA rules ensure that all Working Group meetings are open and that anyone has the right to attend and contribute to the meetings.

4. Drafting the Standard: The Working Group prepares a draft of the proposed standard. Generally, the draft follows the IEEE Standards Style Manual that sets guidelines for the clauses and format of the standards document.

5. Balloting: Once a draft of the standard is finalized in the Working Group, the draft is submitted for Balloting approval. The IEEE Standards Department sends an invitation-to-ballot to any individual who has expressed an interest in the subject matter of the standard. Anyone who responds positively to the invitation-to-ballot becomes a member of the balloting group, as long as the individual is an IEEE Standards Association member or has paid a balloting fee. The IEEE requires that a proposed draft of the standard receive a response rate of 75% (i.e., at least 75% of potential ballots are returned) and that, of the responding ballots, at least 75% approve the proposed draft of the standard. If the standard is not approved, the process returns to the drafting of the standard step in order to modify the standard document to gain approval of the balloting group.

6. Review Committee: After getting 75% approval, the draft standard, along with the balloting comments, are submitted to the IEEE-SA Standards Board Review

Committee (RevCom). The RevCom reviews the proposed draft of the standard against the IEEE-SA Standards Board Bylaws and the stipulations set forth in the IEEE-SA Standards Board Operations Manual. The RevCom then makes a recommendation about whether to approve the submitted draft of the standard document.

7. Final Vote: Each member of the IEEE-SA Standards Board places a final vote on the submitted standard document. In some cases external members are invited to vote. It takes a majority vote of the Standards Board to gain final approval of the standard. In general, if the RevCom recommends approval, the Standards Board will vote to approve the standard.

The Patent Policy

Because the IEEE's standards often incorporate technologies that are covered by one or more patent claims, the IEEE-SA has developed and added to its governing bylaws a patent policy to ensure both that the implementers using the standard-essential patented technology in their standard-compliant products have access to that technology and that the patent holders that voluntarily contribute those technologies to the standard receive adequate compensation for the implementers' use. An important part of the IEEE patent policy is the FRAND commitment, which is a voluntary contractual commitment signifying that a patent holder with patented technology that has been adopted into one of the IEEE's standards will accept as adequate compensation a fair, reasonable, and non-discriminatory royalty for third-party use of that technology. Most standard-setting organizations have developed similar patent policies with similar commitments.

In 2014, the IEEE-SA became the center of a large academic debate among economic and legal scholars when it appointed an ad hoc committee to recommend and subsequently draft amendments to the IEEE patent policy, to which the IEEE Board of Governors gave final approval in February 2015 and which went into effect in March 2015. The IEEE said that the reason for the amendments was to increase the clarity of the patent policy and the obligations that the patent policy's FRAND commitment imposes on patent holders seeking to enforce their standard-essential patents. One particularly controversial amendment was a provision that prohibited patent holders from seeking injunctions and exclusion orders (from the ITC) against infringers of standard-essential patents.

The Antitrust Division stated its support for the 2015 patent policy revisions in a business review letter that it issued in January 2015, upon request from the IEEE-SA. In the letter, the Antitrust Division said that the provisions would unambiguously produce net benefits for consumers with insignificant anticompetitive implications. At least one commentator has criticized the Antitrust Division's legal and economic analysis put forth in its business review letter of the revisions, claiming that the Antitrust Division exaggerated the patent policy's procompetitive benefits and wrongly dismissed as unlikely some of its potential anticompetitive costs.

IEEE 802.4 Standard

In token bus Computer network station must have possession of a token before it can transmit on the computer network. The IEEE 802.4 Committee has defined token bus standards as broadband computer networks, as opposed to Ethernet's baseband transmission technique. Physically, the token bus is a linear or tree-shape cable to which the stations are attached.

The topology of the computer network can include groups of workstations connected by long trunk cables. Logically, the stations are organized into a ring. These workstations branch from hubs in a star configuration, so the network has both a bus and star topology. Token bus topology is well suited to groups of users that are separated by some distance. IEEE 802.4 token bus networks are constructed with 75-ohm coaxial cable using a bus topology. The broadband characteristics of the 802.4 standard support transmission over several different channels simultaneously.

When the logical ring is initialized, the highest numbered station may send the first frame. The token and frames of data are passed from one station to another following the numeric sequence of the station addresses. Thus, the token follows a logical ring rather than a physical ring. The last station in numeric order passes the token back to the first station. The token does not follow the physical ordering of workstation attachment to the cable. Station 1 might be at one end of the cable and station 2 might be at the other, with station 3 in the middle.

In such a case, there is no collision as only one station possesses a token at any given time. In token bus, each station receives each frame; the station whose address is specified in the frame processes it and the other stations discard the frame.

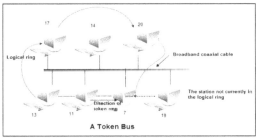

A Token Bus

Physical Layer of the Token Bus

The conventional 75 ohm coaxial cable used for the cable TV can be used as the physical layer of the token bus. The different modulation schemes are used. They are, phase continuous frequency shift keying, phase coherent frequency shift keying, and the multilevel duo binary amplitude-modulated phase shift keying. Signal speeds in the range 1 Mbps, 5 Mbps, and 10 Mbps are achievable. The physical layer of the token bus is totally incompatible to the IEEE 802.3 standard.

MAC Sublayer Function

- When the ring is initialized, stations are inserted into it in order of station address, from highest to lowest.

- Token passing is done from high to low address.

- Whenever a station acquires the token, it can transmit frames for a specific amount of time.

- If a station has no data, it passes the token immediately upon receiving it.

- The token bus defines four priority classes, 0, 2, 4, and 6 for traffic, with 0 the lowest and 6 the highest.

- Each station is internally divided into four substations, one at each priority level i.e. 0,2,4 and 6.

- As input comes in to the MAC sublayer from above, the data are checked for priority and routed to one of the four substations.

- Thus each station maintains its own queue of frames to be transmitted.

- When a token comes into the station over the cable, it is passed internally to the priority 6 substation, which can begin transmitting its frames, if it has any.

- When it is done or when its time expires, the token is passed to the priority 4 substation, which can then transmit frames until its timer expires. After this the token is then passed internally to priority 2 substation.

- This process continues until either the priority 0 substation has sent all its frames or its time expires.

- After this the token is passed to the next station in the ring.

Frame Format of Token Bus

The various fields present in the frame format are-

1 byte	1 byte	1 byte	2-6 byte	2-6 byte	0.8182	4 Byte	1 byte
Preamble	Start De-limiter	Frame Control	Destination Address	Source Address	Data	Checksum	End De-limiter

Frame format of IEEE 802.4:

- Preamble: This field is at least 1 byte long. It is used for bit synchronization.

- Start Delimiter: This one byte field marks the beginning of frame.

- Frame Control: This one byte field specifies the type of frame. It distinguishes data frame from control frames. For data frames it carries frame's priority. For control frames, it specifies the frame type. The control frame types include. token passing and various ring maintenance frames, including the mechanism for letting new station enter the ring, the mechanism for allowing stations to leave the ring.

- Destination address: It specifies 2 to 6 bytes destination address.

- Source address: It specifies 2 to 6 bytes source address.

- Data: This field may be upto 8182 bytes long when 2 bytes addresses are used & upto 8174 bytes long when 6 bytes address is used.

- Checksum: This 4 byte field detects transmission errors.

- End Delimiter: This one byte field marks the end of frame.

The various control frames used in token bus are:

Farme Control Field	Name	Meaning
00000000	Claim_token	Claim token during ring initialization.
00000001	Solicit successor_1	Allow station to enter the ring.
00000010	Solicit successor_1	Allow station to enter the ring.
00000011	Who_follows	Recover from lost token.
00000100	Resolve_contention	Used when multiple stations want to enter.
00001000	Token	Pass the taken.
00001100	Set successor	Allow station to leave the ring.

Maintaining the Ring

Control frames Control frames are frames used for controlling and maintaining the logical ring. The format is same as the format specified in Figure, except the presence of an info field. There are different bit patterns used in the frame control field to define different types of control frames.

Adding a new station to add a new station to the logical ring, the station which currently holds the token broadcasts periodically sends a special control frame called a Solicit-successor frame. This frame contains the address of the sending station and its successor. This intimates the stations within the specified range to join the ring. Hence, the ring remains sorted.

Leaving the logical ring A station can simply leave the ring by sending its successor address to its predecessor and asks it to set this as its successor. To perform this, it passes a special control frame called set successor. The frame contains the address of predecessor as destination address and the address of the successor as sending address.

Ring initialization when the network is powered on, initially, all the stations are off. As soon as the first station is initiated, it checks the channel for the presence of any contenders, by sending a special control frame called claim-token. If there is no response, it generates a new token; thereby, creating a new logical ring with a single station. Periodically it transmits solicit successor tokens, hence, new stations are added frequently, making 'the logical ring grow.

Failure of a successor station when a station finishes the transmission, it passes the token to the next station (successor). If the successor station fails to claim the token, then other stations in the network may not be able to claim the token. Allowing stations to watch their successor's activity after passing the token to them, can rectify this problem. If nothing takes place, until a predetermined time, it retransmits the token. If again there is no response, the successor station is disconnected from the logical ring and a new control frame set-successor is sent to the successor of the failed station.

Failure of multiple successors If a station is not able to pass the token to its successor, or if the successor of its successor also failed, then it sends a special control frame called solicit successor-2, to check the availability of other stations on the network. The network is then relatively established, by running the contention algorithm for the second time.

Failure of token holder if the token holder fails, none of the other stations can get the token. Each station in the ring has a timer internally. They wait until the timer expires and transmits a claim-token frame, and the network is reestablished.

Multiple tokens if the token holder detects the transmission of frames from some other station, it discards its token. If multiple tokens are present in the network, the above process is repeated until only one token is present in the network. If all the tokens in the network are discarded, then one or more stations transmit claim-token frame, and restart the network activity.

The Token-passing Bus Protocol Functions

The following functions provided by the token bus protocol:

- Ring initialization performed when the network is first powered up and after a catastrophic error.

- Station addition optionally performed when a station, holding the token accepts the insertion of a new successor station, (that is, a new station with an address) that is between that of the station holding the token and its current successor station.

- Station removal is achieved by sending new successor identification to its predecessor, or by just disconnecting from the LAN. In the latter case, recovery mechanisms establish the proper new logical ring configuration.

- Recovery and Management, including recovery from failures such as bus idle (lack of activity on the bus) token-passing failure (lack of valid frame transmission), the presence of duplicate token, and detection of a station with a faulty receiver.

When the network is first powered up, or after a catastrophic error, the logical ring needs to be initialized. The idle bus timer, expiring in a LAN station, triggers this process. The detecting station sends a Claim Token MAC control frame.

Each participating station knows the address of its predecessor (the station that transmitted the token to it and its successor) and station to which the token should send next. After a station has completed transmitting data frames and has completed other logical ring maintenance functions, the station passes the token to its successor by sending it a token MAC control frame. Any failure in reaching a successor station triggers a staged recovery mechanism, using other MAC control frames (set solicitor 1and set solicitor 2). If the token holder does not receive a valid token after sending the token the first time, it repeats the token pass operation. If the successor does not transmit after a second token frame, the sender assumes that its successor has failed and sends a Who Follows the MAC control frame, containing its successor's address in the data field. The station, detecting a match between its predecessor and the address in the Who Follows frame data field, respond by sending its address in a Set Successor MAC control frame. In this way, the token holding station establishes a new successor, excluding the failing station from the logical ring. Stations are added to the logical ring through a controlled contention process, using response windows, a specific interval of the time typical to all stations, and based on numerical address comparisons. The actual procedure referred to as the Solicit Successor Procedure.

This procedure raises a concern concerning excessive delay experienced by a station before gaining access to the LAN when many stations attempt to insert into the logical ring and perform the solicit successor procedure. The time a station has to wait between successive passes of the token is called the token rotation time (TRT).To avoid excessive TRT, every station measures the rotation time of the token. If the time exceeds a predefined value set by the station management, the station defers initiation of the solicit successor procedure and verify, at the next appearance of the token, whether it is now rotating fast enough to perform the procedure.

A station can remove itself from the logical ring only by not responding anymore to the token passed to it. Ring station sequence recovery procedures adjust the successor and predecessor information in the predecessor and successor stations, respectively. A more efficient way of leaving the logical ring is to have the exiting station send a Set Successor MAC control frame to its predecessor, containing the address of its successor.

Access priority the token-passing bus protocol provides an optional8-level priority mechanism by which higher layer data frames, LLC sublayer or higher-level protocols, are assigned to eight different service classes, according to their desired transmission priority. Service classes range from 0 (low) to 7 (high). The purpose of this priority mechanism is to allocate bandwidth to the higher priority frames and to send lower priority frames only when there is sufficient bandwidth left. Similarly, each access class is assigned a target token rotation time (TTRT).

Each station measures the time it takes the token to circulate the logical ring. If the token returns to a station in less than the target token rotation time, the station can transmit more frames until the expiration of the TTRT. If the token takes more than the TTRT for a specific priority level, no frames of this priority class can send at this pass of the token.

IEEE 802.5 Standard

The IEEE 802.5 standard specifies the characteristics for Token Ring networks. Token Ring was introduced by IBM in the mid-1980s and quickly became the network topology of choice until the rise in popularity of Ethernet. It is unlikely that you will encounter a ring network in your travels and even more unlikely that you will be implementing a ring network as a new installation. For what it's worth, Token Ring is a solid network system, but Ethernet has all but eliminated it.

The following is a list of the specific characteristics specified in the 802.5 standard:

- Speed The 802.5 Token Ring specifies network speeds of 4 and 16Mbps.

- Topology Token Ring networks use a logical ring topology and most often a physical star. The logical ring is often created in the multi-station access unit (MSAU).

- Media Token Ring networks use unshielded twisted pair cabling or shielded twisted pair.

- Access method 802.5 specifies an access method known as token passing. On a Token Ring network, only one computer at a time can transmit data. When a computer has data to send, it must use a special type of packet known as a token. The token travels around the network looking for computers with data to send. The computer's data is passed along with the token until it gets to the destination computer at which point, the data is removed from the token and the empty token placed back on the ring.

Token Ring

Token Ring is a LAN protocol defined in the IEEE 802.5 where all stations are connected in a ring and each station can directly hear transmissions only from its immediate neighbor. Permission to transmit is granted by a message (token) that circulates around the ring. A token is a special bit pattern (3 bytes long). There is only one token in the network.

Token-passing networks move a small frame, called a token, around the network. Possession of the token grants the right to transmit. If a node receiving the token in order to transmit data, it seizes the token, alters 1 bit of the token (which turns the token into a start-of-frame sequence), appends the information that it wants to transmit, and sends this information to the next station on the ring. Since only one station can possess the token and transmit data at any given time, there are no collisions.

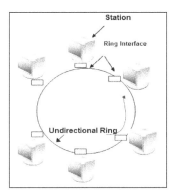

A Ring Network

There are two operating modes of ring interfaces. There are listen and transmit. In listen mode, the input bits are simply copied to output with a delay of 1- bit time. In transmit mode the connection between input and output is broken by the interface so that is can insert its own data. The station comes in transmit mode when it captures the token.

The frames are acknowledged by the destination in a very simple manner. The sender sends frames to receiver with ACK bit 0. The receiver on receiving frames, copies data into its buffer, verifies the checksum and set the ACK bit to 1. The verified frames come back to sender, where they are removed from the ring.

The information frame circulates the ring until it reaches the intended destination station, which copies the information for further processing. The information frame continues to circle the ring and is finally removed when it reaches the sending station. The sending station can check the returning frame to see whether the frame was seen and subsequently copied by the destination.

A station can hold a token for a specific duration of time. During this time, it has to complete its transmission and regenerates the token in ring. Whenever a station finishes its transmissions, the other station grabs the token and starts its own transmission.

Handling Cable Breakage in Ring Networks

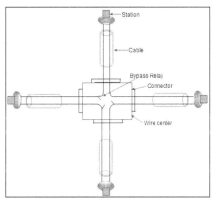

Four stations connected via a wire centres

- If the cable breaks, the entire ring network goes down. This can completely stop the propagation of token in the ring.

- This problem can be solved by using wire centre as shown in figure.

- This wire centre bypasses the terminal that has gone down in following manner:

  o Each station is connected to wire center by a cable containing two twisted pairs, one for data to station and one for data from the station.

  o Inside the wire center are bypass relays that are energized by the current from the stations.

  o If the ring breaks or a station goes down loss of drive current will release the relay and bypass the station.

Physical Layer of Token Ring

The cable recommended for a token ring by IEEE 802.5 contains two pairs of twisted-cables covered by a shield. Signal speed of this media is 1 Mbps or 4 Mbps. But IBM released a Token ring version that can operate at a speed of 16Mbps. The adapter for this also supports 4 Mbps. Differential 'Manchester' encoding scheme is used for encoding the digital data. Any single point failure on the cable may cause the ring to disappear instantly. Special devices called wire centers are used to bypass the bad segment of the cable or the problematic stations.

MAC Sublayer Protocol

The MAC sub layer is on the top of the physical layer. The protocol is defined as follows-

"When there is no traffic on the ring, a 3-byte token circulates continuously until some station grabs it. The station, which acquires the token, changes a specific 0 bit into a 1 bit, thus converts a token frame into a start of frame sequence. The station then transmits the normal data frame sequence. The length of the frame may be long or short. When it is long, the first bit of the transmitted frame completes the round trip through the ring and comes back to the sender before the completion of the current frame. The sender has to remove the bits that have completed their round trip. The maximum time a station is permitted to hold the token is known as token holding time. A station can send any number of frames within the time. As soon as the time is over, it should regenerate the token and put it on the ring".

IEEE 802.5 Token Ring Frame Format

Start of frame and end of frame: Used to mark the beginning and end of the frame. The patterns used do not contain the differential Manchester coded patterns. Hence, these patterns can be distinguished from the useful data field.

1. Access control- The access control field is used to represent the three-byte token along with the start of frame and end of frame. When the station starts transmitting, this field is used to perform monitoring, reservation, priority.

2. Frame control- This field is used to discriminate the data field from the other fields.

3. Source address and destination address- These fields are same as IEEE802.3 and IEEE 802.4 protocol.

4. Check sum- This field is also same as the check sum field of earlier protocols.

Token Ring Maintenance

The following are a few ring management activities:

1. Monitor stations- Each ring has a monitor station that performs monitoring the ring. It also takes appropriate action when the ring is broken. It also clears the ring when there are garbled frames on the ring. If the monitor station fails, some other station is chosen by means of a special contention protocol.

Ring Initialization When the network is powered up, initially there is no monitor. The first station on the network transmits a claim-token frame. If there is nothing else, a claim-token frame is setup the first station becomes the token owner as well as the monitor.

2. Lost tokens- The monitor station has an internal timer that is set for the longest possible time interval without a token. If the token is not produced within the period, the monitor station clears the ring and issues a new token.

3. Orphan frames- Stations crashed after transmitting a short frame form orphan frames. The transmitted frame simply circulates around the ring. The monitor station sets the monitor bit in the access control byte whenever a frame passes through it. If a frame already contains this bit set that means the frame is passing through the monitor for the second time. The monitor immediately removes it from the ring.

Token Ring Protocol

Token ring LAN is an ideal network in a typical office environment — all the stations connected in the form of a ring. A station has to acquire a token before the start of transmission. The frame transmitted by a station makes a full circulation and comes back to the originating station. All intermediate stations receive and retransmit the frame.

MAC protocol- All stations connected in the form of a ring. Only one station seizes the token, and all the other stations must wait for the token. Every transmitted frame revolves around the ring and finally absorbed by the transmitting station. If the frame is shorter, the first bit of the frame completes its round trip transit and comes back to the sender after the release of the last bit. In this case, the transmitting station inserts a new token into the ring after the completion of the current frame transmission. However, for frames with the longer length, the station completes the transmission after the leading edge is received. In case, the station releases the token immediately after the release of the last bit, then the method of release is known as an early release. When a station releases a token, the immediate next station waiting with the data seizes the token and starts the transmission. Token ring scheme is inefficient if there are very few stations ready with data. When all stations are busy, fairly proper utilization of the ring is possible. The main drawback of the token ring is ring maintenance. Loss of token and duplicate tokens are significant issues in token maintenance.

The IBM Token Ring Network

The IBM Token Ring Network is a Local Area Network, based on a token-passing access method. This Token passing method consists of a particular frame, called a token, which continuously circles the network medium, known as the ring. A station that needs to communicate with another station must obtain the token, change it from free to busy, append any relevant data, and transmit the information. The receiving station recognizes that the frame directed toward it by addressing information embedded in the data, and it copies the data into its internal buffers and then releases the frame back onto the ring. The station that initially sent the data, on receipts of the frame that is transmitted, examine any frame status information that was set by the second station, remove the data from the ring, and release a free token. The next station on the ring then have the opportunity to transmit data if necessary, or else it passes the free token onto the next station. This procedure continues indefinitely.

The token ring operation does not suffer from the well-known collision problem because only one station has access to the token at one point in time. It does not imply that only one station may have data on the ring at one time. The IBM Token Ring Network allows multiple frames to be present on the ring at the same time, but access to the free token is still mutually exclusive. In addition to that, IBM's network also ensures that data frames do not circle the ring indefinitely and that all stations on the network are uniquely addressable. The Token ring adapter uses a particular chipset to ensure the integrity and smooth operation of the token-ring network. Some of its functions described below-

- Ring monitor: The adapter acts as an active monitor to perform duties such as token monitoring and ring clock. These duties include removing frames that circulate the ring indefinitely. It also lowers the priority of a free token if the station that released the token has failed to lower its priority. In case, the active monitor fails, it acts as a standby monitor.

- Ring Error Monitor (REM): Collects errors, which occur, on the token ring. These include hard errors, which may indicate ring and station failures and soft errors, which do not affect the integrity of the network.

- Ring Parameter Server (RPS): When stations inserted into the ring, the token ring adapter chipset provides the initialization values.

- Configuration Report Server (CRS): To record the current ring in case of failure of one or more stations, the chipset sends requests to collect status information from various stations. This feature can use in conjunction with a higher-level LAN management function.

The token ring is a compatible superset of the standard that is put forth by the Institute of Electrical and Electronics Engineers (IEEE) Standards Board and the American National Standards Institute (ANSI) standard for a ring, utilizing token passing as the access method. IEEE standard 802.5 formed in the year 1989. Data rates for the IBM Token Ring are 4 Mbps and 16 Mbps. Logic to improve throughput further, known as the early token release, is also covered by the latest version of the standard.

IBM Token Ring Frame Formats

This section presents the frame structures of the IBM Token Ring network. The IBM token ring has two basic formats, or frames, for transmitted information. The first format, known as the Token Format, consists of three bytes of data and represents the free token. Included within this frame is one byte each for Starting Delimiter (SD) and Ending Delimiter (ED), and one byte for Access Control (AC), used to differentiate between a free token and a data frame. The second format, known as the Frame Format, is used for the transmission of network management and user information. This frame, like the free token, consists of start and end delimiters and Access Control to identify a non-token frame, but it also includes the following additional fields for network management and user information transmission.

- Frame Control (FC): Identifies the type of underlying information.

- Destination Address (DA): Identifies the receiving station, the frame.

- Source Address (SA): Identifies the sender.

- Routing Information (RI): Optionally includes source route paths.

- Information (INFO): Includes the actual data that transmitted over the token ring network.

- Frame Check Sequence (FCS): Includes a Cyclic Redundancy Check (CRC) for detecting transmission errors.

- Frame Status (FS): Designates the actions performed on the frame by the remote stations to which it addressed.

1. Medium Access Control (MAC): MAC performs all the network management actions discussed above. It is also a sublayer to the overall Data Link Control (DLC), which is used for lower layer communication activities in various data communication and network architecture models such as the Open Systems Interconnect (OSI) reference model from the International Standards Organization (ISO), Systems Network Architecture (SNA) from IBM, and Transmission Control Protocol/Internet Protocol (TCP/IP).

2. Logical Link Control (LLC): LLC is a sublayer of Data Link Control that defines frame formats and protocols for the transmission of connectionless or connection-oriented services. The information generated by the architectures referenced above transmitted within the LLC Protocol Data Unit (PDD) frames. LLC described in IEEE Standard 802.2/1So 8802.2 The LLC frame format is shown in Figure. LLC frames consist of a Destination Service Access Point (DSAP), a Source Service Access Point (SSAP), one or two bytes of Control Information, and zero or more bytes of Data Information. The Service Access Points (SAPs) used as logical ports, or addresses, from the higher-level communication and network models, such as OSI SNA, and TCP/IP into the LLC sublayer. Communication between two entities on an IBM token ring network will be between addressable MAC/LLC entities.

Addressing

Medium access control address: The IEEE802.5 standard provides two address formats for token ring networks, 16 bits (2-byte) and 48 bit (6-byte). All nodes on a network must use the same addressing scheme. Nearly all networks use the 6-byte format shown in Figure.

Three types of addresses used with the IBM token ring network. They are Ring Station Address, Group Address, and Functional Address.

Ring station address: It is used to identify stations on the token ring uniquely. A 0 in bit 0 of byte 0 represents a Ring Station Address. A 'I' in this bit position would indicate that the address is a group address. When the ring station address is a source address, this group address indicator bit is no longer relevant for group address identification purposes, since frames can only send from individual ring stations. Instead, a value of 'I' in this field indicates that there is source routing information present in the frame.

The bit 1 of byte 0 can be used to select one of the following address administration methods. They are local administration and global administration. In local administration, the network administrator or local management entity manages the addresses. In the globally administered case, the addressing scheme uses the default values that have been assigned by the IEEE and guaranteed as unique. The choice of locally or globally administered addresses is a decision of the network manager; only one of the two schemes should use for an IBM Token Ring Network. In general, globally administered addresses have the benefit of ensuring that all the addresses for ring stations on the network are unique, while locally administered addresses are useful when various network management facilities are in use. An example of this latter case would be to embed an office number in a station address so that the particular device could physically locate through its MAC address alone.

- Group addresses: A group address is specified only within the Destination Address field. It is used to identify multiple stations on the token ring. Default group addresses are known as broadcast addresses. All stations on a particular token ring receive when broadcast addresses are specified. The user may choose to define additional group addresses.

- Functional addresses: Functional address is a particular type of Group address; functional addresses are identified by bytes 0 and 1 of the O A set to a predefined pattern. Bit 0 of byte 2 is set to '0', and one or more of the remaining 31 bits in bytes 2 through 5 is set, as necessary. Each of these 31 bits represents network management functions such as RPS and REM, in addition to representing optional features such as token ring bridges.

- Logical link control addresses: Logical Link Control (LLC) addresses represented by Service Access Points (SAPs) and are one byte in length.

Each LLC POU consists of two SAPs, one destination and one source (OSAP and SSAP). The bits are defined as follows. Bits 0 to 5 are the actual address bits. Bit 6 identifies whether the SAP address is user-defined if set to '0', or defined by the IEEE if set to 'I.' Bit 7 identifies whether the SAP is an individual SAP if set to '0', or a group SAP if set to '1'.

Source Routing and Multi-Ring Operation

Rather than have all stations on an IBM Token Ring Network located on a single physical ring, the IBM Token Ring architecture allows for interconnection of multiple rings via token ring bridges. A token ring bridge is a specially configured ring station that interconnects two physical token ring networks. A ring station that has a frame to transmit decide whether the frame is to be transmitted on the local (source) ring or is to additionally transmitted to all rings. The decision to execute a multi-ring transmission depends on the higher-level protocols that exist on the ring station. To have a multi-ring transmission, the originating ring station inserts source routing information into the frame. The presence of source routing information is indicated by bit 0 of byte 0 of the MAC source address is set to 1. This bit position is usually the group address indicator, but group addresses are irrelevant in a source address field since all transmissions are from one station only. Three types of source routes used in an IBM token ring network. They are non-broadcast, all-routes-broadcast, and single route broadcast.

1. Non-broadcast: Used when a ring station on a remote token ring network knows a route. The originating station transmits the frame with the non-broadcast source route

attached. The token ring bridge, depending on how it configured, optionally transmit the frame on its second ring. Configuration issues that determine whether to transmit to the second ring include internal bridge congestion; matching ring and bridge numbers; and most solid frame passable by the bridge.

2. AII-routes-broadcast: Used when the path to the destination ring station is not known. A bridge is receiving an all-routes-broadcast frame append segment field information, depending on whether or not that specific segment already occurs in the route. Therefore, multiple copies of the original frame, each with different source routing information, may arrive at the destination ring and may also occur more than once on the same ring. The originating station must be prepared to receive multiple responses (usually non-broadcast) and then select the optimum route, depending on such parameters as frame sizes allowable by bridges, the total number of bridges that must cross (that is, number of hops), and response time.

3. Single-route-broadcast: Used when the path to the destination ring is not known. Bridges are needed to be configured for the single-route-broadcast feature, to use this mode. Single route broadcast bridges communicate with one another and form a spanning tree protocol to represent and continuously update the topology of the network. The result is that the transmitted frame only occurs once per ring and the destination rings only receive one copy of the frame. The destination may then respond to the originating station with a non-broadcast frame, containing the routing information of the frame that it just received, or with all-routes-broadcast frame.

IEEE 802.11 Standard

The wired LAN provides reliable service to users, working in a fixed environment. Once installed, the workstations and the servers of a wired LAN are fixed in their native locations. For users who are highly mobile or in a rough terrain, where there is no possibility to install and lay down the cables of a wired LAN, a good solution is to install a wireless LAN. Wireless LANs transmit and receive data over the atmosphere, using radio frequency (RF) or infrared optical technology, thereby, eliminating the need for fixed wired connections. Wireless LANs provides dual advantage of connectivity and mobility. Wireless LANs have gained strong popularity in applications like health-care, retail, manufacturing, warehousing, and academic. These applications use hand-held terminals and notebook computers to transmit real-time information to centralized 'hosts' for processing. Figure shows simple wired and wireless networks.

Wireless LANs have limitations when compared with wired LANs. Wireless LANs are slower than wired LAN. Also, they have limitations with their range of operation. When a station is moved out of its range, it suffers from noise and error in the received data due to the poor signal strength.

IEEE formed a working group to develop a Medium Access Control (MAC) and Physical Layer (PHY) standard for wireless connectivity for stationary, portable, and mobile computers within a local area. This working group is IEEE 802.11. The recommendations of the 802.11 committee have become the standard for wireless networking.

Need for Wireless LANs

Networking and Internet services are essential requirements for today's business computing. An increasing number of LAN users are becoming mobile. These mobile users require connectivity to a network, regardless of where they are because they want simultaneous access to the network. With wireless LANs, users can access shared information without looking for a place to plug in their systems and do not need network managers to set up networks to install cable and other equipment.

Advantages of Wireless LANs

Wireless LANs offer the following advantages over traditional wired networks. Mobility Users on a wireless LAN systems can access to real-time information from anywhere within their organization. This mobility supports productivity and service opportunities, which are not possible with wired networks.

1. Fast Installation and Simplicity: Installing a wireless LAN system can be fast and easy and can eliminate the need to pull cables through walls, floor, and ceilings.

2. Installation Flexibility: Wireless network is suitable for any kind of geographical conditions. Installation requires to properly setup the transmitter and the receiver antenna (RF) or infrared system. This is much easier than cable installation of a wired LAN. If a company decided to move to a new location, the wireless system is much easier to move.

3. Reduced Cost: The initial investment required for wireless LAN hardware is higher than the cost of wired LAN hardware. However, the overall installation expenses and life cycle costs are significantly lower. Long-term cost benefits are greatest in dynamic environments, requiring frequent moves and changes.

Scalability Wireless LAN systems can be configured in a variety of topologies to cater to the need for specific applications and installations. Configurations can be easily changed. They scale well. New nodes can be added to the existing wireless LAN without much degradation of performance.

Uses of Wireless LANs

Wireless LANs frequently act as a substitute rather than replacement for a wired LAN network. They often provide the final few meters of connectivity between a wired network and the mobile user. The following list describes some of the many applications made possible through the power and flexibility of wireless LANs:

1. Doctors and nurses in hospitals can be more productive because wireless handheld terminals or notebook computers with wireless LAN capability can deliver patient information instantly.

2. Consulting or accounting audit teams or small workgroups can increase the productivity with quick wireless network setup.

3. Students or research scholars, attending a class inside an institute campus can instantly access the Internet to consult the catalog of the net digital library.

4. Network managers in dynamic environments minimize the overhead caused by moves, extensions to networks, and other changes with wireless LANs.

5. Training sites at corporations and students at universities use wireless connectivity to ease access to information, information exchanges, and learning.

6. Network managers installing networked computers in older buildings find that wireless LANs are a cost-effective network infrastructure solution.

7. Travelers and tourists can book their ticket through the net during their travel.

8. Warehouse workers use wireless LANs to exchange information with central databases.

9. Network managers implement wireless LANs to provide backup for mission-critical applications, running on wired networks.

10. Senior executives in meetings make quicker decisions because they have real-time information at their fingertips.

Component of a Wireless LAN

Apart from the components needed by the conventional wired LAN, a wireless LAN needs additional components. They are the transmitters and receivers at radio frequency (RF) or infrared (IR). The RF transmitter and receivers need antennas to perform two-way communication. This area requires a wide knowledge about antenna and propagation. Usually a trial installation is carried out before actual implementation. Hubs, bridges, network operating system, servers, and other components are functioning exactly as they were, on a wired LAN.

Mobile Clients

Mobile clients are portable computing devices that act as clients. The following are some of the mobile systems-

1. Laptop computers: Laptop PCs with two-way communication facility (Transceiver);

2. Palmtops or Personal Digital Assistants (PDA) with communication capability;

3. Portable FAX;

4. Cellular phones.

Special Units

For network management and efficient communication, a wireless LAN needs additional equipments.

They are:

- Communication units: These units perform communications within the network and also with other networks.

- Data collecting units: These units collect data from other systems.

- Security Units: These units take care of the network security.

- Transceivers: A transceiver is a half-duplex device. It performs transmission and reception of data within a wireless LAN. It can be able to transmit in one direction at a time.

- Portable bridges: Portable Bridge can support internet-working functions. Two wireless LANs can communicate with each other using a bridge. It can be a transceiver or a satellite port or other communication unit that provides a bridge service.

Working of Wireless LANs

Wireless LANs use electromagnetic waves (radio or infrared technology) to communicate information from one point to another without relying on any physical connection. Radio waves are often referred as radio carriers because they simply perform the function of delivering energy to a remote receiver. The data being transmitted is superimposed on the radio carrier so that it can be accurately extracted at the receiving end. This is generally referred to as modulation of the carrier by the information being transmitted. Once data is superimposed (modulated) onto the radio carrier, the radio signal occupies more than a single frequency, since the frequency or bit rate of the modulating information adds to the carrier. Multiple radio carriers can exist in the same space at the same time without interfering with each other if the radio waves are transmitted on different radio frequencies. To extract data, a radio receiver tunes in one radio frequency while rejecting all other frequencies. In a typical wireless LAN configuration, a transmitter/receiver (transceiver) device, called an access point, connects to the wired network from a fixed location, using standard cabling. The access point receives, buffers, and retransmits data between the wireless LAN and the wired network infrastructure. A single access point can support a small group of users and can function within a range of less than one hundred to several hundred feet. The access point (or the antenna attached to the access point) is usually mounted high but may be mounted essentially anywhere that is practical as long as the desired radio coverage is obtained.

End users access the wireless LAN through wireless LAN adapters, which are implemented as add-on cards in notebook or palmtop computers, as cards in desktop computers, or integrated within hand-held computers. Wireless LAN adapters provide an interface between the client network operating system (NOS) and the airwaves via an antenna. The nature of the wireless connection is transparent to the NOS.

There are two types of wireless networks:

- Type networks Ad Hoc, where stations communicate directly;

- Infrastructure type networks where stations communicate through access points.

To communicate, each station must of course be equipped with an adapter WiFi and a radio antenna (often integrated into the adapter). More and more computer equipment come with a built-in WiFi adapter. Except not the case, you must buy one and connect it to the station. The connection is very varied: there are WiFi USB adapters, PCMCIA, PCI, etc.

There are several variations of WiFi. In short, 802.11b and 802.11g are compatible them and both operate with the radio waves of a frequency of 2.4 GHz. The 802.11b reached a speed of 11 Mb/s and 802.11g rises to 54 Mb/s. The 802.11a is not compatible with 802.11b and 802.11g, because it works with the waves a radio frequency of 5 GHz. It can reach 54 Mb/s. The 802.11n allows to achieve a real flow rate greater than 100 Mb/s. It is capable of operating at 2.4 GHz or 5 GHz and is compatible with the 802.11b/g and 802.11a. Unfortunately, most 802.11n equipment available today use only tape 2.4 GHz (and are therefore not compatible with the 802.11a).

Today the WiFi version of the most used is far 802.11g. It should be rapidly overtaken by 802.11n.

The fact that WiFi is originally designed to perform WLAN does not prevent not also be used in other contexts. For example, a myriad of products, such as electronic organizers (PDAs) or Personal Data Assistant (PDAs), printers, computer monitors, VCRs or even Hi-Fi, are now equipped with WiFi connections allowing them to be linked together without any wire. In this case, the WLAN is used to achieve a WPAN. Conversely, many local authorities do not have access to top speed (ADSL is not available everywhere) are turning to WiFi to cover a town or towns with the same wireless network. This can be called Wireless MAN (WMAN).

Finally, companies are deploying wireless networks, called hotspots1 that allow anyone to connect to the Internet wirelessly slightly across the US and around the world. So one sees now what might be called WWAN (Wireless Wide Area Networks) based on WiFi technology (WiFi technology itself, however, carries data over short distances).

802.11 Architecture

The 802.11architecture defines two types of services and three different types of stations.

802.11 Services

The two types of services are-

1. Basic Services Set (BSS)

- The basic services set contain stationary or mobile wireless stations and a central base station called access point (AP).

- The use of access point is optional.

- If the access point is not present, it is known as stand-alone network.

Such a BSS cannot send data to other BSSs. This type of architecture is known as adhoc architecture.

- The BSS in which an access point is present is known as an infrastructure network.

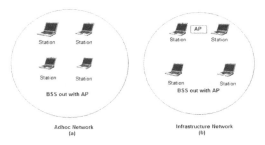

Basics Service Sets

2. Extend Service Set (ESS)

- An extended service set is created by joining two or more basic service sets (BSS) having access points (APs).

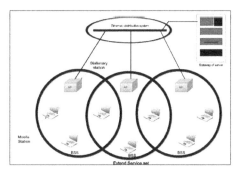

- These extended networks are created by joining the access points of basic services sets through a wired LAN known as distribution system.

- The distribution system can be any IEET LAN.

There are two types of stations in ESS:

(i) Mobile stations: These are normal stations inside a BSS.

(ii) Stationary stations: These are AP stations that are part of a wired LAN.

- Communication between two stations in two different BSS usually occurs via two APs.

- A mobile station can belong to more than one BSS at the same time.

802.11 Station Types

IEEE 802.11 defines three types of stations on the basis of their mobility in wireless LAN. These are:

- No-transition mobility: These types of stations are either stationary i.e. immovable or move only inside a BSS.

- BSS-transition mobility: These types of stations can move from one BSS to another but the movement is limited inside an ESS.

- ESS-transition mobility: These types of stations can move from one ESS to another. The communication mayor may not be continuous when a station moves from one ESS to another ESS.

Physical Layer Functions

- As we know that physical layer is responsible for converting data stream into signals, the bits of 802.11 networks can be converted to radio waves or infrared waves.

- These are six different specifications of IEEE 802.11. These implementations, except the first one, operate in industrial, scientific and medical (ISM) band. These three banks are unlicensed and their ranges are:

  o 902-928 MHz

  o 2.400-4.835 GHz

  o 5.725-5.850 GHz.

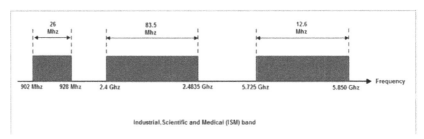

The different implementations of IEE802.11 are given below:

IEEE 802.11 Infrared

- It uses diffused (not line of sight) infrared light in the range of 800 to 950 nm.

- It allows two different speeds: I Mbps and 2Mbps.

- For a I-Mbps data rate, 4 bits of data are encoded into 16 bit code. This 16 bit code contains fifteen as and a single 1.

- For a 2-Mbps data rate, a 2 bit code is encoded into 4 bit code. This 4 bit code contains three Os and a single 1.

- The modulation technique used is pulse position modulation (PPM) i.e. for converting digital signal to analog.

IEEE 802.11 FHSS

- IEEE 802.11 uses Frequency Hoping Spread Spectrum (FHSS) method for signal generation.

- This method uses 2.4 GHz ISM band. This band is divided into 79 subbands of 1MHz with some guard bands.

- In this method, at one moment data is sent by using one carrier frequency and then by some other carrier frequency at next moment. After this, an idle time is there in communication. This cycle is repeated after regular intervals.

- A pseudo random number generator selects the hopping sequence.

- The allowed data rates are 1 or 2 Mbps.

- This method uses frequency shift keying (two levels or four level) for modulation i.e. for converting digital signal to analogy.

IEEE 802.11 DSSS

- This method uses Direct Sequence Spread Spectrum (DSSS) method for signal generation. Each bit is transmitted as 11 chips using a Barker sequence.

- DSSS uses the 2.4-GHz ISM band.

- It also allows the data rates of 1 or 2 Mbps.

- It uses phase shift keying (PSK) technique at 1 M baud for converting digital signal to analog signal.

IEEE 802.11a OFDM

- This method uses Orthogonal Frequency Division Multiplexing (OFDM) for signal generation.

- This method is capable of delivering data upto 18 or 54 Mbps.

- In OFDM all the subbands are used by one source at a given time.

- It uses 5 GHz ISM band.

- This band is divided into 52 subbands, with 48 subbands for data and 4 sub-bands for control information.

- If phase shift keying (PSK) is used for modulation then data rate is 18 Mbps. If quadrature amplitude modulation (QAM) is used, the data rate can be 54 Mbps.

IEEE 802.11b HR-OSSS

- It uses High Rate Direct Sequence Spread Spectrum method for signal generation.

- HR-DSSS is similar to DSSS except for encoding method.

- Here, 4 or 8 bits are encoded into a special symbol called complementary code key (CCK).

- It uses 2.4 GHz ISM band.

- It supports four data rates: 1,2,5.5 and 11 Mbps.

- 1 Mbps and 2 Mbps data rates uses phase shift modulation.

- The 5.5. Mbps version uses BPSK and transmits at 1.375 Mbaud/s with 4-bit CCK encoding.

- The 11 Mbps version uses QPSK and transmits at 1.375 Mbps with 8-bit CCK encoding.

IEEE 802.11g OFDM

- It uses OFDM modulation technique.

- It uses 2.4 GHz ISM band.

- It supports the data rates of 22 or 54 Mbps.

- It is backward compatible with 802.11 b.

MAC sublayer Functions

802.11 support two different modes of operations. These are:

- Distributed Coordination Function.

- The DCF is used in BSS having no access point.

- DCF uses CSMA/CA protocol for transmission.

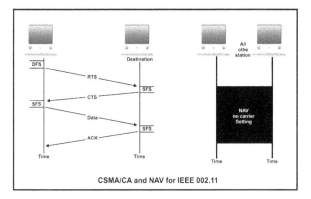

CSMA/CA and NAV for IEEE 002.11

The following steps are followed in this method:

- When a station wants to transmit, it senses the channel to see whether it is free or not.

- If the channel is not free the station waits for back off time.

- If the station finds a channel to be idle, the station waits for a period of time called distributed inter frame space (DIFS).

- The station then sends control frame called request to send (RTS) as shown in figure.

- The destination station receives the frame and waits for a short period of time called short inter frame space (SIFS).

- The destination station then sends a control frame called clear to send (CTS) to the source station. This frame indicates that the destination station is ready to receive data.

- The sender then waits for SIFS time and sends data.

- The destination waits for SIFS time and sends acknowledgement for the received frame.

Collision Avoidance

802.11 standards use Network Allocation Vector (NAV) for collision avoidance.

The procedure used in NAV is explained below:

- Whenever a station sends an RTS frame, it includes the duration of time for which the station will occupy the channel.

- All other stations that are affected by the transmission create a timer caned network allocation vector (NAV).

- This NAV (created by other stations) specifies for how much time these stations must not check the channel.

- Each station before sensing the channel, check its NAV to see if has expired or not.

- If its NAV has expired, the station can send data, otherwise it has to wait.

There can also be a collision during handshaking i.e. when RTS or CTS control frames are exchanged between the sender and receiver. In this case following procedure is used for collision avoidance:

- When two or more stations send RTS to a station at same time, their control frames collide.

- If CTS frame is not received by the sender, it assumes that there has been a collision.

- In such a case sender, waits for back off time and retransmits RTS.

Point Coordination Function

- PCF method is used in infrastructure network. In this Access point is used to control the network activity.

- It is implemented on top of the DCF and IS used for time sensitive transmissions.

- PCF uses centralized, contention free polling access method.

- The AP performs polling for stations that wants to transmit data. The various stations are polled one after the other.

- To give priority to PCF over DCF, another inter frame space called PIFS is defined. PIFS (PCF IFS) is shorter than DIFS.

- If at the same time, a station is using DCF and AP is using PCF, then AP is given priority over the station.

- Due to this priority of PCF over DCF, stations that only use DCF may not gain access to the channel.

- To overcome this problem, a repetition interval is defined that is repeated continuously. This repetition interval starts with a special control frame called beacon frame.

- When a station hears beacon frame, it start their NAV for the duration of the period of the repetition interval.

Frame Format of 802.11

The MAC layer frame consists of nine fields.

Frame Control (FC): This is 2 byte field and defines the type of frame and some control information. This field contains several different subfields.

These are listed in the table below:

Field	Explanation
Version	The Current Version is 0.
Type	Specifies the type of information in the frame body 00. Management, 01-control, and 10-Data.

Frame Format of IEEE 802.11

- D: It stands for duration and is of 2 bytes. This field defines the duration for which the frame and its acknowledgement will occupy the channel. It is also used to set the value of NA V for other stations.

- Addresses: There are 4 address fields of 6 bytes length. These four addresses represent source, destination, source base station and destination base station.

- Sequence Control (SC): This 2 byte field defines the sequence number of frame to be used in flow control.

- Frame body: This field can be between 0 and 2312 bytes. It contains the information.

- FCS: This field is 4 bytes long and contains 'cRC-32 error detection sequence.

IEEE 802.11 Frame Types

There are three different types of frames:

- Management frame: These are used for initial communication between stations and access points.

- Control frame: These are used for accessing the channel and acknowledging frames. The control frames are RTS and CTS.

- Data frame: These are used for carrying data and control information.

802.11 Addressing

There are four different addressing cases depending upon the value of To DS and from DS subfields of FC field. Each flag can be 0 or 1, resulting in 4 different situations.

- If To DS = 0 and From DS = 0, it indicates that frame is not going to distribution system and is not coming from a distribution system. The frame is going from one station in a BSS to another.

- If To DS = 0 and From DS = 1, it indicates that the frame is coming from a distribution system. The frame is coming from an AP and is going to a station. The address 3 contains original sender of the frame (in another BSS).

- If To DS = 1 and From DS = 0, it indicates that the frame is going to a distribution system. The frame is going from a station to an AP. The address 3 field contains the final destination of the frame.

- If To DS = 1 and From DS = 1, it indicates that frame is going from one AP to another AP in a wireless distributed system.

The table below specifies the addresses of all four cases-

TO DS	From DS	Address 1	Address 2	Address 3	Address 4
0	0	Destination	Source	BSS ID	N/A
0	1	Destination	Sending AP	Source	N/A
1	0	Receiving AP	Source	Destination	N/A
1	1	Receiving AP	Sending AP	Destination	Source

Protocols for Wireless LAN

The CSMA protocol is very difficult to implement for wireless LAN. Hence special protocols are needed to avoid collision. MACA and MACAW are the two widely used protocols.

MACA Protocol

During 1990, Kam developed the MACA (Multiple Access with Collision Avoidance) protocol for wireless transmission. The protocol is very simple to implement and works in the following manner. Station X, willing to transmit data to the nearby station Y, sends a short frame called RTS (Request to Send) first. On hearing this short frame, all stations other than the receiving station, avoid transmission, thereby allowing the communication to take place without interference. The receiving station sends a CTS

(Clear to Send) frame to the calling station. After receiving the CTS frame, station X begins transmission. When simultaneous transmission of RTS by two stations W and X to station Y occurs, both frames collide with each other and are lost. When there is no CTS from station Y, both stations wait for a random amount of time (binary exponential back off) and start the whole process again.

MACAW Protocol

Bhargavan investigated the behavior of MACA protocol and refined it with modifications. The first modification was the acknowledgment frame for the successful receipt of each frame. This modification adds carrier sense to stations. The second modification was to apply the binary exponential back off algorithm to source-destination pair. This improves the fairness of the protocol. They have also added to stations, the ability to exchange information, regarding congestion.

Network Protocol

A network protocol defines rules and conventions for communication between network devices. Network protocols include mechanisms for devices to identify and make connections with each other, as well as formatting rules that specify how data is packaged into sent and received messages. Some protocols also support message acknowledgment and data compression designed for reliable and/or high-performance network communication.

Modern protocols for computer networking all generally use packet switching techniques to send and receive messages in the form of packets — messages subdivided into pieces that are collected and reassembled at their destination. Hundreds of different computer network protocols have been developed, each designed for specific purposes and environments.

Internet Protocols

The Internet Protocol (IP) family contains a set of related (and among the most widely used) network protocols. Beside Internet Protocol itself, higher-level protocols like TCP, UDP, HTTP, and FTP all integrate with IP to provide additional capabilities. Similarly, lower-level Internet Protocols like ARP and ICMP also coexist with IP. In general, higher-level protocols in the IP family interact more closely with applications like web browsers, while lower-level protocols interact with network adapters and other computer hardware.

Wireless Network Protocols

Thanks to Wi-Fi, Bluetooth, and LTE, wireless networks have become commonplace.

Network protocols designed for use on wireless networks must support roaming mobile devices and deal with issues such as variable data rates and network security.

Network Routing Protocols

Routing protocols are special-purpose protocols designed specifically for use by network routers on the internet. A routing protocol can identify other routers, manage the pathways (called routes) between sources and destinations of network messages, and make dynamic routing decisions. Common routing protocols include EIGRP, OSPF, and BGP.

Network Protocols Implementation

Modern operating systems contain built-in software services that implement support for some network protocols. Applications like web browsers contain software libraries that support the high-level protocols necessary for that application to function. For some lower-level TCP/IP and routing protocols, support is implemented in direct hardware (silicon chipsets) for improved performance.

Each packet transmitted and received over a network contains binary data (ones and zeros that encode the contents of each message). Most protocols add a small header at the beginning of each packet to store information about the message's sender and its intended destination. Some protocols also add footer at the end. Each network protocol has the ability to identify messages of its own kind and process the headers and footers as part of moving data among devices.

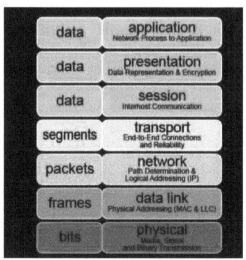

OSI Model

A group of network protocols that work together at higher and lower levels is often called a protocol family.

Types of Network Protocols and their Functions

TCP and UDP

The Transmission Control Protocol (TCP) and the User Datagram Protocol (UDP) are used to transmit network data to and from server and client applications. The main difference between the two protocols is that TCP uses a connection-oriented transport, while UDP uses a connectionless type of communication. When the TCP protocol is used, a special connection is opened up between two network devices, and the channel remains open to transmit data until it is closed.

On the other hand, a UDP transmission does not make a proper connection and merely broadcasts its data to the specified network address without any verification of receipt. For certain types of applications and services, a TCP connection makes more sense, while other types are more efficiently provided by UDP communication. The advantage of TCP is that the transmission is much more reliable because it uses acknowledgement packets to ensure delivery. The advantage of UDP is that there is no connection, so it is much faster without all the checks and acknowledgements going on, but is also less reliable. In Table some common TCP/IP applications are shown with the type of protocol they use.

Protocol	Common Port
FTP (File Transfer Protocol)	20, 21
SSH (Secure Shell)	22
Telnet	23
SMTP (Simple Mail Transfer Protocol)	25
DNS (Domain Name Service)	53
TFTP (Trivial File Transfer Protocol)	69
HTTP (Hypertext Transfer Protocol)	80
POP3 (Post Office Protocol version 3)	110
NNTP (Network News Transport Protocol)	119
NTP (Network Time Protocol)	123
IMAP4 (Internet Message Access Protocol version 4)	143
HTTPS (Hypertext Transfer Protocol Secure).	443

DNS

TCP/IP networks communicate with hosts using their IP addresses. It would be very difficult for someone to have to memorize the different IP addresses for the hosts they want to connect to on the network. A Domain Name Service (DNS) makes it easier to identify a host by a domain name. A domain name uses words rather than numbers to identify Internet hosts. Suppose you want to connect to the Comitial Web site by using your Web browser.

NAT (Network Address Translation)

NAT translates one IP address to another. This can be a source address or a destination address. Two basic implementations of NAT can be used: static and dynamic.

Static NAT

With static NAT, a manual translation is performed by an address translation device, translating one IP address to a different one. Typically, static NAT is used to translate destination IP addresses in packets as they come into your network, but you can translate source addresses also.

Dynamic NAT

With static address translation, you need to build the translations manually. If you have 1000 devices, you need to create 1000 static entries in the address translation table, which is a lot of work. Typically, static translation is done for inside resources that outside people want to access. When inside users access outside resources, dynamic translation is typically used. In this situation, the global address assigned to the internal user isn't that important, since outside devices don't directly connect to your internal users—they just return traffic to them that the inside user requested.

ICS (Internet Connection Sharing)

ICS (Internet Connection Sharing) is a built-in feature of Windows 98 Second Edition, Windows 2000, Windows Me, and Windows Xp. ICS provides networked computers with the capability to share a single connection to the Internet. Multiple users can use ICS to gain access to the Internet through a single connection by using Dial-Up Networking or local networking.

WINS (Windows Internet Name Service)

While DNS resolves host names to IP addresses, WINS resolves NetBIOS names to IP addresses. Windows Internet Name Service provides a dynamic database of IP address to NetBIOS name resolution mappings. WINS, determines the IP address associated with a particular network computer. This is called name resolution. WINS supports network client and server computers running Windows. WINS uses a distributed database that is automatically updated with the names of computers currently available and the IP address assigned to each one. DNS is an alternative for name resolution suitable for network computers with fixed IP addresses.

SNMP (Simple Network Management Protocol)

Simple Network Management Protocol is a TCP/IP protocol for monitoring networks and network components. SNMP uses small utility programs called agents to monitor behavior and traffic on the network, in order to gather statistical data. These agents can be loaded onto managed devices such as hubs, NIC's, servers, routers, and bridges. The gathered data is stored in a MIB (management information base). To collect the information in a usable form, a management program console polls these agents and downloads the information from their MIB's, which then can be displayed as graphs, charts and sent to a database program to be analyzed.

NFS (Network File System)

Network File System (NFS) is a distributed file system that allows users to access files and directories located on remote computers and treat those files and directories as if they were local.

Zeroconf (Zero configuration)

Zero Configuration Networking is a set of techniques that automatically create a usable IP network without configuration or special servers. This allows unknowledgeable users to connect computers, networked printers, and other items together and expect them to work automatically. Without Zeroconf or something similar, a knowledgeable user must either set up special servers, like DHCP and DNS, or set up each computer's network settings manualy.

Zeroconf currently solves three problems:

- Choose numeric network addresses for networked items;

- Figure out which computer has a certain name;

- Figure out where to get services, like printing;

- SMB (Server Message Block).

A file-sharing protocol designed to allow networked computers to transparently access files that reside on remote systems over a variety of networks. The SMB protocol defines a series of commands that pass information between computers. SMB uses four message types: session control, file, printer, and message. It is mainly used by Microsoft Windows equipped computers. SMB works through a client-server approach, where a client makes specific requests and the server responds accordingly. One section of the SMB protocol is specifically for file system access, such that clients may make requests to a file server. The SMB protocol was optimised for local subnet usage, but one could use it to access different subnets across the Internet on which MS Windows file-and-print sharing exploits usually focus. Client computers may have their own hard disks, which are not publicly shared, yet also want access to the shared file systems and printers on the server, and it is for this primary purpose that SMB is best known and most heavily used.

AFP (Apple File Protocol)

The file sharing protocol used in an AppleTalk network. In order for non-Apple networks to access data in an AppleShare server, their protocols must translate into the AFP language. AFP versions 3.0 and greater rely exclusively on TCP/IP (port 548 or 427) for establishing communication, supporting AppleTalk only as a service discovery protocol. The AFP 2.x family supports both TCP/IP and AppleTalk for communication and service discovery.

LPD (Line Printer Daemon) and Samba

LPD is the primary UNIX printing protocol used to submit jobs to the printer. The LPR component initiates commands such as "print waiting jobs," "receive job," and "send queue state," and the LPD component in the print server responds to them. The most common implementations of LPD are in the official BSD UNIX operating system and the Loping project. The Common Unix Printing System (or CUPS), which is more common on modern Linux distributions, borrows heavily from LPD. Unix and Mac OS X Servers use the Open Source SAMBA to provide Windows users with Server Message Block (SMB) file sharing.

WAN (Wide Area Networks) Technologies

Circuit-switched

Services provide a temporary connection across a phone circuit. In networking, these are typically used for backup of primary circuits and for temporary boosts of bandwidth.

Dedicated Circuit

Dedicated circuit is a permanent connection between two sites in which the bandwidth is dedicated to that company's use. These circuits are common when a variety of services, such as voice, video, and data, must traverse the connection and you are concerned about delay issues with the traffic and guaranteed bandwidth.

Cell-switched

Cell-switched services can provide the same features that dedicated circuits offer. Their advantage over dedicated circuits is that a single device can connect to multiple devices on the same interface. The downside of these services is that they are not available at all locations, they are difficult to set up and troubleshoot, and the equipment is expensive when compared to equipment used for dedicated circuits.

Packet Switching

Packet-switched services are similar to cell-switched services. Whereas cell-switched services switch fixed-length packets called cells, packet-switched services switch variable-length packets. This feature makes them better suited for data services, but they can nonetheless provide some of the QoS features that cell-switched services provide. Packet switching offers more efficient use of a telecommunication provider's network bandwidth. With packet switching, the switching mechanisms on the network route each data packet from switch to switch individually over the network using the best-available path. Any one physical link in a packet-switched network can carry packets from many different senders and for many different destinations. Where as in a circuit switched connection, the bandwidth is dedicated to one sender and receiver only.

ISDN (Integrated Services Digital Network)

Integrated Services Digital Network adapters can be used to send voice, data, audio, or video over standard telephone cabling. ISDN adapters must be connected directly to a digital telephone network. ISDN adapters are not actually modems, since they neither modulate nor demodulate the digital ISDN signal. Like standard modems, ISDN adapters are available both as internal devices that connect directly to a computer's expansion bus and as external devices that connect to one of a computer's serial or parallel ports. ISDN can provide data throughput rates from 56 Kbps to 1.544 Mbps using a T1 service. ISDN hardware requires a NT (network termination) device, which converts network data signals into the signaling protocols used by ISDN. Sometimes, the NT interface is included, or integrated, with ISDN adapters and ISDN-compatible routers. In other cases, an NT device separate from the adapter or router must be implemented. ISDN works at the physical, data link, network, and transport layers of the OSI Model.

FDDI (Fiber Distributed Data Interface)

Fiber Distributed Data Interface, shares many of the same features as token ring, such as a token passing, and the continuous network loop configuration. But FDDI has better fault tolerance because of its use of a dual, counter-rotating ring that enables the ring to reconfigure itself in case of a link failure. FDDI also has higher transfer speeds, 100 Mbps for FDDI, compared to 4 - 16 Mbps for Token Ring. Unlike Token Ring, which uses a star topology, FDDI uses a physical ring. Each device in the ring attaches to the adjacent device using a two stranded fiber optic cable. Data travels in one direction on the outer strand and in the other direction on the inner strand. When all devices attached to the dual ring are functioning properly, data travels on only one ring. FDDI transmits data on the second ring only in the event of a link failure.

Media	MAC Method	Signal Propagation Method	Speed	Topologies	Maximum Connections
Fiber-optic	Token passing	Forwarded from device to device (or port to port on a hub) in a closed loop	100 Mbps	Double ring Star	500 nodes

T1 (T Carrier Level 1)

A 1.544 Mbps point to point dedicated, digital circuit provided by the telephone companies. T1 lines are widely used for private networks as well as interconnections between an organizations LAN and the telco. A T1 line uses two pairs of wire one to transmit, and one to receive. and time division multiplexing (TDM) to interleave 24 64-Kbps voice or data channels. The standard T1 frame is 193 bits long, which holds 24 8-bit voice samples and one synchronization bit with 8,000 frames transmitted per second. T1 is not restricted to digital voice or to 64 Kbps data streams. Channels may be combined and the total 1.544 Mbps capacity can be broken up as required.

T3 (T Carrier Level 3)

A T3 line is a super high-speed connection capable of transmitting data at a rate of 45 Mbps. A T3 line represents a bandwidth equal to about 672 regular voice-grade telephone lines, which is wide enough to transmit real time video, and very large databases over a busy network. A T3 line is typically installed as a major networking artery for large corporations, universities with high-volume network traffic and for the backbones of the major Internet service providers.

OCx (Optical Carrier)

Optical Carrier, designations are used to specify the speed of fiber optic networks that conforms to the SONET standard.

Level	Speed
OC-1	51.85 Mbps
OC-3	155.52 Mbps
OC-12	622.08 Mbps
OC-24	1.244 Gbps
OC-48	2.488 Gbps

X.25

X.25 is a network layer protocol that runs across both synchronous and asynchronous physical circuits, providing a lot of flexibility for your connection options. X.25 was actually developed to run across unreliable medium. It provides error detection and correction, as well as flow control, at both the data link layer (by LAPB) and the network layer (by X.25). In this sense, it performs a function similar to what TCP, at the transport layer, provides for IP. Because of its overhead, X.25 is best delegated to asynchronous, unreliable connections. If you have a synchronous digital connection, another protocol, such as Frame Relay or ATM, is much more efficient. An X.25 network transmits data with a packet-switching protocol, bypassing noisy telephone lines. This protocol relies on an elaborate worldwide network of packet-forwarding nodes that can participate in delivering an X.25 packet to its designated address.

Internet Access Technologies

XDSL (Digital Subscriber Line)is a term referring to a variety of new Digital Subscriber Line technologies. Some of these varieties are asymmetric with different data rates in the downstream and upstream directions. Others are symmetric. Downstream speeds range from 384 Kbps (or "SDSL") to 1.5-8 Mbps (or "ADSL").

Asymmetric Digital Subscriber Line

A high-bandwidth digital transmission technology that uses existing phone lines and also allows voice transmissions over the same lines. Most of the traffic is transmitted downstream to the user, generally at rates of 512 Kbps to about 6 Mbps.

Broadband Cable (Cable modem)

Cable modems use a broadband connection to the Internet through cable television infrastructure. These modems use frequencies that do not interfere with television transmission.

POTS/PSTN

(Plain Old Telephone Service/Public Switched Telephone Network) POTS / PSTN use modem's which is a device that makes it possible for computers to communicate over telephone lines. The word modem comes from Modulate and Demodulate. Because standard telephone lines use analog signals, and computers digital signals, a sending modem must modulate its digital signals into analog signals. The computers modem on the receiving end must then demodulate the analog signals into digital signals. Modems can be external, connected to the computers serial port by an RS-232 cable or internal in one of the computers expansion slots. Modems connect to the phone line using standard telephone RJ-11 connectors.

Wireless

A wireless network consists of wireless NICs and access points. NICs come in different models including PC Card, ISA, PCI, etc. Access points act as wireless hubs to link multiple wireless NICs into a single subnet. Access points also have at least one fixed Ethernet port to allow the wireless network to be bridged to a traditional wired Ethernet network, such as the organization's network infrastructure. Wireless and wired devices can coexist on the same network.

- WLAN (Wireless Local Area Network)- A group of computers and associated devices that communicate with each other wirelessly.

- WPA (Wi-Fi Protected Access)- A security protocol for wireless networks that builds on the basic foundations of WEP. It secures wireless data transmission by using a key similar to WEP, but the added strength of WPA is that the key changes dynamically. The changing key makes it much more difficult for a hacker to learn the key and gain access to the network.

- WPA2 (Wi-Fi Protected Access 2)- WPA2 is the second generation of WPA security and provides a stronger encryption mechanism through Advanced Encryption Standard (AES), which is a requirement for some government users.

- WPA-Personal- A version of WPA that uses long and constantly changing encryption keys to make them difficult to decode.

- WPA-Enterprise- A version of WPA that uses the same dynamic keys as WPA-Personal and also requires each wireless device to be authorized according to a master list held in a special authentication server.

A MAC address is 48 bits long and is represented as a hexadecimal number. Represented in hex, it is 12 characters in length, where each character is 4 bits. To make it easier to read, the MAC address is represented in a dotted hexadecimal format, like this: FFFF. FFFF.FFFF.

Some formats use a colon (:) instead; and in Some cases, the colon separator is spaced after every two hexadecimal digits, like this: FF:FF:FF:FF:FF:FF. the first six digits of a MAC address are associated with the vendor, or maker, of the NIC.

Each vendor has one or more unique sets of six digits. These first six digits are commonly called the organizationally unique identifier (OUI). The last six digits are used to represent the NIC uniquely within the OUI value. In theory, each NIC has a unique MAC address. In reality however, this is probably not true. What is important for your purposes is that each of your NICs has a unique MAC address within the same physical or logical segment.

A logical segment is a virtual LAN (VLAN) and is referred to as a broadcast domain. Some devices, such as Cisco routers, might allow you to change the MAC address for a NIC, while others won't.

Every data link layer frame has two MAC addresses: a source MAC address of the host creating the frame and a destination MAC address for the device (or devices, in the cast of a broadcast or multicast) intended to receive the frame.

If only one device is to receive the frame, a unicast destination MAC address is used. If all devices need to receive the frame, a destination broadcast address is used.

When all the binary bits are enabled for a MAC address, this is referred to as a local broadcast address: FFFF.FFFF.FFFF.

Network protocols in terms of routing, addressing schemes, interoperability and naming conventions.

TCP/IP

Transmission Control Protocol, A connection based Internet protocol responsible for breaking data into packets, which the IP protocol sends over the network. IP is located at the TCP/IP Internet layer which corresponds to the network layer of the OSI Model. IP is responsible for routing packets by their IP address.

IP is a connectionless protocol which means, IP does not establish a connection between source and destination before transmitting data, thus packet delivery is not guaranteed by IP. Instead, this must be provided by TCP. TCP is a connection based protocol and, is designed to guarantee delivery by monitoring the connection between source and destination before data is transmitted. TCP places packets in sequential order and requires acknowledgment from the receiving node that they arrived properly before any new data is sent.

TCP/IP Model

Application layer	DHCP - DNS - FTP - HTTP - IMAP4 - IRC - NNTP - XMPP - MIME - POP3 - SIP - SMTP - SNMP - SSH - TELNET - BGP - RPC - RTP - RTCP - TLS/SSL - SDP - SOAP - L2TP – PPTP.
Transport layer	This layer deals with opening and maintaining connections, ensuring that packets are in fact received. This is where flow-control and connection protocols exist, such as: TCP - UDP - DCCP - SCTP – GTP.
Network layer	IP (IPv4 - IPv6) - ARP - RARP - ICMP - IGMP - RSVP - IPSec - IPX/SPX.
Data link layer	ATM - DTM - Ethernet - FDDI - Frame Relay - GPRS – PPP.
Physical layer	Ethernet physical layer - ISDN - Modems - PLC - RS232 - SONET/SDH - G.709 - Wi-Fi.

IPX/SPX

IPX/SPX is the primary protocol of Novell NetWare (in particular, versions 4.0 and earlier, though it can be used on all versions). Internetwork Packet Exchange/Sequenced Packet Exchange developed by Novell and is used primarily on networks that use the Novell NetWare network operating system. The IPX and SPX protocols provide services similar to those offered by IP and TCP. Like IP, IPX is a connectionless network layer protocol. SPX runs on top of IPX at the transport layer and, like TCP, provides connection oriented, guaranteed delivery. IPX/SPX provides many of the same features as TCP/IP, and is a routable transport protocol that allows networks to be segmented. However, network segmentation with IPX/SPX is done with network numbers and not with subnet masks. IPX/SPX is also similar to TCP/IP because IPX/SPX relies on internal protocols for network communication.

IPX

IPX is similar to the operation of UDP of TCP/IP. IPX is a connectionless datagram transfer service. Because it is connectionless, like UDP, it does not require any preliminary connection setup to transmit the data packets. A disadvantage to connectionless communication is that flow control and error correction are not provided during network communication. In addition, packet delivery is not guaranteed. IPX also provides addressing and routing of packets within and between network segments.

SPX

SPX is similar to the operation of TCP of TCP/IP. SPX is connection-oriented data transfer over IPX. Because SPX is connection oriented, flow control and error correction are provided along with packet delivery acknowledgments. SPX allows a single packet to remain unacknowledged at one time. If a packet is unacknowledged, the packet is retransmitted a total of 8 times. If there's no acknowledgment, SPX considers the connection failed.

SPXII

SPXII is an enhancement to SPX. SPXII has several improvements over SPX. SPXII allows more than one packet to remain unacknowledged. SPXII also allows for a larger packet size, which improves network performance by reducing the number of acknowledgment packets placed on the network.

NetBEUI

NetBIOS Enhanced User Interface was designed as a small, efficient protocol for use in department-sized LANs of 20-200 computers that do not need to be routed to other subnets. NetBEUI is used almost exclusively on small, non-routed networks. A LAN-only (non-routable) protocol used in early Windows networks based on the NetBIOS API, NetBEUI is a Windows protocol that even Microsoft doesn't recommend for any but the most isolated networks. NetBEUI isn't required for NetBIOS functionality. As an extension of NetBIOS, NetBEUI is not routable, therefore networks supporting NetBEUI must be connected with bridges, rather than routers, like NetBIOS, the NetBEUI interface must be adapted to routable protocols like TCP/IP for communication over WANs.

AppleTalk

The AppleTalk routing protocol is, amazing as it may sound, used by Macintosh networks. There are two important factors to understand about the AppleTalk protocol: zones and network numbers. AppleTalk network numbers assign AppleTalk networks unique numerical values that identify them as segments. Clients and servers can be part of only one network number. Because AppleTalk is routable, clients can access servers from any network number. AppleTalk also uses zones to aid clients in browsing an AppleTalk network. Zones allow servers, printers, and clients to be grouped logically for the purpose of resource access. Unlike network numbers, servers, printers, and clients can be part of more than one zone. Having membership in more than one zone allows clients easier access to network resources. Clients need not use the Chooser to view the resources of multiple zones.

TCP (Transmission Control Protocol)

Transmission Control Protocol uses a reliable delivery system to deliver layer 4 segments to the destination. This would be analogous to using a certified, priority, or next-day service with the Indian Speed Post; Service.

For example, with a certified letter, the receiver must sign for it, indicating the destination actually received the letter: proof of the delivery is provided. TCP operates under a similar premise: it can detect whether or not the destination received a sent segment. With the postal example, if the certified letter got lost, it would be up to you to resend it; with TCP, you don't have to worry about what was or wasn't received—TCP will take care of all the tracking and any necessary resending of lost data for you.

TCP's main responsibility is to provide a reliable full-duplex, connection-oriented, logical service between two devices.

TCP goes through a three-way handshake to establish a session before data can be sent. Both the source and destination can simultaneously send data across the session. It uses windowing to implement flow control so that a source device doesn't overwhelm a destination with too many segments. It supports data recovery, where any missed or corrupted information can be re-sent by the source. Any packets that arrive out of order, because the segments traveled different paths to reach the destination, can easily be reordered, since segments use sequence numbers to keep track of the ordering.

UDP (User Datagram Protocol)

UDP uses a best-effort delivery system, similar to how first class and lower postal services of the Indian Postal Service work. With a first class letter (post card), you place the destination address and put it in your mailbox, and hope that it arrives at the destination.

With this type of service, nothing guarantees that the letter will actually arrive at the destination, but in most instances, it does. If, however, the letter doesn't arrive at the destination, it's up to you, the letter writer, to resend the letter: the post office isn't going to perform this task for you.

UDP operates under the same premise: it does not guarantee the delivery of the transport layer segments. While TCP provides a reliable connection, UDP provides an unreliable connection.

UDP doesn't go through a three-way handshake to set up a connection—it simply begins sending the data. Likewise, UDP doesn't check to see whether sent segments were received by a destination; in other words, it doesn't use an acknowledgment

Some Commonly used Ports

Port Number	Service
80	HTTP
21	FTP
110	POP3
25	SMTP
23	Telnet

FTP (File Transfer Protocol)

One of the earliest uses of the Internet, long before Web browsing came along, was transferring files between computers. The File Transfer Protocol (FTP) is used to connect to remote computers, list shared files, and either upload or download files between local and remote computers.

FTP runs over TCP, which provides a connection-oriented, guaranteed data-delivery service. FTP is a character-based command interface, although many FTP applications have graphical interfaces. FTP is still used for file transfer purposes, most commonly as a central FTP server with files available for download. Web browsers can make FTP requests to download programs from links selected on a Web page.

You should become familiar with the basic commands available in an FTP session. To begin a character based command session on a Windows computer, follow these steps-

- Open a Command prompt window, type ftp at the prompt, and press Enter.

- This will begin an FTP session on the local machine but will not initialize a connection to another machine.

- Without a connection to another machine, you will not be able to do anything. To connect, type open example.com or open 10.10.10.1, in which exmple.com or 10.10.10.1 is the name or IP address of a host that is available as an FTP server. Most FTP servers require a logon id and password, or they will accept anonymous connections. At this point you will be prompted for a logon ID and password.

- Once you are connected, you can list the files on the remote server by typing dir.

- If you have created privileges on the remote server, you can create a new directory by typing modern.

- To download a file, type gets filename.txt where filename.txt is the name of the file you are downloading.

- To upload a file, type put filename.txt.

SFTP (Secure File Transfer Protocol)

SSH File Transfer Protocol or SFTP is a network protocol that provides file transfer and manipulation functionality over any reliable data stream.

TFTP (Trivial File Transfer Protocol)

TFTP is used when a file transfer does not require an acknowledgment packet during file transfer. TFTP is used often in router configuration. TFTP is similar in operation to FTP. TFTP is also a command-line-based utility.

One of the two primary differences between TFTP and FTP is speed and authentication. Because TFTP is used without acknowledgment packets, it is usually faster than FTP. TFTP does not provide user authentication like FTP and therefore the user must be logged on to the client and the files on the remote computer must be writable. TFTP supports only unidirectional data transfer (unlike FTP, which supports bi-directional transfer). TFTP is operated over port 69.

SMTP (Simple Mail Transfer Protocol)

SMTP is a standard electronic-mail protocol that handles the sending of mail from one SMTP to another SMTP server. To accomplish the transport, the SMTP server has its own MX (mail exchanger) record in the DNS database that corresponds to the domain for which it is configured to receive mail.

When equipped for two-way communication, mail clients are configured with the address of a POP3 server to receive mail and the address of an SMTP server to send mail. The clients can configure server parameters in the properties sheets of the mail client, basing the choices on an FQDN or an IP address.

SMTP uses TCP for communication and operates on port 25. Simple Mail Transfer Protocol (SMTP) is the application-layer protocol used for transmitting e-mail messages. SMTP is capable of receiving e-mail messages, but it's limited in its capabilities. The most common implementations of SMTP are in conjunction with either POP3 or IMAP4. For example, users download an e-mail message from a POP3 server, and then transmit messages via an SMTP server

HTTP (Hypertext Transfer Protocol)

HTTP is often called the protocol of the Internet. HTTP received this designation because most Internet traffic is based on HTTP. When a user requests a Web resource, it is requested using HTTP.

When a client enters this address into a Web browser, DNS is called to resolve the Fully Qualified Domain Name (FQDN) to an IP address. When the address is resolved, an HTTP get request is sent to the Web server. The Web server responds with an HTTP send response. Such communication is done several times throughout a single session to a Web site. HTTP uses TCP for communication between clients and servers. HTTP operates on port 80.

HTTPS (Hypertext Transfer Protocol Secure)

HTTP is for Web sites using additional security features such as certificates. HTTPS is used when Web transactions are required to be secure. HTTPS uses a certificate based technology such as VeriSign.

Certificate-based transactions offer a mutual authentication between the client and the server. Mutual authentication ensures the server of the client identity, and ensures the client of the server identity. HTTPS, in addition to using certificate-based authentication, encrypts all data packets sent during a session.

Because of the encryption, confidential user information cannot be compromised. To use HTTPS, a Web site must purchase a certificate from a third-party vendor such as VeriSign, CertCo, United States Postal Service, or other certificate providers. When the certificate is issued to a Web site from a third-party vendor, the Web site is using trusted communication with the client. The communication is trusted because the third party is not biased toward either the Web site or the client. To view a certificate during a HTTPS session, simply double-click the lock icon in the lower-right area of the Web browser. HTTPS operates on port 443 and uses TCP for communication.

POP3 / IMAP4 (Post Office Protocol Version 3 / Internet Message Access Protocol Version 4)

Post Office Protocol 3 (POP3) and Internet Message Access Protocol 4 (IMAP4) are two application-layer protocols used for electronic messaging across the Internet. POP3 is a protocol that involves both a server and a client. A POP3 server receives an e-mail message and holds it for the user. A POP3 client application periodically checks the mailbox on the server to download mail. POP3 does not allow a client to send mail, only to receive it. POP3 transfers e-mail messages over TCP port 110.

IMAP4 is an alternate e-mail protocol- IMAP4 works in the same way as POP3, in that an e-mail message is held on a server and then downloaded to an e-mail client application. Users can read their e-mail message locally in their e-mail client application, but they can't send an e-mail message using IMAP4. When users access e-mail messages via IMAP4, they have the option to view just the message header, including its title and the sender's name, before downloading the body of the message. Users can create, change, or delete folders on the server, as well as search for messages and delete them from the server.

To perform these functions, users must have continued access to the IMAP server while they are working with e-mail messages. With IMAP4, an e-mail message is copied from the server to the e-mail client. When a user deletes a message in the e-mail client, the message remains on the server until it is deleted on the server. POP3 works differently in that an e-mail message is downloaded and not maintained on the server, unless configured otherwise. Therefore, the difference between POP3 and IMAP4 is that IMAP4 acts like a remote file server, while POP3 acts in a store-and-forward manner in its default configuration. (You can configure POP3 clients to leave copies of messages on the server, if you prefer).

Both Microsoft and Netscape Web browsers have incorporated POP3. In addition, the Eudora and Microsoft Outlook Express e-mail client applications support both POP3 and IMAP4.

Telnet

Short for Telecommunication Network, a virtual terminal protocol allowing a user logged on to one TCP/IP host to access other hosts on the network. Many people use remote control applications to access computers at their workplace from outside the network. In remote control, a session appears in which the user is able to manage the files on the remote computer, although the session appears to be functioning locally. Telnet is an early version of a remote control application.

Telnet is very basic; it offers solely character-based access to another computer. If you want to see a person's graphical desktop, you would need a different type of protocol, such as Remote Desktop Protocol (RDP), Independent Computing Architecture (ICA), or X Windows. Telnet acts as a user command with an underlying Transmission Control Protocol/Internet Protocol (TCP/IP) protocol that handles the establishment, maintenance, and termination of a remote session. The difference between using Telnet and a protocol such as File Transfer Protocol (FTP), is that Telnet logs you directly on to the remote host, and you see a window into that session on your local computer. A typical Telnet command might be as follows: telnet example.com.

Because this particular host is invalid, this command will have no result. However, if it were a valid host the remote computer would ask you to log on with a user ID and password. A correct ID and password would allow you to log on and execute Telnet commands.

You can often use Telnet to manage equipment that lacks a monitor. For example, most routers have Telnet enabled so that the administrator can log in and manage the router. Telnet also provides a quick check to make certain that network connectivity is functioning. Because Telnet sits at the application layer, if it can connect to a remote host, you can be certain that network connectivity between the two hosts is operational, as well as all lower-layer protocols.

SSH (Secure Shell)

SSH is a program for logging in to and executing commands on a remote machine. It provides secure encrypted communications between two untrusted hosts over an insecure network. X11 connections and arbitrary TCP/IP ports can also be forwarded over the secure channel. When SSH connects and logs in to a specified computer, the user must prove his/her identity to the remote machine which is transmitted across the connection using one of three forms of data encryption. This process makes SSH impervious to Internet eavesdroppers who might otherwise steal account information.

ICMP (Internet Control Message Protocol)

ICMP provides network diagnostic functions and error reporting. One of the most used IP commands is the Packet Internet Grouper (PING) command. When a host PINGS another client, it sends an ICMP ECHO request, and the receiving host responds with an ICMP ECHO REPLY. PING checks network connectivity on clients and routers. ICMP also provides a little network help for routers. When a router is being overloaded with route requests, the router sends a source quench message to all clients on the network, instructing them to slow their data requests to the router.

ARP / RARP (Address Resolution Protocol / Reverse Address Resolution Protocol)

The Address Resolution Protocol (ARP) is an Internet layer protocol that helps TCP/IP network components find other devices in the same broadcast domain. ARP uses a local broadcast (255.255.255.255) at layer 3 and FF:FF:FF:FF:FF:FF at layer 2 to discover neighboring devices. Basically stated, you have the IP address you want to reach, but you need a physical (MAC) address to send the frame to the destination at layer 2.

ARP resolves an IP address of a destination to the MAC address of the destination on the same data link layer medium, such as Ethernet. Remember that for two devices to talk to each other in Ethernet (as with most layer 2 technologies), the data link layer uses a physical address (MAC) to differentiate the machines on the segment. When Ethernet devices talk to each other at the data link layer, they need to know each other's MAC addresses.

RARP is sort of the reverse of an ARP. In an ARP, the device knows the layer 3 address, but not the data link layer address. With a RARP, the device doesn't have an IP address and wants to acquire one. The only address that this device has is a MAC address. Common protocols that use RARP are BOOTP and DHCP.

NTP (Network Time Protocol)

The Network Time Protocol is used to synchronize the time of a computer client or server to another server or reference time source, such as a radio or satellite receiver or modem. It provides accuracy's typically within a millisecond on LANs and up to a few tens of milliseconds on WANs.

SNMP

SNMP is a two-way network management protocol. SNMP consists of two components, the SNMP Agent, and the SNMP Management Console. The SNMP Management Console is the server side for SNMP. The management console sends requests to the SNMP Agents as get commands that call for information about the client.

The SNMP Agent responds to the Management Console's get request with a trap message. The trap message has the requested information for the Management Console to evaluate. Security can be provided in many ways with SNMP; however, the most common form of security for SNMP is the use of community names, associations that link SNMP Agents to their Management Consoles.

Agents, by default, respond only to Management Consoles that are part of the same community name. If an SNMP Agent receives a request from a Management Console that is not part of the same community name, then the request for information is denied.

Because SNMP is an industry-standard protocol, heterogeneous environments are common. Many vendors provide versions of SNMP Management Consoles. Hewlett Packard, for example provides HP Open View (one of the most popular Management Consoles on the market); Microsoft provides SNMP Server with the Windows NT and 2000 Resource Kits and Systems Management Server. SNMP Management Consoles request information according to a Management Information Base (MIB) format. An MIB is a numeric value that specifies the type of request, and to which layer of the OSI model the request is being sent.

SCP (Secure Copy Protocol)

Secure Copy or SCP is a means of securely transferring computer files between a local and a remote host or between two remote hosts, using the Secure Shell (SSH) protocol. The protocol itself does not provide authentication and security; it expects the underlying protocol, SSH, to secure this.

The SCP protocol implements file transfers only. It does so by connecting to the host using SSH and there executes an SCP server (SCP). The SCP server program is typically the very same program as the SCP client.

LDAP (Lightweight Directory Access Protocol)

Lightweight Directory Access Protocol, or LDAP, is a networking protocol for querying and modifying directory services running over TCP/IP.

A directory is a set of information with similar attributes organized in a logical and hierarchical manner. The most common example is the telephone directory, which consists of a series of names organized alphabetically, with an address and phone number attached.

An LDAP directory often reflects various political, geographic, and/or organizational boundaries, depending on the model chosen. LDAP deployments today tend to use Domain Name System (DNS) names for structuring the topmost levels of the hierarchy. Deeper inside the directory might appear entries representing people, organizational units, printers, documents, groups of people or anything else which represents a given tree entry.

IGMP (Internet Group Multicast Protocol)

The Internet Group Management Protocol is a communications protocol used to manage the membership of Internet Protocol multicast groups. IGMP is used by IP hosts and adjacent multicast routers to establish multicast group memberships. It is an integral part of the IP multicast specification, like ICMP for unicast connections. IGMP can be used for online video and gaming, and allows more efficient use of resources when supporting these uses.

LPR (Line Printer Remote)

The Line Printer Daemon protocol/Line Printer Remote protocol (or LPD, LPR) also known as the Berkeley printing system, is a set of programs that provide printer spooling and network print server functionality for Unix-like systems.

The most common implementations of LPD are the official BSD UNIX operating system and the LPRng project. The Common UNIX Printing System (or CUPS), which is more common on modern Linux distributions, borrows heavily from LPD.

A printer that supports LPD/LPR is sometimes referred to as a "TCP/IP printer" (TCP/IP is used to establish connections between printers and workstations on a network), although that term seems equally applicable to a printer that supports CUPS.

Network Protocols 1.3 become Standards

Management Focus

There are many standards organizations around the world, but perhaps the best known is the Internet Engineering Task Force (IETF). IETF sets the standards that govern how much of the Internet operates.

The IETF, like all standards organizations, tries to seek consensus among those involved before issuing a standard. Usually, a standard begins as a protocol (i.e., a language or set of rules for operating) developed by a vendor (e.g., HTML [Hypertext mark-up Language]). When a protocol is proposed for standardization, the IETF forms a working group of technical experts to study it. The working group examines the protocol to identify potential problems and possible extensions and improvements then issues a report to the IETF.

If the report is favorable, the IETF issues a request for comment (RFC) that describes the proposed standard and solicits comments from the entire world. Most large software companies likely to be affected by the proposed standard prepare detailed responses. Many "regular" Internet users also send their comments to the IETF.

The IETF reviews the comments and possibly issues a new and improved RFC, which again is posted for more comments. Once no additional changes have been identified, it becomes a proposed standard.

Usually, several vendors adopt the proposed standard and develop products based on it. Once at least two vendors have developed hardware or software based on it and it has proven successful in operation, the proposed standard is changed to a draft standard. This is usually the final specification, although some protocols have been elevated to Internet standards, which usually signifies mature standards not likely to change.

The process does not focus solely on technical issues; almost 90 percent of the IETF's participants work for manufacturers and vendors, so market forces and politics often complicate matters. One former IETF chairperson who worked for a hardware manufacturer has been accused of trying to delay the standards process until his company had a product ready, although he and other IETF members deny this. Likewise, former IETF directors have complained that members try to standardize every product their firms produce, leading to a proliferation of standards, only a few of which are truly useful.

Institute of Electrical and Electronics Engineers the Institute of Electrical and Electronics Engineers (IEEE) is a professional society in the United States who's Standards Association (IEEE-SA) develops standards. The IEEE-SA is probably most known for its standards for LANs. Other countries have similar groups; for example, the British counterpart of IEEE is the Institution of Electrical Engineers (IEE).

Internet Engineering Task Force the IETF sets the standards that govern how much of the Internet will operate. The IETF is unique in that it doesn't really have official memberships. Quite literally anyone is welcome to join its mailing lists, attend its meetings, and comment on developing standards.

Open System Interconnection (OSI) Model

Open System Interconnection (OSI) model is an ISO standard for worldwide communication Networks that defines a networking framework for implementing protocols in seven layers. Layering the communications process means breaking down the communication process into Smaller and Easier to handle interdependent categories. The convention and rules used in such communications are collectively known as Layer protocol. Open Systems Interconnection (OSI) model is developed by ISO (International organization for standardization) in 1984. ISO is the organization dedicated to defining global communication and standards.

This model is called Open System Interconnection (OSI) because this model allows any two different systems to communicate regardless of their underlying architecture. Therefore OSI reference model allows open communication between different systems without requiring changes' to the logic of the underlying hardware and software.

The International standard organization (ISO), in an effort to encourage open networks, developed an open systems interconnect reference model. The model logically groups the functions and sets rules, called protocols, necessary to establish and conduct communication between two or more parties. The model consists of seven functions, often referred to as layers. Every layer added its own header to the packet from previous layer.

OSI reference model is a logical framework for standards for the network communication. OSI reference model is now considered as a primary standard for internetworking and inter computing. Today many network communication protocols are based on the standards of OSI model. In the OSI model the network/data communication is defined into seven layers. The seven layers can be grouped into three groups - Network, Transport and physical layer.

Application

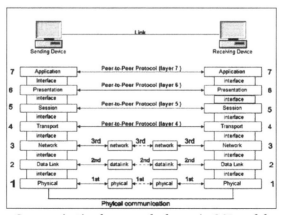

Communication between the layers in OSI model

- Layer 1, 2 and 3 i.e. physical, data link, and network are network support layers.

- Layer 4, Transport layer provides end to end reliable data transmission.

- Layer 5, 6 and 7 i.e. Session, Presentation, and Application layer are user support layers.

It is important to note that OSI model is just a model. It is not a protocol that can be installed or run on any system. To remember the names of seven layers in order one conman mnemonic used is - "All People Seem to Need Data Processing".

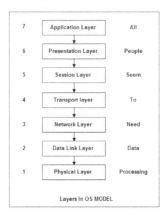

7	Application Layer	All
6	Presentation Layer	People
5	Session Layer	Seem
4	Transport layer	To
3	Network Layer	Need
2	Data Link Layer	Data
1	Physical Layer	Processing

Layers In OS MODEL

The last three layers are mainly concerned with the organization of terminal software and are not directly the concern of communications engineers. The transport layer is the one which links the communication processes to this software-oriented protocol.

Layer 7 – Application Layer

The application layer serves as the window for users and application processes to access network services. It is implemented in End system. The application layer makes the interface between the program that is sending or is receiving data and the protocol stack. When you download or send emails, your e-mail program contacts this layer. This layer provides network services to the end-users like Mail, ftp, telnet, DNS.

1.	FTH	File Transfer Protocol
2.	DHCP	Dynamic Host Configuration Protocol
3.	DNS	Domain Name System
4.	NFS	Network File System
5.	SMTP	Simple Mail Transfer Protocol
6.	POP3	Post Office Protocol-3
7.	SNMP	Simple Network Management Protocol
8.	HTTP	Hyper Text Transfer Protocol
9.	BGP	Border Gateway Protocol
10.	RIP	Routing Information Protocol

Function of Application Layer

- Resource sharing and device redirection.

- Remote file access.

- Remote printer access.

- Inter-process communication.

- Network management.

- Directory services.

- Electronic messaging (such as mail).

Network Virtual Terminal

A network virtual terminal is a software version of a physical terminal and allows a user to log on to a remote host. For this, application layer creates a software emulation of a terminal at the remote host. The user's computer talks to the software terminal which, in turn, talks to the host and vice-versa. The remote host believes it is communicating with one of its own terminals and allows the user to log on.

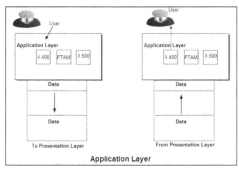

Application Layer

File transfer, access and management (FTAM): This application allows a user to access a file in a remote host to make changes or to read data, to retrieve files from remote computer for use in local computer, and to manage or control files in a remote computer locally.

- Mail services: This application provides various e-mail services such as email forwarding and storage.

- Directory services: This application provides the distributed database sources and access for global information about various objects and services.

- Protocols used at application layer are FTP, DNS, SNMP, SMTP, FINGER, and TELNET.

Layer 6 – Presentation Layer

Presentation Layer is also called Translation layer. The presentation layer presents the data into a uniform format and masks the difference of data format between two dissimilar systems. The presentation layer formats the data to be presented to the application layer. It can be viewed as the translator for the network. This layer may translate data from a format used by the application layer into a common format at the sending station, and then translate the common format to a format known to the application layer at the receiving station.

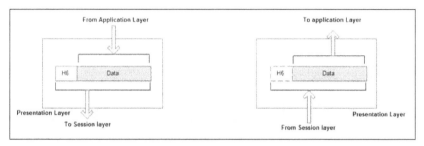

Functions of Presentation Layer-

- Character code translation: for example, ASCII to EBCDIC.

- Data conversion: bit order, CR-CR/LF, integer-floating point, and so on.

- Data compression: reduces the number of bits that need to be transmitted on the network.

- Data encryption: encrypt data for security purposes. For example, password encryption.

Layer 5 - Session Layer

Session layer has the primary responsibility of beginning, maintaining and ending the communication between two devices, which is called Session. It also provides for orderly communication between devices by regulating the flow of data.

The session protocol defines the format of the data sent over the connections. Session layer establish and manages the session between the two users at different ends in a network. Session layer also manages who can transfer the data in a certain amount of time and for how long.

The examples of session layers and the interactive logins and file transfer sessions. Session layer reconnect the session if it disconnects. It also reports and logs and upper layer errors. The session layer allows session establishment between processes running on different stations. The dialogue control and token management are responsibility of session layer.

Functions of Session Layer

Session establishment, maintenance and termination allows two application processes on different machines to establish, use and terminate a connection, called a session.

Session support performs the functions that allow these processes to communicate over the network, performing security, name recognition, logging and so on.

Dialog control Dialog control is the function of session layer that determines which device will communicate first and the amount of data that will be sent.

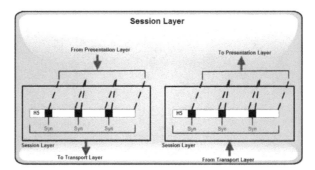

When a device is contacted first, the session layer is responsible for determining which device participating in the communication will transmit at a given time as well as controlling the amount of data that can be sent in a transmission. This is called dialog control.

The types of dialog control that can take place include simplex, half duplex and full duplex.

Dialog separation or Synchronization: The session layer is also responsible for adding checkpoint or markers within the message. This process of inserting markers to the stream of data is known as dialog separation.

The protocols that work on the session layer are NetBIOS, Mail Slots, Names Pipes, and RPC.

Layer 4 – Transport Layer

Transport layer (also called end-to-end layer) manages end to end (source to destination) (process to process) message delivery in a network and also provides the error checking and hence guarantees that no duplication or errors are occurring in the data transfers across the network. It makes sure that all the packets of a message arrive intact and in order.

Transport layer also provides the acknowledgement of the successful data transmission and retransmits the data if error is found. The transport layer ensures that messages are delivered error-free, in sequence, and with no losses or duplications.

The size and complexity of a transport protocol depends on the type of service it can get from the network layer. Transport layer is at the core of OSI model. Transport layer provides services to application layer and takes services from network layer.

Transport layer divides the message received from upper layer into packets at source and reassembles these packets again into message at the destination.

Transport layer provides two types of services-

Connection Oriented Transmission

- In this type of transmission the receiving device sends an acknowledgment, back to the source after a packet or group of packet is received.

- This type of transmission is also known as reliable transport method.

- Because connection oriented transmission requires more packets be sent across network, it is considered a slower transmission method.

- If the data that is sent has problems, the destination requests the source for retransmission by acknowledging only packets that have been received and are recognizable.

- Once the destination computer receives all of the data necessary to reassemble the packet, the transport layer assembles the data in the correct sequence and then passes it up, to the session layer.

Connectionless Transmission

- In this type of transmission the receiver does not acknowledge receipt of a packet.

- Sending device assumes that packet arrive just fine.

- This approach allows for much faster communication between devices.

- The trade-off is that connectionless transmission is less reliable than connection oriented.

Functions of Transport Layer

Segmentation of message into packet and reassembly of packets into message: accepts a message from the (session) layer above it, splits the message into smaller units (if not already small enough), and passes the smaller units down to the network layer. The transport layer at the destination station reassembles the message.

- Message acknowledgment: provides reliable end-to-end message delivery with acknowledgments.

- Message traffic control: tells the transmitting station to "back-off" when no message buffers are available.

- Session multiplexing: multiplexes several message streams, or sessions onto one logical link and keeps track of which messages belong to which sessions.

- Service point addressing: The purpose of transport layer is to delivery message from one process running on source machine to another process running on destination machine. It may be possible that several programs or processes are running on both the machines at a time. In order to deliver the message to correct process, transport layer header includes a type of address called service point address or port address. Thus by specifying this address, transport layer makes sure that the message is delivered to the correct process on destination machine.

- Flow control: Like Data link layer, transport layer also performs flow control. Transport layer makes sure that the sender and receiver communicate at a rate they both can handle. Therefore flow control prevents the source from sending data packets faster than the destination can handle. Here, flow control is performed end-to-end rather than across a link.

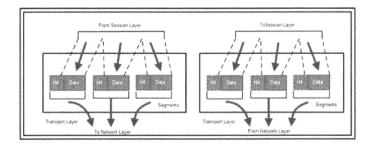

- Error control: Like Data link layer, Transport layer also performs error control. Here error control is performed end-to-end rather than across a single link. The sending transport layer ensures that the entire message arrives at the receiving transport layer without error (damage, loss or duplication). Error correction is achieved through retransmission.

- Protocols: These protocols work on the transport layer TCP, SPX, NETBIOS, ATP and NWLINK.

Layer 3 – Network Layer

This layer is in charge of packet addressing, converting logical addresses into physical addresses. It is responsible for the source-to-destination delivery of a packet across multiple networks (links). This layer is also in charge of setting the routing. The packets will use to arrive at their destination, based on factors like traffic and priorities. The network layer determines that how data transmits between the network devices.

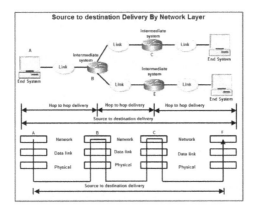

If two systems are connected to same link, then there is no need for network layer. And if two systems are attached to different networks with connecting devices like routers between the networks, then there is need for the network layer.

It also translates the logical address into the physical address e.g computer name into MAC address. It is also responsible for defining the route, it managing the network problems and addressing The network layer controls the operation of the subnet, deciding which physical path the data should take based on network conditions, priority of service, and other factors. The X.25 protocols works at the physical, data link, and network layers.

The network layer lies between data link kyer and transport layer. It takes services from Data link and provides services to the transport layer.

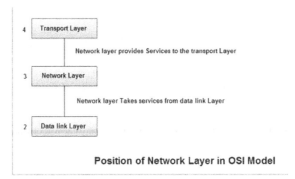

Position of Network Layer in OSI Model

Functions of Network Layer

- Subnet Traffic Control: Routers (network layer intermediate systems) can instruct a sending station to "throttle back" its frame transmission when the router's buffer fills up.

- Logical-Physical Address Mapping: translates logical addresses, or names, into physical addresses.

- Subnet Usage Accounting: has accounting functions to keep track of frames forwarded by subnet intermediate systems, to produce billing information.

- In the network layer and the layers below, peer protocols exist between a node and its immediate neighbor, but the neighbor may be a node through which data is routed, not the destination station. The source and destination stations may be separated by many intermediate systems.

Internetworking

- One of the main responsibilities of network layer is to provide internetworking between different networks.

- It provides logical connection between different types of network.

- It is because of this layer, we can combine various different networks to form a bigger network.

Logical Addressing

- Large number of different networks can be combined together to from bigger networks or internetwork.

- In order to identify each device on internetwork uniquely, network layer defines an addressing scheme.

- Such an address distinguishes each device uniquely and universally.

Routing

- When independent networks or links are combined together to create internet works, multiple routes are possible from source machine to destination machine.

- The network layer protocols determine which route or path is best from source to destination. This function of network layer is known as routing.

- Routes frames among networks.

Packetizing

- The network layer receives the data from the upper layers and creates its own packets by encapsulating these packets. The process is known as packetizing.

- This packetizing in done by Internet Protocol (IP) that defines its own packet format.

Fragmentation

- Fragmentation means dividing the larger packets into small fragments.

- The maximum size for a transportable packet in defined by physical layer protocol.

- For this, network layer divides the large packets into fragments so that they can be easily sent on the physical medium.

- If it determines that a downstream router's maximum transmission unit (MTU) size is less than the frame size, a router can fragment a frame for transmission and re-assembly at the destination station.

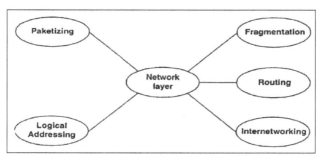

Functions of Network Layer

- Protocols: These protocols work on the network layer IP, ICMP, ARP, RIP, OSI, IPX and OSPF.

Layer 2 - Data Link Layer

It is responsible for reliable node-to-node delivery of data. It receives the data from network layer and creates frames, add physical address to these frames and pass them to physical layer.

The data link layer provides error-free transfer of data frames from one node to another over the physical layer, allowing layers above it to assume virtually error-free transmission over the link. Data Link layer defines the format of data on the network. A network data frame, packet, includes checksum, source and destination address, and data.

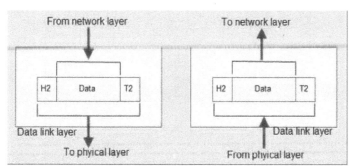

The data link layer handles the physical and logical connections to the packet's destination, using a network interface. This layer gets the data packets send by the network layer and convert them into frames that will be sent out to the network media, adding the physical address of the network card of your computer, the physical address of the network card of the destination, control data and a checksum data, also known as CRC. The X.25 protocols works at the physical, data link, and network layers.

Data Link Layer Consists of Two Sub-layers

1. Logical Link Control (LLC) sublayer: LLC sublayer provides interface between the media access methods and network layer protocols such as Internet protocol which is a part of TCP/IP protocol suite. LLC sublayer determines whether the communication is going to be connectionless or connection-oriented at the data link layer.

2. Medium Access Control (MAC) sublayer: MAC sublayer is responsible for connection to physical media. At the MAC sublayer of Data link layer, the actual physical address of the device, called the MAC address is added to the packet. Such a packet is called a Frame that contains all the addressing information necessary to travel from source device to destination device.

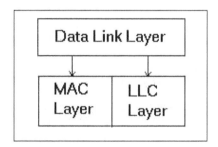

MAC address is the 12 digit hexadecimal number unique to every computer in this world. A device's MAC address is located on its Network Interface Card (NIC). In these 12 digits of MAC address, the first six digits indicate the NIC manufacturer and the last six digits are unique. For example, 32-14-a6-42-71-0c is the 12 digit hexadecimal MAC address. Thus MAC address represents the physical address of a device in the network.

Functions of Data Link Layer

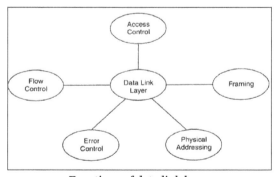

Functions of data link layer

1. Link Establishment and Termination: Establishes and terminates the logical link between two nodes.

2. Physical addressing: After creating frames, Data link layer adds physical addresses (MAC address) of sender and receiver in the header of each frame.

3. Frame Traffic Control: Tells the transmitting node to "back-off algorithm" when no frame buffers are available.

4. Frame Sequencing: Transmits/receives frames sequentially.

5. Frame Acknowledgment: Provides/expects frame acknowledgments. Detects and recovers from errors that occur in the physical layer by retransmitting non-acknowledged frames and handling duplicate frame receipt.

6. Frame Delimiting: Creates and recognizes frame boundaries.

7. Frame Error Checking: Checks received frames for integrity.

8. Media Access Management: determines when the node "has the right" to use the physical medium.

9. Flow control: It is the traffic regulatory mechanism implemented by Data Link layer that prevents the fast sender from drowning the slow receiver. If the rate at which data is absorbed by receiver is less that the rate produced in the sender, the data link layer imposes this flow control mechanism.

10. Error control: Data link layer provides the mechanism of error control in which it detects and retransmits damaged· or lost frames. It also deals with the problem of duplicate frame, thus providing reliability to physical layer.

11. Access control: When a single communication channel is shared by multiple devices, MAC sub-layer of data link layer helps to determine which device has control over the channel at a given time.

12. Feedback: After transmitting the frames, the system waits for the feedback. The receiving device then sends the acknowledgement frames back to the source providing the receipt of the frames.

Layer 1 – Physical Layer

The physical layer, the lowest layer of the OSI model, is concerned with the transmission and reception of the unstructured raw bit stream over a physical medium. It describes the electrical/optical, mechanical, and functional interfaces to the physical medium, and carries the signals for all of the higher layers. Physical layer defines the cables, network cards and physical aspects.

It is responsible for the actual physical connection between the devices. Such physical connection may be made by using twisted pair cable, fiber-optic, coaxial cable or wireless communication media. This layer gets the frames sent by the Data Link layer and converts them into signals compatible with the transmission media. If a metallic cable is used, then it will convert data into electrical signals; if a fiber optical cable is used, then it will convert data into luminous signals; if a wireless network is used, then it will convert data into electromagnetic signals; and so on.

When receiving data, this layer will get the signal received and convert it into 0s and 1s and send them to the Data Link layer, which will put the frame back together and check for its integrity The X.25 protocols works at the physical, data link, and network layers.

Functions of Physical Layer

Data Encoding: Modifies the simple digital signal pattern (1s and 0s) used by the PC to better accommodate the characteristics of the physical medium, and to aid in bit and frame synchronization. It determines:

- What signal state represents a binary 1?

- How the receiving station knows when a "bit-time" starts?

- How the receiving station delimits a frame?

1. Physical medium attachment, accommodating various possibilities in the medium.

- Will an external transceiver (MAU) be used to connect to the medium?

- How many pins do the connectors have and what is each pin used for?

- Transmission Technique: determines whether the encoded bits will be transmitted by baseband (digital) or broadband (analog) signaling.

- Physical Medium Transmission: transmits bits as electrical or optical signals appropriate for the physical medium, and determines:

  o What physical medium options can be used?

  o How many volts/db should be used to represent a given signal state, using a given physical medium.

2. Protocols used at physical layer are ISDN, IEEE 802 and IEEE 802.2.

- Bit synchronization: The physical layer provides the synchronization of the bits by providing a clock. This clock controls both transmitter as well as receiver thus providing synchronization at bit level.

- Provides physical characteristics of interfaces and medium: Physical layer manages the way a device connects to network media. For example, if the physical connection from the device to the network uses coaxial cable, the hardware that functions at the physical layer will be designed for that specific type of network. All components including connectors are also specified at physical layer.

- Bit rate control: Physical layer defines the transmission rate i.e. the number of bits sent in one second. Therefore it defines the duration of a bit.

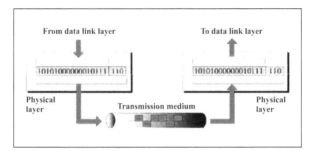

- Line configuration: Physical layer also defines the way in which the devices are connected to the medium. Two different line configurations are used point to point configuration and multipoint configuration. To activate, maintain and deactivate the physical connection.

- Transmission mode: Physical layer also defines the way in which the data flows between the two connected devices. The various transmission modes possible are: Simplex, half-duplex and full-duplex.

- Physical topologies: Physical layer specifies the way in which the different, devices/nodes are arranged in a network i.e. bus, star or mesh.

- Multiplexing: Physical layer can use different techniques of multiplexing, in order to improve the channel efficiency.

- Circuit switching: Physical layer also provides the circuit switching to interconnect different networks.

Advantages of OSI Model Layered Architecture

OSI model has various advantages:

- It is a truly generic model. And it is considered as a standard model in computer networking.

- Layers in OSI model architectures are distinguished according to the services, interfaces, and protocols.

- Since the protocols are hidden, any protocols can be implemented in this model. So I call it as a generic model. It has all flexibility to adapt to many protocols.

- It supports connection-oriented as well as connectionless services. So we can use the connection-oriented model when we need reliability and connection-less services when we need a faster data transmission over the internet.

- It follows the divide and conquers technique. All the services are distinguished in various layers. So administration and maintenance for these OSI model architecture are straightforward and easy.

- This layered architecture follows abstraction principle. Change in one layer does not impact much on other layers.

- It is more secure and adaptable than having all services bundled in a single layer.

These are all advantages of OSI model layered architecture. However, there are some disadvantages of this Layered Architecture as well.

Disadvantages of OSI Model Layered Architecture

- It doesn't define any particular protocol.

- It may find sometimes difficult to fit a new protocol in this model. This is because this model was created before the invention of any of these protocols.

- The session layer is used for session management. Presentation layer deals with user interaction. Though they are useful, not as much as other layers in the OSI model.

- There is some duplication of services at various layers. Such as, both transport and data link layer have error control mechanisms.

- There is also interdependence among the layers. These layers cannot work in parallel. They have to be in wait to receive data from its predecessor.

References

- Electrical-and-electronics: techopedia.com, Retrieved 7 April, 2019

- Ulf-Daniel Ehlers, Jan Martin Pawlowski (2006). Handbook on quality and standardization in e-learning. ISBN 9783540327882. Retrieved 2010-11-17, Retrieved 27 July, 2019

- What-is-ieee-8024-protocol, computer-network: ecomputernotes.com, Retrieved 23 January, 2019

- IEEE-Standard, Networking: brainbell.com, Retrieved 25 April, 2019

- What-is-ieee-8025-protocol, communication-networks: ecomputernotes.com, Retrieved 15 January, 2019

- Wireless-lan, communication-networks: ecomputernotes.com, Retrieved 14 June, 2019

- Definition-of-protocol-network: lifewire.com, Retrieved 8 August, 2019

- Types-of-network-protocols-explained-with-functions: computernetworkingnotes.com, Retrieved 18 February, 2019

- Osi-layers, communication-networks: ecomputernotes.com, Retrieved 9 July, 2019

- Advantages-disadvantages-of-osi-model-layered-architecture: csestack.org, Retrieved 19 March, 2019

3

Network Topology and its Types

The topological structure of a network is known as network topology. It can be depicted either physically or logically. Some of the different types of network topologies are bus network topology, ring network topology and tree network topology. The topics elaborated in this chapter will help in gaining a better perspective about these branches of network topology.

The term Network Topology defines the geographic Physical or logical arrangement of computer networking devices. The term Topology refers to the way in which the various nodes or computers of a network are linked together. It describes the actual layout of the computer network hardware. Two or more devices connect to a link; two or more links form a topology. Topology determines the data paths that may be used between any pair of devices of the network.

The selection of a Network Topology for a network can not be done in isolation as it affects the choice of media and the access method used. Because it determines the strategy used in wiring a building for a network and deserves some careful study.

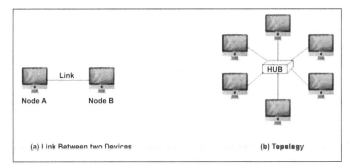

(a) Link Between two Devices   (b) Topology

The following factors are considered while selecting a topology:

1. Cost,

2. Reliability,

3. Scalability,

4. Bandwidth capacity,

5. Ease of installation,

6. Ease of troubleshooting,

7. Delay involved in routing information from one node to another.

Types of Topologies

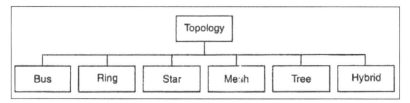

While making a selection of a particular topology we consider the relative status of different devices that are to be linked.

The nodes in a network can have following two relationships:

Peer to Peer

In this relationship, all the devices in the network have equal status in sharing the link. For example, Ring & Mesh topology.

Primary-Secondary

In this, one device controls the traffic and all other devices transmit through primary device. e.g. Star topology.

Logical Topology

A network's logical topology can also be referred to as its signal topology. This type of topology is not interested in how devices on the network are connected but how they communicate with each other. Logical topologies are created by the network protocols on NICs that determine the movement of data on the physical topology. Examples of these are:

- Ethernet - logical bus topology.
- LocalTalk - logical bus or star topology.
- IBM Token Ring - logical ring.

To add to this seeming confusion it may be the case that a network's logical topology is not always the same as its physical topology.

Physical Topology

A network's physical topology is the arrangement or layout of computers, cables, and other components on the network.

The physical topology of a network directly affects its capabilities. The choice of one topology over another will have an impact on the following:

- Type of equipment the network needs.

- Capabilities of the equipment.

- Growth of the network.

- The way the network is managed.

Before computers can either share resources or perform other communications tasks, they must be connected. Most networks use cable to connect one computer to another. It is not as simple as just plugging a computer into a cable connecting other computers. There are many different types of cable, network cards, network operating systems, and other components, all of which require different types of arrangements.

To work properly, a network topology takes a lot of careful planning, determining not only the type of cable to be used but also how it runs through floors, ceilings, and walls.

Bus Network Topology

Bus Topology is multipoint electrical circuits that can be implemented using coaxial cable, UTP, or STP. Data transmission is bidirectional, with the attached devices transmitting in both directions. While generally operating at a raw data rate of 10 Mbps, actual throughput is much less.

It is employed frequently in the LANs with distributed control. In all nodes, as shown in Figure, share the shared bus. Messages placed on the bus transmitted to all nodes. Nodes must be able to recognize their address to receive messages. However; unlike nodes in a ring, they do not have to repeat and forward messages intended for other nodes. As a result, there is none of the delay and overhead associated with re-transmitting messages at each intermediate node. Because of the passive role node play in transmission on the bus, network operation continues in the event of node failures. This makes distributed BUS networks inherently resistive to single-point failures.

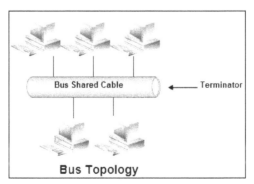

Bus Topology

Bus networks employ a decentralized method of media access control known as CSMA (Carrier Sense Multiple Access) that allows the attached devices to make independent decisions relative to media access and initiation of transmission. This approach results in data collisions and requires frequent retransmission. However, networks specified in the IEEE 802.3 standard, and generally, have a maximum specified length of 1.5 miles (2.5 km). Ethernet is based on a bus topology. A tree topology is a variation on the bus topology, with multiple branches of the trunk of the central bus. Bus networks also suffer from the vulnerability of the bus, as if, one node is down, all nodes in the bus down. Similarly, tree networks are dependent on the integrity of the root bus.

Examples of Bus Topology

Ethernet - Ethernet is the least expensive high-speed LAN alternative. It transmits and receives data at a speed of 10 million bits per second. Data transferred between wiring closets using either a heavy coaxial cable (thick net) or fiber optic cable. Thick net coaxial still used for medium-long distances where medium levels of reliability are needed. Fiber goes farther and has more excellent reliability but a higher cost. To connect several workstations within the same room, a light-duty coaxial cable called thin net commonly used. These other media reflect an older view of workstation computers in a laboratory environment. The figure shows the scheme of Ethernet where a sender transmits a modulated carrier wave that propagates from the sender toward both ends of the cable.

Ethernet was first designed and installed by Xerox Corporation at its Palo Atto Research Center (PARe) in the mid-1970. In the year 1980, DEC Intel and Xerox came out with a joint specification which has become the de facto standard. Ethernet from this period is often called DIX after its corporate sponsors Digital, Intel, and Xerox. Ethernet as the most popular protocol for LAN technology.

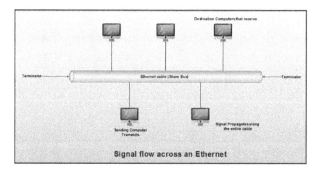

Signal flow across an Ethernet

Local Talk

LocalTalk is a LAN that employs bus topology. Apple Computer Corporation invented it for use with Apple's PCs LocalTalk uses ordinary telephone wire with standard RJ-l1 telephone connectors, the same as used to plug in a telephone and modem. Each connector plugs into a LocalTalk transceiver, which connects to a PC's LocalTalk interface card. LocalTalk transceivers that connect to a PC's parallel port are also available. Multiple computers can connect in a daisy chain, like the way railroad cars connected on a train. Hub can also be used for the same purpose.

LocalTalk does have some limitations over Ethernet. For one, LocalTalk is slower than Ethernet. LocalTalk has a bandwidth of230.4 Kbits/second, while Ethernet has a bandwidth of 10MB per second. In practice, Ethernet runs about 4-to-5 times faster, than LocalTalk. Another limitation of LocalTalk is that it cannot run TCP/IP protocols directly.

LocalTalk significant advantages are that it is simple and very inexpensive. The hardware and software required for LocalTalk already built into every Macintosh computer to connect with a LocalTalk network except the iMac(tm). LocalTalk is also cheaper in terms of cabling than Ethernet. Many Macintosh computer owners use a printer cable to create a temporary network between two Macintosh Computers. There is no software to install beyond the Macintosh operating system itself and LocalTalk work with any current version of the Macintosh operating system as well as versions from several years ago. For cabling of a LocalTalk network, standard RJ-II phone cable is used which is cheaper than the cable used for Ethernet. Many printers on the market come with built-in LocalTalk support, making them easy to share on such a network.

Bus Network Terminators

The terminator is a device that supplies electrical resistance at the end of a transmission line to absorb the signals of the line, thus preventing them from bouncing and being received again by the network stations.

The best cable that can use in the bus network is the coaxial cable for that it is the safest and gives you higher speed and resistance in the network.

Features of Bus Network

1. Simplicity is the simplest and most common method used in Ethernet networks.

2. A long cable acts as a backbone network that connects all devices in the network.

3. Use less cable than any other topology.

4. The bus topology has all its nodes connected directly to a link and has no other connection between nodes.

5. Physically, each host connected to a standard cable, so they can communicate directly, although breaking the cable causes the hosts to be disconnected.

6. There is no signal generation on each node or router.

7. The number of devices connected to the bus affects the performance of the network.

Functionality of Bus Network

1. The type of wiring used can be coaxial, twisted pair, or optical fiber.

2. The information travels through the cable in both directions at an approximate speed of 10/100 Mbps or has resistance at its two ends (terminator).

3. Network data sent in the form of electronic signals to all computers in the network. Only one computer at a time can send messages in this topology.

4. Computers connected to a bus, or transmit data to other computers on the network or expect to receive data from other computers.

5. The bus topology is not responsible for transmitting data from one computer to another. Consequently, if a computer fails, it does not affect the rest of the network.

6. To prevent the signal from bouncing throughout the cable, a terminator is placed on each end of the cable to absorb all the signals. It allows the cable to be released from these signals so that other computers can send data.

Advantages of Bus Topology

1. It is Easy to Connect a Device to the Network:

If the computer or peripheral has the appropriate connection mechanism, then it can be easily added to the network. The new device connects to the linear bus topology and becomes part of the network immediately. For those who need a temporary network that can be setup quickly, there isn't a better option that is available right now. If several users need mutual access to a printer, adding the printer to the network meets that need immediately.

2. It is Cheaper than other Network Options:

Compared to ring, star, or hybrid networks, bus topology is the cheapest to implement. That is because it requires less cable length than the other network options. Although terminators are required at both ends of the backbone to ensure the network can function properly, it is still easy and affordable to install when a small network is required.

3. The Failure of one Station does not Affect the Rest of the Network:

If one computer or peripheral should fail when using bus topology, the rest of the network is not affected by this change in performance. The linear nature of the network means that each unit transmits to the backbone and that data is then available to the other units that remain connected. This makes it an effective way to share uninterrupted communication.

4. No Hubs or Switches are Required:

With bus topology, the linear nature of the network allows data to flow freely throughout the network. Although this limits outside connections, it does create a localized network that can effectively work with each terminal that has been connected. A central file server is used instead of hubs and switches, which means there are fewer points of potential failure that must be managed with this setup compared to others.

5. Extensions can be Made to the Network:

The size and scope of bus topology is naturally limited. It can, however, be extended quite easily. Joining cable with a repeater or connector allows for additional peripherals or computers to be added to the network. Although this can increase the number of packet collisions that may occur, it is a simplified solution that can get people up and working quickly and for a minimal overall cost.

6. Multiple Nodes can be Installed without Difficulty:

For a small network, another option that is often considered is point-to-point topology. Bus topology has an advantage here because it supports multiple nodes instead of just 2 nodes. That is how the original form of an Ethernet network came about. 10Base2, which is popularly known as "thinnet," utilizes bus topology to create a local area network that can be used to form departments or working groups.

7. Multiple Peripherals can be Supported Through Bus Topology:

Routers, printers, and other data devices can be connected to this network in addition to computers or terminals. This can increase the speed of productivity because instead of sending commands to a centralized network, a command can be sent directly to the needed peripheral. A print command from a computer, for example, can stay local and improve production speed, which keeps workers more productive over time.

8. Wiring Terminators Take no Power Requirements:

The terminators that are used for most bus topology systems are passive devices. They're made of resistors and capacitors, which means there isn't a power requirement that must be met. This makes it easy to install a simple LAN at virtually any location where networking would be beneficial to a department or working group.

Disadvantages of Bus Topology

1. Additional Devices Slow the Network Down:

Because bus topology links every computer and peripheral through a backbone, additional devices will slow down the entire network since only one cable is being used. That also places the entire network at-risk should something happen to that cable. If the backbone is damaged for some reason, it can either cause the entire network to fail or have it split into two networks instead of one.

2. Size Limitations are Always Present:

A backbone has limited length, which means there is a maximum number of computers and peripherals that can be added to the network. That size limitation also increases the risk that collisions will occur within the bus topology because communication spacing is at such a premium.

3. Security Options are Limited with Bus Topology:

Any computer that is connected to the backbone of a bus topology network will be able to see all the data transmissions that occur on all the other computers. Each terminal has full access to every other terminal. That means security options are difficult to install on such a setup because everyone can see what everyone else is doing.

4. Maintenance Costs are Higher:

Although bus topology is cheaper to setup, the costs of maintaining this network are higher in the long run. It may be a good network for those with small, short-term needs. Because it is not scalable and the costs increase over time, however, it may not be the best choice for those who anticipate growth occurring within their network.

5. A break in the Backbone can Cause an Entire Network to Collapse:

Because the size of bus topology is limited, a break in the backbone causes the entire network to collapse in some way. Full communication cannot be restored until the issue is repaired or the backbone is completely replaced. That means it cannot be used as a stand-alone solution. A breakage event will cause any computer or peripheral to lose its communication with devices on the other side of the network. Without a second terminator in place, the likely result is network collapse.

6. The Quality of the Data is Placed At-risk on Large Bus Topology Setups:

In addition to the speed issues that occur with a larger network using bus topology, there are data quality issues that must be considered. When data packets collide with one another, the outcome is data loss. Increasing the number of nodes that are present on the network has a direct impact on the quality of communication that occurs. That is why the size of these networks is naturally limited.

7. Bus Termination Issues can Lead to Network Issues:

Communication problems in bus topology can occur when there is improper termination. Terminators are required by ISO 11898 to be at the two extreme ends of the network, which tends to be the controller node and the node which is furthest away from the controller. Even if termination is not appropriately used, certain baud rates can still be successful in their port-to-port communication, which can lead to a lengthy identification process of the network issue.

8. The Computers may Share Data, but they don't Communicate:

Bus topology would be much more efficient if the computers on the network could co-ordinate with one another regarding transmission times. They do not coordinate, however, which means multiple transmissions can occur simultaneously and this creates heavy network traffic with a high potential of data loss. Even if the backbone is extended with repeaters to boost the signal, there is too much simplicity in this network setup to make it an effective system for a large setup.

9. A T-connection Failure Immediately Limits Access:

Because each node is independently connected to the backbone, bus topology doesn't provide a secondary connection resource. If there is a T-connection failure for the connection, then there is no way for data to be shared along the network or to the computer or peripheral that has been separated from the backbone.

It is clear to see that small networks that require a temporary solution benefit from the advantages and disadvantages of bus topography. In theory, there is no limit to the number of nodes that can be added to the backbone of this system, though additional units come with the risks of slow data speeds and quality issues can be encountered. Satellite offices and other small network areas can benefit from a permanent installation of this type as well.

Mesh Network Topology

Mesh network topology is one of the key network architectures in which devices are connected with many redundant interconnections between network nodes such as routers and switches. In a mesh topology, if any cable or node fails, there are many other ways for two nodes to communicate. While ease of troubleshooting and increased reliability are definite pluses, mesh networks are expensive to install because they use a lot of cabling. Often, a mesh topology will be used in conjunction with other topologies (such as Star, Ring and Bus) to form a hybrid topology. Some WAN architecture, such as the Internet, employ mesh routing. Therefore, the Internet allows sites to communicate even during a war.

There are two types of mesh topologies: full mesh and partial mesh.

1. Full mesh topology occurs when every node has a circuit connecting it to every other node in a network. Full mesh is very expensive to implement and yields the greatest amount of redundancy, so in the event that one of those nodes fails, network traffic can be directed to any of the other nodes. Full mesh is usually reserved for backbone networks.

2. With partial mesh, some nodes are organized in a full mesh scheme but others are only connected to one or two in the network. Partial mesh topology is commonly found in peripheral networks connected to a full meshed backbone. It is less expensive to implement and yields less redundancy than full mesh topology.

Ring Network Topology

A ring topology is a network configuration in which device connections create a circular data path. Each networked device is connected to two others, like points on a circle. Together, devices in a ring topology are referred to as a ring network.

In a ring network, packets of data travel from one device to the next until they reach their destination. Most ring topologies allow packets to travel only in one direction, called a unidirectional ring network. Others permit data to move in either direction, called bidirectional.

The major disadvantage of a ring topology is that if any individual connection in the ring is broken, the entire network is affected.

Ring topologies may be used in either LANs (local area networks) or WANs (wide area networks). Depending on the type of network card used in each computer of the ring topology, a coaxial cable or an RJ-45 network cable is used to connect computers together.

Ring Topology

In the past, the ring topology was most commonly used in schools, offices, and smaller buildings where networks were smaller. However, today, the ring topology is seldom used, having been switched to another type of network topology for improved performance, stability, or support.

Advantages of ring topology:

1. All data flows in one direction, reducing the chance of packet collisions.
2. A network server is not needed to control network connectivity between each workstation.
3. Data can transfer between workstations at high speeds.
4. Additional workstations can be added without impacting performance of the network.

Disadvantages of ring topology:

1. All data being transferred over the network must pass through each workstation on the network, which can make it slower than a star topology.

2. The entire network will be impacted if one workstation shuts down.

3. The hardware needed to connect each workstation to the network is more expensive than Ethernet cards and hubs/switches.

Star Network Topology

A star topology is a network topology in which all the network nodes are individually connected to a central switch, hub or computer which acts as a central point of communication to pass on the messages.

In a star topology, there are different nodes called hosts and there is a central point of communication called server or hub. Each host or computer is individually connected to the central hub. We can also term the server as the root and peripheral hosts as the leaves.

In this topology, if nodes want to communicate with a central node, then they pass on the message to the central server and the central server forwards their messages to the different nodes. Thus, they form a topology like the representation of a star.

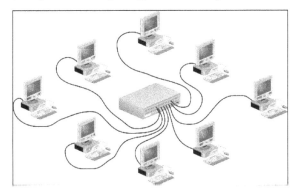

Communication in a Star topology

Let's say all the computers of a floor are connected to a common hub or switch. The switch maintains a CAM table in this case. The CAM table is Content Addressable Memory where hardware addresses of the all the connected devices are stored inside a memory in the switch.

For example, if computer A wants to send a data packet to computer B then computer A will forward the message to the switch. The switch will check the address of the destination computer and forward the message to the same.

In the case of a hub, a hub has no memory of its own. So when computer A sends a message to computer B, then hub announces "Hello all the ports connected to me, you have got a packet for this address. Who of you has this address?" This procedure is called ARP (Address Resolution Protocol) and using this network protocol the hub is able to find the address of the intended machine and hence, it transfers the packet to the destination machine.

Advantages of Star Topology:

- Less damage in case of a single computer failure as it does not affect the entire network.

Disadvantages of Star topology:

- More cables are required to be connected because each computer individually connects to the central server.

- Single points of failure in case the server get down.

Tree Network Topology

A tree topology is a special type of structure in which many connected elements are arranged like the branches of a tree. For example, tree topologies are frequently used to organize the computers in a corporate network, or the information in a database.

In a tree topology, there can be only one connection between any two connected nodes. Because any two nodes can have only one mutual connection, tree topologies form a natural parent and child hierarchy.

Tree Topology in Computer Networking

In computer networks, a tree topology is also known as a star bus topology. It incorporates elements of both a bus topology and a star topology. Below is an example network diagram of a tree topology, in which the central nodes of two star networks are connected to one another.

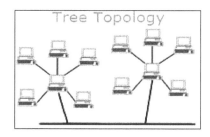

In the picture above, if the main cable or trunk between each of the two star topology networks were to fail, those networks would be unable to communicate with each other. However, computers on the same star topology would still be able to communicate.

Tree Topology in Computer Programming

In computer programming, tree topologies can be used to structure many kinds of data, including a computer program itself.

For example, this is a computer program written in Lisp:

```
(+ 1 2 (if (> p 10) 3 4))
```

This program says "If p is greater than 10, add the numbers 1, 2, and 3. Otherwise, add the numbers 1, 2, and 4." Like all Lisp programs, it has an inherent tree topology structure. If we draw it as a graph, it looks like the tree shown at right. Representing a program this way can be useful because it clearly shows how all the operations and data are connected.

Programs in this kind of structure also have special uses. For instance, genetic programming techniques can evolve new computer programs by exchanging branches between existing programs structured as trees.

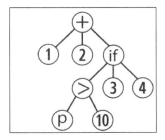

Tree Topology in Binary Trees

A binary tree is a tree topology in which every node has a maximum of two children. The child nodes are labeled as "left child" or "right child." This type of data structure is often used for sorting and searching large amounts of data. In the binary tree shown below, each parent's left child has a value less than the right child.

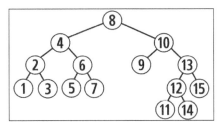

B-trees

A B-tree is a variation of a binary tree that was invented by Rudolf Bayer and Ed Mc-Creight at Boeing Labs in 1971. Its nodes have children that fall within a predefined minimum and maximum, usually between 2 and 7. A B-tree graph might look like the image below.

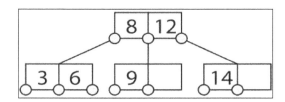

B-trees are "self-balancing," meaning the height of the branches is managed so that they do not get arbitrarily large. Each node contains partitioning "key values" that indicate the values of the children. Their design is optimized for handling very large data files, and for writing data to memory or disk. They are used extensively in database systems like MySQL, PostgreSQL, and Redis, and filesystems such as NTFS, HFS+, and ext4.

Advantages of Tree Topology:

1. It is an extension of Star and bus Topologies, so in networks where these topologies can't be implemented individually for reasons related to scalability, tree topology is the best alternative.

2. Expansion of Network is possible and easy.

3. Here, we divide the whole network into segments (star networks), which can be easily managed and maintained.

4. Error detection and correction is easy.

5. Each segment is provided with dedicated point-to-point wiring to the central hub.

6. If one segment is damaged, other segments are not affected.

Disadvantages of Tree Topology:

1. Because of its basic structure, tree topology, relies heavily on the main bus cable, if it breaks whole network is crippled.

2. As more and more nodes and segments are added, the maintenance becomes difficult.

3. Scalability of the network depends on the type of cable used.

Hybrid Network Topology

The hybrid network topology includes a mix of bus topology, mesh topology, ring topology, star topology, and tree topology. The combination of topologies depends on the need of a company.

For example, if there is a Mesh topology in one office department while a Ring topology in another department, connecting these two with bus topology will result in Hybrid topology. Combination of Star-Ring and Star-Bus networks is the most common examples of the hybrid network topology.

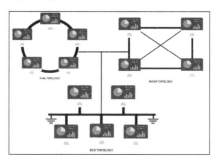

Types of Hybrid Network Topologies

There are different types of hybrid network topologies depending on the basic requirement of an organization but the most commonly used one is Star-Ring and Star-Bus topologies that make up the hybrid.

1. Star-Ring Network Topology:

In a Star-Ring topology, a set of star topologies are connected with a ring topology as the adjoining topology. Joining each star topology to the ring topology is a wired connection.

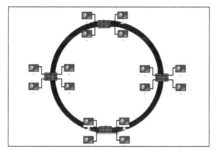

Figure: Demonstrates the Star-Ring topology

Information from a given star topology reaching a connecting node in the main ring topology and the data can flow either in a bidirectional or unidirectional manner. A Uni-directional ring topology can transfer data in either clockwise or counter clockwise direction. Thus, a uni-direction ring topology is a half-duplex, whereas a Bi-directional ring topology can transfer and receive data at the same time. Thus, a bidirectional ring topology can be called a full-duplex network.

2. Star-Bus Network Topology:

A Star-Bus topology is the combination of star network topology and bus network topology, in Star-Bus network a set of star topologies are interconnected by a central bus network. Joining each star topology to the bus topology results the Star-Bus topology.

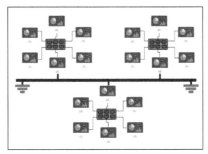

Figure: Demonstrates the Star-Bus topology.

Advantages of Hybrid Network Topology

- Reliable: Unlike other networks, fault detection and troubleshooting is easy in this type of topology. The part in which fault is detected can be isolated from the rest of network and required corrective measures can be taken, without affecting the functioning of rest of the network.

- Scalable: It's easy to increase the size of network by adding new components, without disturbing existing architecture.

- Flexible: Hybrid Network can be designed according to the requirements of the organization and by optimizing the available resources. Special care can be given to nodes where traffic is high as well as where chances of fault are high.

- Effective: Hybrid topology is the combination of two or more topologies, so we can design it in such a way that strengths of constituent topologies are maximized while there weaknesses are neutralized. For example we saw Ring Topology has good data reliability (achieved by use of tokens) and Star topology has high tolerance capability (as each node is not directly connected to other but through central device), so these two can be used effectively in hybrid star-ring topology.

Disadvantages of Hybrid Topology

- Complexity of Design: One of the biggest drawback of hybrid topology is its design. Its not easy to design this type of architecture and its a tough job for designers. Configuration and installation process needs to be very efficient.

- Costly Hub: The hubs used to connect two distinct networks, are very expensive. These hubs are different from usual hubs as they need to be intelligent enough to work with different architectures and should be function even if a part of network is down.

- Costly Infrastructure: As hybrid architectures are usually larger in scale, they require a lot of cables, cooling systems, sophisticate network devices, etc.

References

- What-is-lan-topologies-explain-each-topology, computer-network: ecomputernotes.com, Retrieved 2 February, 2019

- Bus-topologies, computer-network: ecomputernotes.com, Retrieved 12 May, 2019

- Advantages-and-disadvantages-of-bus-topology: vittana.org, Retrieved 17 July, 2019

- Mesh-Network: edrawsoft.com, Retrieved 7 April, 2019

- Ringtopo: computerhope.com, Retrieved 15 July, 2019

- Star-topology-advantages-disadvantages-star-topology: fossbytes.com, Retrieved 16 August, 2019
- Treetopo: computerhope.com, Retrieved 29 January, 2019

- Hybrid-topology: computernetworktopology.com, Retrieved 15 June, 2019

- Hybrid-topologies: top10electrical.blogspot.com, Retrieved 2 March, 2019

4

Computer Networking Devices

Computer networking devices, also called nodes, are devices which originate, route and terminate the data. A few common devices which function as nodes are hubs, bridges and routers. The chapter closely examines these key types of computer networking devices to provide an extensive understanding of the subject.

Network devices are physical devices that are required for communication and interaction between hardware on a computer network. They are units that mediate data in a computer network and are also called network equipment. Units which are the last receiver or generate data are called hosts or data terminal equipment.

Hub

Hub in computer network is used for connecting multiple computers or segments of a LAN. Normally, it is used for Peer to Peer small Home Network. LAN Hub receive data packets (frames) through one port and broadcasts them through all other ports, so that all other computers or other network devices can see all packets.

That is, a LAN configures with Ethernet hub physically falls under the category of a star type topology. In the star topology hub work as a central controller. However, logically, it falls under the category of a bus type topology. Commercially available network hub normally have eight or sixteen ports. Networking hub operate at the physical layer of the OSI model. Traditional Networking hubs support 10 Mbps rated speeds (data rate or bandwidth) only, but Newer technology Dual-speed hub support 100 Mbps. There is no routing table in hub, as you find in router or switch.

Working of Network Hubs

Network hubs are categorized as Layer 1 devices in the Open Systems Interconnection (OSI) reference model. They connect multiple computers together, transmitting data received at one port to all of its other ports without restriction. Hubs operate in half-duplex.

This model raises security and privacy concerns, because traffic could not be safeguarded or quarantined. It also presents a practical issue in terms of traffic management. Devices on a hub function as a network segment and share a collision domain. Thus, when two devices connected to a network hub transmit data simultaneously, the packets will collide, causing network performance problems. This is mitigated in switches or routers, as each port represents a separate collision domain.

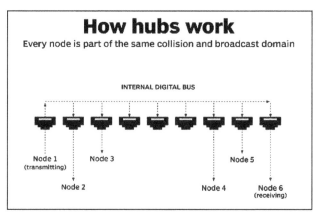

Networking hub

All devices connected to a network hub share all available bandwidth equally. This differs from a switch environment, where each port is allotted a dedicated amount of bandwidth.

Technical Information

Physical Layer Function

A network hub is an unsophisticated device in comparison with a switch. As a *multiport repeater* it works by repeating bits (symbols) received from one of its ports to all other ports. It is aware of physical layer packets, that is it can detect their start (preamble), an idle line (interpacket gap) and sense a collision which it also propagates by sending a jam signal. A hub cannot further examine or manage any of the traffic that comes through it: any packet entering any port is rebroadcast on all other ports. A hub/repeater has no memory to store any data in – a packet must be transmitted while it is received and it is lost when a collision occurs (the sender should detect this and retry the transmission). Due to this, hubs can only run in half duplex mode. Consequently, due to a larger collision domain, packet collisions are more frequent in networks connected using hubs than in networks connected using more sophisticated devices.

Connecting Multiple Hubs

The need for hosts to be able to detect collisions limits the number of hubs and the total size of a network built using hubs (a network built using switches does not have these limitations). For 10 Mbit/s networks built using repeater hubs, the 5-4-3 rule must be followed: up to five segments (four hubs) are allowed between any two end stations. For 10BASE-T networks, up to five segments and four repeaters are allowed between any two hosts. For 100 Mbit/s networks, the limit is reduced to 3 segments (2 Class II hubs) between any two end stations, and even that is only allowed if the hubs are of Class II.

Some hubs have manufacturer specific stack ports allowing them to be combined in a way that allows more hubs than simple chaining through Ethernet cables, but even so, a large Fast Ethernet network is likely to require switches to avoid the chaining limits of hubs.

Additional Functions

Most hubs detect typical problems, such as excessive collisions and jabbering on individual ports, and *partition* the port, disconnecting it from the shared medium. Thus, hub-based twisted-pair Ethernet is generally more robust than coaxial cable-based Ethernet (e.g. 10BASE2), where a misbehaving device can adversely affect the entire collision domain. Even if not partitioned automatically, a hub simplifies troubleshooting because hubs remove the need to troubleshoot faults on a long cable with multiple taps; status lights on the hub can indicate the possible problem source or, as a last resort, devices can be disconnected from a hub one at a time much more easily than from a coaxial cable.

To pass data through the repeater in a usable fashion from one segment to the next, the framing and data rate must be the same on each segment. This means that a repeater cannot connect an 802.3 segment (Ethernet) and an 802.5 segment (Token Ring) or a 10 Mbit/s segment to 100 Mbit/s Ethernet.

Fast Ethernet Classes

100 Mbit/s hubs and repeaters come in two different speed grades: Class I delay the signal for a maximum of 140 bit times (enabling translation/recoding between 100BASE-TX, 100BASE-FX and 100BASE-T4) and Class II hubs delay the signal for a maximum of 92 bit times (enabling installation of two hubs in a single collision domain).

Dual-speed Hub

In the early days of Fast Ethernet, Ethernet switches were relatively expensive devices. Hubs suffered from the problem that if there were any 10BASE-T devices connected then the whole network needed to run at 10 Mbit/s. Therefore, a compromise between a hub and a switch was developed, known as a dual-speed hub. These devices make use of an internal two-port switch, bridging the 10 Mbit/s and 100 Mbit/s segments. When a network device becomes active on any of the physical ports, the device attaches it to either the 10 Mbit/s segment or the 100 Mbit/s segment, as appropriate. This obviated the need for an all-or-nothing migration to Fast Ethernet networks. These devices are considered hubs because the traffic between devices connected at the same speed is not switched.

Gigabit Ethernet Hub

Repeater hubs have been defined for Gigabit Ethernet but commercial products have failed to appear due to the industry's transition to switching.

Active Hub

Active hub is a hub that includes a signal amplifier or concentrator. It is also known as multi-port repeater. An active hub works on the physical layer. Active hubs can regenerate signals. You can also define in simple ways, A central connecting device in a network that regenerates signals on the output side to keep the signal strong. Also called a "multiport repeater". Contrast with passive hub and intelligent hub.

Uses of Active Hub

- When a switch is accessible for end users to make connections, e.g. In a conference room, an inexperienced or careless user can bring down the network by connecting two ports together, causing a switching loop. This can be prevented by using a hub, where a loop will break other users on the hub, but not the rest of the network (more precisely, it will break the current collision domain up to the next switch/bridge port). This hazard can also be avoided by using switches that can detect and deal with loops, for example by implementing the spanning tree protocol.

- A hub with an AUI port can be used to connect to a 10BASE5 network.

- For inserting a protocol analyzer into a network connection, a hub is an alternative to a network tap or port mirroring.

- A hub with a 10BASE2 port can be used to connect devices that only support 10BASE2 to a modern network.

Functions of Active Hub

Devices can be disconnected from a hub one at a time much more easily than from a coaxial cable. Hub-based twisted-pair Ethernet is generally more robust than coaxial cable-based Ethernet , where a misbehaving device can adversely affect the entire collision domain. Even if not partitioned automatically, a hub simplifies troubleshooting because hubs remove the need to troubleshoot faults on a long cable with multiple taps; status lights on the hub can indicate the possible problem source or, as a last resort. To pass data through the repeater in a usable fashion from one segment to the next, the framing and data rate must be the same on each segment.

Passive Hub

A central connecting device in a network that joins wires from several stations in a star configuration. It does not provide any processing or regeneration of signals. Contrast with active hub and intelligent hub.

Physical networks build by these hubs called node to node contact between physical networks. Assume an example of a punch-down block that is made of simple plastic, un-powered box used to plug network cables into. These are called repeater who can give support to connect multi devices but cannot use electricity for this purpose.

Intelligent Hub

An intelligent hub however, adds extra features to an active hub that is crucial to the success of businesses. On account of their low cost and cost effective solutions, hubs are significant to the needs of the contemporary businesses.

Intelligent hub is another form of hub that is increasingly being used. An advanced version that comprises the best of both active and passive hubs, it provides with the ability to manage the network from one central location. With the help of an intelligent hub, one can easily identify, diagnose problems and even come up with remedial solutions. This troubleshooting of a large enterprise scale network is possible with the help of an intelligent hub.

In addition to, an intelligent hub can offer flexible transmission rates to various devices. With standard transmission rates of 10, 16 and 100Mbps to desktop systems using popular technologies like Ethernet, FDDI or Token Ring, an intelligent hub easily incorporates the better of the other two hubs in terms of features and benefits. No wonder, hubs have become an integral part of the current networking systems.

Moreover, an intelligent hub also provides with a boost in the flexibility in configuration and management of the networks. With support for the technologies like terminal servers, routers and switches, an intelligent hub today provides with the best of solutions to the current needs of the home and business computing.

In the physical form, a hub is a small rectangular box usually made of plastic. A hub that joins multiple computers and networks receives its power from an ordinary wall outlet and forms a single network segment. Hub as a facility provides for a direct communication channel which all computers on the same network can access to and use the system accordingly.

A networking hub that provides direct accessibility to all computers on the system comprises of a series of ports. Each of such ports accepts a network cable and hence provide for the accessibility of all the linked computers. A reasonably advanced IT infrastructure, literacy, multi-language capabilities, professionals with communication skills and creativity, credibility and rapport with the user community and series of ports are important components that form part of hubs.

One has to understand the usefulness of a hub in the context of his own requirements. Factors like the number of ports that a hub features, rating of the bandwidth, the manufacturer and its market credibility are important to determine if the hub is right for one. For instance, a simple Large Area Network (LAN) would require a four port hub while a five port hub if provided with an unlinking facility, offers a positive compromise between up-front cost and future extensibility. On the whole, one has to go for a hub that matches his needs perfectly and one that can be upgraded depending upon future needs.

Bridge

A computer networking device which creates a single associated network by multiple communication networks known as computer Network Bridge.

Bridges are connection devices between networks that operate in the data link layer of the OSI model. It means that bridges have more functionality (in terms of connection) than Layer 1 devices, such as repeaters and hubs. Bridges are used to segment networks that have grown to a point where data traffic through the physical environment of the network slows down the global transfer of information.

Like repeaters, bridges are used to connect similar LANs together, for example, Ethernet-to-Ethernet and operate at the bottom two layers of the OSI model, i.e. physical layer and data link layer. As it operates on second layer of the OSI model,' it relays only necessary data to other signals. MAC addresses (physical addresses) are used to determine whether data is necessary or not.

Bridges (which usually include bridge hardware and some bridge operating system software) can examine MAC addresses (also called hardware addresses; these recorded in the NIC of each computer on the network) in each data packet that circulates through the segments of the network that connects the bridge. By knowing which MAC addresses reside in each of the segments of the network, the bridge can prevent data traffic from a specific segment from passing to another segment of the network that also connected to the bridge.

It passes information from one LAN segment to another based on the destination address of the packet. In other words, when a bridge receives data through one of its ports, it checks the data for a MAC address. If this address matches that of the node connected to other port, the bridge sends this data through this port. This action is called forwarding. If the address does not match with any node connected to other port, the bridge discards it. This action is called filtering. Unlike repeaters, bridges have buffers to store and forward packets in the event that the destination link is congested with traffic.

Therefore, bridges offer a segmentation strategy to recover and preserve bandwidth in a broad homogeneous network (by homogeneous, we mean a network that only uses a defined network architecture, such as Ethernet). For example, a broad network can be divided into three distinct segments using a bridge.

Bridges divide broad networks into segments to keep data traffic between segments isolated.

Although installing a bridge between networks may seem the definitive answer to maximize the adequate performance of the network, the truth is that it has some disadvantages. The bridges send the broadcast packets from the different nodes of the network to all segments of the network (such as NETBIOS and other systems). Also, in those cases in which the bridge cannot resolve a MAC address for a particular segment of the network, it sends the packets to all the segments it connects.

Transparent Bridges Build a Routing Table

Transparent bridges are used in Ethernet networks to forward packets (and isolate those that are part of the local segment traffic) in the network according to a routing table. The bridge constructs this table by creating samples of the packets received at its different ports until a complete list of the MAC addresses of the network and the particular network segment in which they located obtained.

Bridges with the Routing of Origin

Bridges with source routing in Token Ring networks do not offer as many features as transparent bridges in Ethernet networks. Bridges with source routing receive packets that specify the route that those packets should follow. The bridge has to read the address that each package includes to re-issue it to the corresponding segment.

The main advantage of bridge over repeater is that it has filtering action. If any noise on Ethernet occurs because of collision or disturbance in electrical signal, the bridge will consider it as an incorrectly formed frame and win not forward to the segment connected to other port of the bridge. Note that bridge can relay broadcast packets and packets with unknown destination.

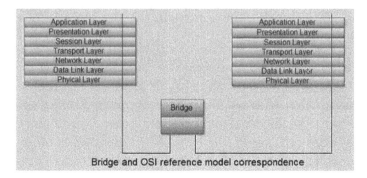

Bridge and OSI reference model correspondence

So far, we have seen that at the maximum four repeaters can be used to connect multiple Ethernet segments. However, if a bridge is provided between repeaters, this limit of four is increased. The maximum number of bridges is not specifically limited.

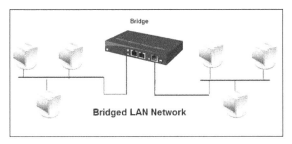

From architecture point of view bridges are protocol independent devices and are very simple. They do not perform complex processes on the data packets traveling through them such as the evaluation of the network as a whole in order to make end-to-end routing decisions. They simply read the destination address of the incoming data packet and forward it along its way to the next link. Therefore, bridges are Inexpensive and fast. There are bridges called cascading bridges, and are used to support multiple LANs connected by multiple media.

Dissimilar LANs such as Ethernet-to-token ring can also be connected with the help of bridge known as encapsulating bridge. The function of encapsulating bridge is also very simple. It encapsulates the originating LAN data along with control information of the end user LAN. Bridges with routing function between LANs are also available.

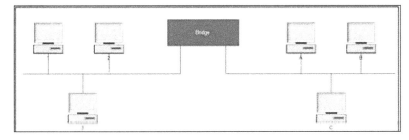

Computer 1 wishes to talk to computer 3 on the same network. The packet sent by computer 1 will contain the physical address of computer 3 that will also be received by the bridge device connecting the two LAN segments. The bridge will read the physical address contained in the packet and observe that this address belongs to the computer on the same LAN segment. Hence, bridge will filter this packet and will not allow it to be transmitted on other side of the network. In case computer 1 wishes to talk with computer C on other segment, the bridge will know from its table of addresses that this address belongs to the computer attached to other segment of the network. In this case this will be forwarded to the other segment of the LAN. The bridge learns location of computers attached the network by watching frames. Note that case of broadcast and multicast packets, bridge forwards these packets to all computers attached to the segment on both sides.

Media Access Control (MAC) Bridge

This is used to connect dissimilar LANs such as Ethernet -to-token ring using encapsulation or translation. This bridge translates the original' packet format from the requesting LAN segment by encapsulating or enveloping with control data specific to the protocol of the destination LAN segment.

Address Table

As explained above, each bridge should have an address table that indicates the location of different computers or nodes on the segments of LAN. More specifically, it indicates the connection between nodes and ports. When a bridge is booted first time, this table is found to be blank. Now, this question arises how this table is filled with appropriate addresses of different nodes attached to ports. Most of the bridges are called adaptive or self-leaning bridges because they learn the location of the node and associated port themselves and make a list of nodes attached to each segment.

When a bridge receives a data packet from a computer, it first copies the physical address of that computer contained in the packet into its list. Afterward, bridge determines whether this packet should be forwarded or not. In other words, the bridge learns the location of the computer on the network as soon as the computer on the network sends some packet.

If a computer does not send a packet, the bridge will never be able to determine its position and unnecessarily forward the packet on network. Fortunately, this cannot happen because a computer with network software attached to a network transmits at least one frame when the system first boots. Furthermore, computer communication being bidirectional, there is always an acknowledgement for each received packets.

Bridge Protocols

Bridge protocols include spanning tree, source routing protocol, and source routing transparent.

Spanning Tree Protocol (STP) Bridge

This is also known as adaptive or self-learning bridges and is defined in IEEE 802.1 standards. It has already been explained in the above section. Ideally, in bridged network, the network tree of the bridge provides only one span (link) for each LAN-to-LAN connection and therefore, no network with bridges can form a loop. Sometimes, looping can occur.

A broadcast data packet sent by the computer attached on segment 1can reach to all computers attached on segment 2 and 3 without a connection between segment 1 and 3 .Sometimes, the bridge connection between segment 1and 3 or like is provided to give the network more redundancy. Now, in this case the same broadcast packet sent by the segment 1 will reach to segment 3 by two routes i.e. from segment 1 to 2 to 3 and another by segment 1 to 3. In this manner the computers on segment 3 will receive duplicate packets. In case of large networks some segments may receive many packets and thus cause looping.

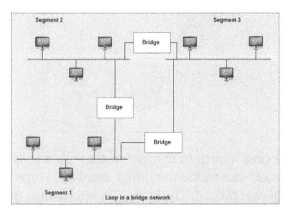

A loop, therefore, can cause a broadcast packet or a packet with an unknown destination to circulate through it, thus rendering the network inoperable. This condition is avoided by making some bridges not to forward frames. An algorithm known as distributed spanning tree (DST) accomplishes this task. This algorithm decides which bridge should forward the packets in the network. Under this scheme bridges exchange a control message known as a hello message to select a single transmission route. Remaining bridges maintain a standby position and provide alternate path in case of the same bridge fails in the selected transmission path. Bridge connecting segment 1 and 3 will be active only if the bridge connecting segment 2 and 3 fails otherwise it acts as a standby bridge for network. In other words, bridges that support the spanning tree algorithm have the ability to automatically reconfigure themselves for alternate paths if a network segment fails, thereby improving overall reliability.

IBM Source Routing Protocol (SRP) Bridge

These are programmed with specific routes for each packet based on considerations such as the physical location of the nodes, and the number of bridges involved.

Source Routing Transparent (SRT)

It is defined in theIEEE802.1 standard. It is effectively a combination of STP and SRP. The SRT router can connect LANs by either method, as programmed.

Translational Bridge

A translational bridge can forward datalink layer frames between local area networks (LANs) which utilize different network protocols. A translational bridge can be used to

connect such as Ethernet to FDDI, or Ethernet to Token Ring, or Ethernet on unshielded twisted pair (UTP) to coax, and between copper wiring, and fiber-optic cable.

The diagram here shows a token ring network and an ethernet network using a translational bridge.

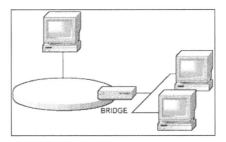

When the host on the ring wishes to communicate with any host on the ethernet, it
transmits the token ring frame which the bridge receives, strips of token ring headers,
and reconstructs in ethernet format. The bridge then transmits the frame to the host on
the destination segment.

Transparent Bridging

Transparent bridging is the augmentation of Ethernet allowing partial segmentation of
the network into two or more collision domains. The IEEE-defined transparent bridging is an industry standard in 802.1D. Transparent bridges improve network performance by allowing devices in the same segmented collision domain to communicate
without that traffic unnecessarily being forwarded to the other collision domain.

Transparent bridges are the predominant bridge type for Ethernet, and it is important
to understand Ethernet switches essentially act as multiport transparent bridges.

Figure shows a transparent bridge supporting Ethernet segments or collision domains.
If Host1 and Host2 are talking to each other, their conversation will use bandwidth only
on their side of the bridge. This allows Host4 and Host5 to also hold a conversation. If
all devices were in the same collision domain, only one conversation would be possible.

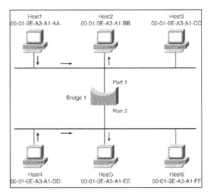

Figure: Host1 to Host2 and Host4 to Host5

However, if Host1 wants to talk to Host4, as shown in figure, the bandwidth will be utilized on both sides of the bridge, allowing only the one conversation.

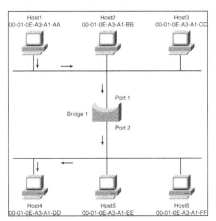

Figure: Host1 to Host4

How does the transparent bridge determine which users are connected to which side of the bridge? Well, transparent bridging has a little more "under the hood" than the example illustrates.

The 802.1D specification for transparent bridging defines five unique processes as part of transparent bridging:

- Learning

- Flooding

- Filtering

- Forwarding

- Aging.

Learning

Learning is the process of obtaining the MAC address of devices. When a bridge is first turned on, it has no entries in its bridge table. As traffic passes through the bridge, the sender's MAC addresses are stored in a table along with the associated port on which the traffic was received. This table is often called a bridge table, MAC table, or content addressable memory (CAM) table.

Table shows a listing of all the devices on the sample network in figure.

Sample Bridge Table		
Hosts	Port 1	Port 2
Host1/ 00-01-0E-A3-A1-AA	X	

Sample Bridge Table		
Host2/ 00-01-0E-A3-A1-BB	X	
Host3/ 00-01-0E-A3-A1-CC	X	
Host4/ 00-01-0E-A3-A1-DD		X
Host5/ 00-01-0E-A3-A1-EE		X
Host6/ 00-01-0E-A3-A1-FF		X

Flooding

When a bridge does not have an entry in its bridge table for a specific address, it must transparently pass the traffic through all its ports except the source port. This is known as flooding. The source port is not "flooded" because the original traffic came in on this port and already exists on that segment. Flooding allows the bridge to learn, as well as stay transparent to the rest of the network, because no traffic is lost while the bridge is learning. Figure shows how the bridge forwards the traffic on all its ports.

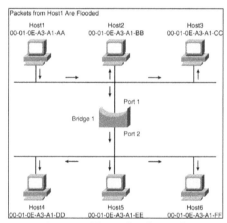

Figure: Bridge1 Floods Traffic

Filtering

After the bridge learns the MAC address and associated port of the devices to which it is connected, the benefits of transparent bridging can be seen by way of filtering. Filtering occurs when the source and destination are on the same side (same bridge port) of the bridge. In Figure, filtering occurs each time Host1 and Host2 talk, as well as when Host4 and Host5 talk.

Forwarding

Forwarding is simply passing traffic from a known device located on one bridge port to another known device located on a different bridge port. Again, referring back to Figure, after the initial devices were learned, forwarding occurs when Host1 and Host4 talk.

Aging

In addition to the MAC address and the associated port, a bridge also records the time that the device was learned. Aging of learned MAC addresses allows the bridge to adapt to moves, adds, and changes of devices to the network. After a device is learned, the bridge starts an aging timer. Each time the bridge forwards or filters a frame from a device, it restarts that device's timer. If the bridge doesn't hear from a device in a preset period of time, the aging timer expires and the bridge removes the device from its table.

Aging ensures that the bridge tracks only active systems, and ensures that the MAC address table does not consume too much system memory.

Shortest Path Bridging

Shortest path bridging (SPB or 802.1aq) is the IEEE's specification for enabling multipath routing in the data center.

Shortest path bridging is similar conceptually to its IETF counterpart, Transparent Interconnection of Lots of Links (TRILL) but differs from TRILL in its use of tree structures. Another difference between TRILL and SPB is that SPB routes are symmetric, meaning that the route from one point to another is the same going back. This allows shortest path bridging to use some of the management and monitoring technologies already in use, such as loopback and traceroute.

Shortest path bridging, which is undergoing IEEE's standardization process, is meant to replace the spanning tree protocol (STP). STP was created to prevent bridge loops by allowing only one path between network switches or ports. When a network segment goes down, an alternate path is chosen and this process can cause unacceptable delays in a data center network. Like TRILL, shortest path bridging is designed to address this problem by applying the Layer 3 routing protocol to Layer 2 devices. This essentially allows Layer 2 devices to route Ethernet frames. Proponents of shortest path bridging claim that by getting rid of STP and freeing up more Layer 2 paths, enterprises will be better able to migrate virtual machines (VMs) across the data center network. There will also be more bandwidth available for intensive applications like real-time communications (RTC) and for the transport of storage traffic across the Ethernet network with Fibre Channel over Ethernet (FCoE) and iSCSI.

Benefits

Shortest Path Bridging - VID (SPBV) and Shortest Path Bridging - MAC (SPBM) is two operating modes of 802.1aq, and are described in more detail below. Both inherit key benefits of link state routing:

- The ability to use all available physical connectivity, because loop avoidance uses a Control Plane with a global view of network topology.

- Fast restoration of connectivity after failure, again because of Link State routing's global view of network topology.

- Under failure, the property that only directly affected traffic is impacted during restoration; all unaffected traffic just continues.

- Rapid restoration of broadcast and multicast connectivity, because IS-IS floods all of the required information in the SPB extensions to IS-IS, thereby allowing unicast and multicast connectivity to be installed in parallel, with no need for a second phase signaling process to run over the converged unicast topology to compute and install multicast trees.

Virtualisation is becoming an increasingly important aspect of a number of key applications, in both carrier and enterprise space, and SPBM, with its MAC-in-MAC datapath providing complete separation between client and server layers, is uniquely suitable for these.

"Data Centre virtualisation" articulates the desire to flexibly and efficiently harness available compute resources in a way that may rapidly be modified to respond to varying application demands, without the need to dedicate physical resources to a specific application. One aspect of this is server virtualisation. The other is connectivity virtualisation, because a physically distributed set of server resources must be attached to a single IP subnet, and modifiable in an operationally simple and robust way. SPBM delivers this; because of its client-server model, it offers a perfect emulation of a transparent Ethernet LAN segment, which is the IP subnet seen at layer 3. A key component of how it does this is implementing VLANs with scoped multicast trees, which means no egress discard of broadcast/unknown traffic, a feature common to approaches that use a small number of shared trees, hence the network does not simply degrade with size as the percentage of frames discarded goes up. It also supports "single touch" provisioning, so that configuration is simple and robust; the port of a virtual server must simply be bound locally to the SPBM I-SID identifying the LAN segment, after which IS-IS for SPB floods this binding, and all nodes that need to install forwarding state to implement the LAN segment do so automatically.

The carrier-space equivalent of this application is the delivery of Ethernet VPN services to Enterprises over common carrier infrastructure. The required attributes are fundamentally the same; complete transparency for customer Ethernet services (both point-to-point and LAN), and complete isolation between one customer's traffic and that of all other customers. The multiple virtual LAN segment model provides this, and the single-touch provisioning model eases carrier operations. Furthermore, the MAC-in-MAC data path allows the carrier to deploy the "best in class" Ethernet OAM suit (IEEE 802.1ag, etc.), entirely transparently and independently from any OAM which a customer may choose to run.

A further consequence of SPBM's transparency in both dataplane and control plane is that it provides a perfect, "no compromise" delivery of the complete MEF 6.1 service set. This includes not only E-LINE and E-LAN constructs, by also E-TREE (hub-and-spoke) connectivity. This latter is clearly very relevant to enterprise customers of carrier VPN/MPLS services which have this network structure internally. It also provides the carrier with the toolkit to support geo-redundant broadband backhaul; in this applications, many DSLAMs or other access equipment's must be backhauled to multiple Broadband Remote Access Server (BRAS) sites, with application-determined binding of sessions to a BRAS. However, DSLAMs must not be allowed to communicate with each other, because carriers then lose the ability to control peer-to-peer connectivity. MEF E-TREE does just this, and further provides an efficient multicast fabric for the distribution of IP TV.

SPBM offers both the ideal multicast replication model, where packets are replicated only at fork points in the shortest path tree that connects members, and also the less state intensive head end replication model where in essence serial unicast packets are sent to all other members along the same shortest path first tree. These two models are selected by specifying properties of the service at the edge which affect the transit node decisions on multicast state installation. This allows for a trade-off to be made between optimum transit replication points (with their larger state costs) v.s. reduced core state (but much more traffic) of the head end replication model. These selections can be different for different members of the same Individual Service ID (I-SID) allowing different trade-offs to be made for different members.

This is a quick way to understand what SPBM is doing on the scale of the entire network. Figure shows how a 7-member E-LAN is created from the edge membership information and the deterministic distributed calculation of per source, per service trees with transit replication. Head end replication is not shown as it is trivial and simply uses the existing unicast FIBs to forward copies serially to the known other receivers.

Operations and Management

802.1aq builds on all existing Ethernet Operations, administration and management (OA&M). Since 802.1aq ensures that its unicast and multicast packets for a given virtual lan (VLAN) follow the same forward and reverse path and use completely standard 802 encapsulations, all of the methods of 802.1ag and Y.1731 operate unchanged on an 802.1aq network.

High Level

802.1aq is the Institute of Electrical and Electronics Engineers (IEEE) sanctioned link state Ethernet control plane for all IEEE VLANs covered in IEEE 802.1Q. Shortest Path Bridging virtual local area network identifier (VLAN ID) or Shortest Path Bridging VID (SPBV) provides capability that is backwards compatible with spanning tree technologies. Shortest Path Bridging Media Access Control (MAC) or (SPBM), (previously known as Provider Backbone Bridge PBB) provides additional values which capitalize on Provider Backbone Bridge (PBB) capabilities. SPB (the generic term for both) combines an Ethernet data path (either IEEE 802.1Q in the case of SPBV, or Provider Backbone Bridges (PBBs) IEEE 802.1ah in the case of SPBM) with an IS-IS link state control protocol running between Shortest Path bridges (network-to-network interface (NNI) links). The link state protocol is used to discover and advertise the network topology and compute shortest path trees (SPT) from all bridges in the SPT Region.

In SPBM, the Backbone MAC (B-MAC) addresses of the participating nodes and also the service membership information for interfaces to non-participating devices (user network interface (UNI) ports) is distributed. Topology data is then input to a calculation engine which computes symmetric shortest path trees based on minimum cost from each participating node to all other participating nodes. In SPBV these trees provide a shortest path tree where individual MAC address can be learned and Group Address membership can be distributed. In SPBM the shortest path trees are then used to populate forwarding tables for each participating node's individual B-MAC addresses and for Group addresses; Group multicast trees are sub trees of the default shortest path tree formed by (Source, Group) pairing. Depending on the topology several different equal cost multi path trees are possible and SPB supports multiple algorithms per IS-IS instance.

In SPB as with other link state based protocols, the computations are done in a distributed fashion. Each node computes the Ethernet compliant forwarding behavior independently based on a normally synchronized common view of the network (at scales of about 1000 nodes or less) and the service attachment points (user network interface (UNI) ports). Ethernet filtering Database (or forwarding) tables are populated locally to independently and deterministically implement its portion of the network forwarding behavior.

The two different flavors of data path give rise to two slightly different versions of this protocol. One (SPBM) is intended where complete isolation of many separate instances of client LANs and their associated device MAC addresses is desired, and it therefore uses a full encapsulation (MAC-in-MAC a.k.a. IEEE 802.1ah). The other (SPBV) is intended where such isolation of client device MAC addresses is not necessary, and it reuses only the existing VLAN tag a.k.a. IEEE 802.1Q on participating network-to-network interface (NNI) links.

Chronologically SPBV came first, with the project originally being conceived to address scalability and convergence of MSTP.

At the time the specification of Provider Backbone bridging was progressing and it became apparent that leveraging both the PBB data plane and a link state control plane would significantly extend Ethernet's capabilities and applications. Provider Link State Bridging (PLSB) was a strawman proposal brought to the IEEE 802.1aq Shortest Path Bridging Working Group, in order to provide a concrete example of such a system. As

IEEE 802.1aq standardization has progressed, some of the detailed mechanisms proposed by PLSB have been replaced by functional equivalents, but all of the key concepts embodied in PLSB are being carried forward into the standard.

The two flavors (SPBV and SPBM) will be described separately although the differences are almost entirely in the data plane.

Shortest Path Bridging-VID

Shortest Path bridging enables shortest path trees for VLAN Bridges all IEEE 802.1 data planes and SPB is the term used in general. Recently there has been a lot of focus on SPBM as explained due to its ability to control the new PBB data plane and leverage certain capabilities such as removing the need to do B-MAC learning and automatically creating individual (unicast) and group (multicast) Trees. SPBV was actually the original project that endeavored to enable Ethernet VLANs to better utilize mesh networks.

A primary feature of Shortest Path bridging is the ability to use Link State IS-IS to learn network topology. In SPBV the mechanism used to identify the tree is to use a different Shortest Path VLAN ID (VID) for each source bridge. The IS-IS topology is leveraged both to allocate unique SPVIDs and to enable shortest path forwarding for individual and group addresses. Originally targeted for small low configuration networks SPB grew into a larger project encompassing the latest provider control plane for SPBV and harmonizing the concepts of Ethernet data plane. Proponents of SPB believe that Ethernet can leverage link state and maintain the attributes that have made Ethernet one of the most encompassing data plane transport technologies. When we refer to Ethernet it is the layer 2 frame format defined by IEEE 802.3 and IEEE 802.1. Ethernet VLAN bridging IEEE 802.1Q is the frame forwarding paradigm that fully supports higher level protocols such as IP.

SPB defines a shortest path Region which is the boundary of the shortest path topology and the rest of the VLAN topology (which may be any number of legacy bridges.) SPB operates by learning the SPB capable bridges and growing the Region to include the SPB capable bridges that have the same Base VID and MSTID configuration digest (Allocation of VIDs for SPB purposes).

SPBV builds shortest path trees that support Loop Prevention and optionally support loop mitigation on the SPVID. SPBV still allows learning of Ethernet MAC addresses but it can distribute multicast address that can be used to prune the shortest path trees according to the multicast membership either through Multiple MAC Registration Protocol (MMRP) or directly using IS-IS distribution of multicast membership.

SPBV builds shortest path trees but also interworks with legacy bridges running Rapid Spanning Tree Protocol and Multiple Spanning Tree Protocol. SPBV uses techniques from MSTP Regions to interwork with non-SPT regions behaving logically as a large distributed bridge as viewed from outside the region.

SPBV supports shortest path trees but SPBV also builds a spanning tree which is computed from the link state database and uses the Base VID. This means that SPBV can use this traditional spanning tree for computation of the Common and Internal Spanning Tree (CIST). The CIST is the default tree used to interwork with other legacy bridges. It also serves as a fall back spanning tree if there are configuration problems with SPBV.

SPBV has been designed to manage a moderate number of bridges. SPBV differs from SPBM in that MAC addresses are learned on all bridges that lie on the shortest path and a shared VLAN learning is used since destination MACs may be associated with multiple SPVIDs. SPBV learns all MACs it forwards even outside the SPBV region.

Shortest Path Bridging-MAC

SPBM reuses the PBB data plane which does not require that the Backbone Core Bridges (BCB) learn encapsulated client addresses. At the edge of the network the C-MAC (client) addresses are learned. SPBM is very similar to PLSB (Provider Link State Bridging) using the same data and control planes but the format and contents of the control messages in PLSB are not compatible.

Individual MAC frames (unicast traffic) from an Ethernet attached device that are received at the SPBM edge are encapsulated in a PBB (mac-in-mac) IEEE 802.1ah header and then traverse the IEEE 802.1aq network unchanged until they are stripped of the encapsulation as they egress back to the non-participating attached network at the far side of the participating network.

Ethernet destination addresses (from UNI port attached devices) perform learning over the logical LAN and are forwarded to the appropriate participating B-MAC address to reach the far end Ethernet destination. In this manner Ethernet MAC addresses are never looked up in the core of an IEEE 802.1aq network. When comparing SPBM to PBB, the behavior is almost identical to a PBB IEEE 802.1ah network. PBB does not specify how B-MAC addresses are learned and PBB may use a spanning tree to control the B-VLAN. In SPBM the main difference is that B-MAC address are distributed or computed in the control plane, eliminating the B-MAC learning in PBB. Also SPBM ensures that the route followed is shortest path tree.

The forward and reverse paths used for unicast and multicast traffic in an IEEE 802.1aq network are symmetric. This symmetry permits the normal Ethernet Continuity Fault Messages (CFM) IEEE 802.1ag to operate unchanged for SPBV and SPBM and has desirable properties with respect to time distribution protocols such as Precision Time Protocol (PTP Version 2). Also existing Ethernet loop prevention is augmented by loop mitigation to provide fast data plane convergence.

Group address and unknown destination individual frames are optimally transmitted to only members of the same Ethernet service. IEEE 802.1aq supports the creation of thousands of logical Ethernet services in the form of E-LINE, E-LAN or E-TREE constructs which are formed between non participating logical ports of the IEEE 802.1aq network. These group address packets are encapsulated with a PBB header which indicates the source participating address in the SA while the DA indicates the locally significant group address this frame should be forwarded on and which source bridge originated the frame. The IEEE 802.1aq multicast forwarding tables are created based on computations such that every bridge which is on the shortest path between a pair of bridges which are members of the same service group will create proper forwarding database (FDB) state to forward or replicate frames it receives to that members of that service group. Since the group address computation produce shortest path trees, there is only ever one copy of a multicast packet on any given link. Since only bridges on a shortest path between participating logical ports create forwarding database (FDB) state the multicast makes the efficient use of network resources.

The actual group address forwarding operation operates more or less identically to classical Ethernet, the backbone destination address (B-DA)+ backbone VLAN identifier (B-VID) combination are looked up to find the egress set of next hops. The only difference compared with classical Ethernet is that reverse learning is disabled for participating bridge backbone media access control (B-MAC) addresses and is replaced with an ingress check and discard (when the frame arrives on an incoming interface from an unexpected source). Learning is however implemented at the edges of the SPBM multicast tree to learn the B-MAC to MAC address relationship for correct individual frame encapsulation in the reverse direction (as packets arrive over the Interface).

Properly implemented an IEEE 802.1aq network can support up to 1000 participating bridges and provide tens of thousands of layer 2 E-LAN services to Ethernet devices. This can be done by simply configuring the ports facing the Ethernet devices to indicate they are members of a given service. As new members come and go, the IS-IS protocol will advertise the I-SID membership changes and the computations will grow or shrink the trees in the participating node network as necessary to maintain the efficient multicast property for that service.

IEEE 802.1aq has the property that only the point of attachment of a service needs configuration when a new attachment point comes or goes. The trees produced by the computations will automatically be extended or pruned as necessary to maintain connectivity. In some existing implementations this property is used to automatically (as opposed to through configuration) add or remove attachment points for dual-homed technologies such as rings to maintain optimum packet flow between a non-participating ring protocol and the IEEE 802.1aq network by activating a secondary attachment point and deactivating a primary attachment point.

Failure Recovery

Failure recovery is as per normal IS-IS with the link failure being advertised and new computations being performed, resulting in new FDB tables. Since no Ethernet addresses are advertised or known by this protocol, there is no re-learning required by the SPBM core and its learned encapsulations are unaffected by a transit node or link failure.

Fast link failure detection may be performed using IEEE 802.1ag Continuity Check Messages (CCMs) which test link status and report a failure to the IS-IS protocol. This allows much faster failure detection than is possible using the IS-IS hello message loss mechanisms.

Both SPBV and SPBM inherit the rapid convergence of a link state control plane. A special attribute of SPBM is its ability to rebuild multicast trees in a similar time to unicast convergence, because it substitutes computation for signaling. When an SPBM bridge has performed the computations on a topology database, it knows whether it is on the shortest path between a root and one or more leaves of the SPT and can install state accordingly. Convergence is not gated by incremental discovery of a bridge's place on a multicast tree by the use of separate signaling transactions. However, SPBM on a node does not operate completely independently of its peers, and enforces agreement on the current network topology with its peers. This very efficient mechanism uses exchange of a single digest of link state covering the entire network view, and does not need agreement on each path to each root individually. The result is that the volume of messaging exchanged to converge the network is in proportion to the incremental change in topology and not the number of multicast trees in the network. A simple link event that may change many trees is communicated by signaling the link event only; the consequent tree construction is performed by local computation at each node. The addition of a single service access point to a service instance involves only the announcement of the I-SID, regardless of the number of trees. Similarly the removal of a bridge, which might involve the rebuilding of hundreds to thousands of trees, is signaled only with a few link state updates.

Commercial offerings will likely offer SPB over multi-chassis lag. In this environment multiple switch chassis appear as a single switch to the SPB control plane, and multiple links between pairs of chassis appear as an aggregate link. In this context a single link or node failure is not seen by the control plane and is handled locally resulting in sub 50ms recovery times.

Equal Cost Multi Tree

Sixteen equal cost multi tree (ECMT) paths are initially defined however there are many more possible. ECMT in an IEEE 802.1aq network is more predictable than with internet protocol (IP) or multiprotocol label switching (MPLS) because of symmetry between the forward and reverse paths. The choice as to which ECMT path will be used is therefore an operator assigned head end decision while it is a local / hashing decision with IP/MPLS.

IEEE 802.1aq, when faced with a choice between two equal link cost paths, uses the following logic for its first ECMT tie breaking algorithm: first, if one path is shorter than the other in terms of hops, the shorter path is chosen, otherwise, the path with the minimum Bridge Identifier { BridgePriority concatenated with (IS-IS SysID) } is chosen. Other ECMT algorithms are created by simply using known permutations of the BridgePriority||SysIds. For example, the second defined ECMT algorithm uses the path with the minimum of the inverse of the BridgeIdentifier and can be thought of as taking the path with the maximum node identifier. For SPBM, each permutation is instantiated as a distinct B-VID. The upper limit of multipath permutations is gated by the number of B-VIDs delegated to 802.1aq operation, a maximum of 4094, although the number of useful path permutations would only require a fraction of the available B-VID space. Fourteen additional ECMT algorithms are defined with different bit masks applied to the BridgeIdentifiers. Since the BridgeIdentifier includes a priority field, it is possible to adjust the ECMT behavior by changing the BridgePriority up or down.

A service is assigned to a given ECMT B-VID at the edge of the network by configuration. As a result, non-participating packets associated with that service are encapsulated with the VID associated with the desired ECMT end to end path. All individual and group address traffic associated with this service will therefore use the proper ECMT B-VID and be carried symmetrically end to end on the proper equal cost multi path. Essentially the operator decides which services go in which ECMT paths, unlike a hashing solution used in other systems such as IP/MPLS. Trees can support link aggregation (LAG) groups within a tree "branch" segment where some form of hashing occurs.

This symmetric and end to end ECMT behavior gives IEEE 802.1aq a highly predictable behavior and off line engineering tools can accurately model exact data flows. The behavior is also advantageous to networks where one way delay measurements are important. This is because the one way delay can be accurately computed as 1/2 the round trip delay. Such computations are used by time distribution protocols such as IEEE 1588 for frequency and time of day synchronization as required between precision clock sources and wireless base stations.

Shown above are three figures which show 8 and 16 equal cost tree (ECT) behavior in different network topologies. These are composites of screen captures of an 802.1aq network emulator and show the source in purple, the destination in yellow, and then all the computed and available shortest paths in pink. The thicker the line, the more shortest paths use that link. The animations shows three different networks and a variety of source and destination pairs which continually change to help visualize what is happening.

The equal cost tree (ECT) algorithms can be almost extended through the use of OPAQUE data which allows extensions beyond the base 16 algorithms more or less infinitely. It is expected that other standards groups or vendors will produce variations on the currently defined algorithms with behaviors suited for different networks styles. It is expected that numerous shared tree models will also be defined, as will hop by hop hash based equal-cost multi-path (ECMP) style behaviors all defined by a VID and an algorithm that every node agrees to run.

Traffic Placement/Engineering

802.1aq does not spread traffic on a hop by hop basis. Instead, 802.1aq allows assignment of a Service ID (ISID) to a Vlan ID (VID) at the edge of the network. A VID will correspond to exactly one of the possible sets of shortest path nodes in the network and will never stray from that routing. If there are 10 or so shortest paths between different nodes, it is possible to assign different services to different paths and to know that the traffic for a given service will follow exactly the given path. In this manner traffic can easily be assigned to the desired shortest path. In the event that one of the paths becomes overloaded it is possible to move some services off that shortest path by reassigning that service's ISID to a different, less loaded, VID at the edges of the network.

The deterministic nature of the routing makes offline prediction/computation/experimentation of the network loading much simpler since actual routes are not dependent on the contents of the packet headers with the exception of the VLAN identifier.

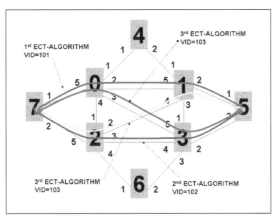

Figure - Equal Cost Shortest Path: assignment to services

Figure shows four different equal cost paths between nodes 7 and 5. An operator can achieve relatively good balance of traffic across the cut between nodes [0 and 2] and [1 and 3] by assigning the services at nodes 7 and 5 to one of the four desired VIDs. Using more than 4 equal cost tree (ECT) paths in the network will likely allow all 4 of these paths to be used. Balance can also be achieved between nodes 6 and 4 in a similar manner.

In the event that an operator does not wish to manually assign services to shortest paths it is a simple matter for a switch vendor to allow a simple hash of the ISID to one of the available VIDS to give a degree of non-engineered spreading. For example, the ISID modulo the number of ECT-VIDs could be used to decide on the actual relative VID to use.

In the event that the ECT paths are not sufficiently diverse the operator has the option of adjusting the inputs to the distributed ECT algorithms to apply attraction or repulsion from a given node by adjusting that node's Bridge Priority. This can be experimented with via offline tools until the desired routes are achieved at which point the bias can be applied to the real network and then ISIDs can be moved to the resulting routes.

Looking at the animations in figure shows the diversity available for traffic engineering in a 66 node network. In this animation there are 8 ECT paths available from each highlighted source to destination and therefore services could be assigned to 8 different pools based on the VID. One such initial assignment in Figure 6 could therefore be (ISID modulo 8) with subsequent fine tuning as required.

Example:

We will work through SPBM behavior on a small example, with emphasis on the shortest path trees for unicast and multicast.

The network shown in figure consists of 8 participating nodes numbered 0 through 7. These would be switches or routers running the IEEE 802.1aq protocol. Each of the 8 participating nodes has a number of adjacencies numbered 1..5. These would likely correspond to interface indexes, or possibly port numbers. Since 802.1aq does not support parallel interfaces each interface corresponds to an adjacency. The port / interface index numbers are of course local and are shown because the output of the computations produce an interface index (in the case of unicast) or a set of interface indexes (in the case of multicast) which are part of the forwarding information base (FIB) together with a destination MAC address and backbone VID.

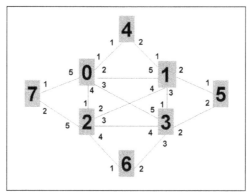

Figure: Example nodes, links and interface indexes

The network has a fully meshed inner core of four nodes (0,1,2,3) and then four outer nodes (4,5,6 and 7), each dual-homed onto a pair of inner core nodes.

Normally when nodes come from the factory they have a MAC address assigned which becomes a node identifier but for the purpose of this example we will assume that the nodes have MAC addresses of the form 00:00:00:00:N:00 where N is the node id (0..7) from figure. Therefore, node 2 has a MAC address of 00:00:00:00:02:00. Node 2 is connected to node 7 (00:00:00:00:07:00) via node 2's interface/5.

The IS-IS protocol runs on all the links shown since they are between participating nodes. The IS-IS hello protocol has a few additions for 802.1aq including information about backbone VIDs to be used by the protocol. We will assume that the operator has chosen to use backbone VIDs 101 and 102 for this instance of 802.1aq on this network.

The node will use their MAC addresses as the IS-IS SysId and join a single IS-IS level and exchange link state packets (LSPs in IS-IS terminology). The LSPs will contain node information and link information such that every node will learn the full topology of the network. Since we have not specified any link weights in this example, the IS-IS protocol will pick a default link metric for all links, therefore all routing will be minimum hop count.

After topology discovery the next step is distributed calculation of the unicast routes for both ECMP VIDs and population of the unicast forwarding tables (FIBs).

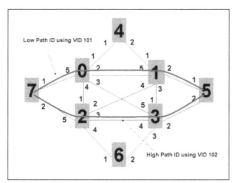

Figure: Two ECMP paths between nodes 7 and 5

Consider the route from Node 7 to Node 5- there are a number of equal cost paths. 802.1aq specifies how to choose two of them: the first is referred to as the Low PATH ID path. This is the path which has the minimum node id on it. In this case the Low PATH ID path is the 7->0->1->5 path (as shown in red in figure). Therefore, each node on that path will create a forwarding entry toward the MAC address of node five using the first ECMP VID 101. Conversely, 802.1aq specifies a second ECMP tie breaking algorithm called High PATH ID. This is the path with the maximum node identifier on it and in the example is the 7->2->3->5 path.

Node 7 will therefore have a FIB that among other things indicates:

- MAC 00:00:00:05:00 / vid 101 the next hop is interface/1.

- MAC 00:00:00:05:00 / vid 102 the next hop is interface/2.

Node 5 will have exactly the inverse in its FIB:

- MAC 00:00:00:07:00 / vid 101 the next hop is interface/1.

- MAC 00:00:00:07:00 / vid 102 the next hop is interface/2.

The intermediate nodes will also produce consistent results so for example node 1 will have the following entries:

- MAC 00:00:00:07:00 / vid 101 the next hop is interface/5.

- MAC 00:00:00:07:00 / vid 102 the next hop is interface/4.

- MAC 00:00:00:05:00 / vid 101 the next hop is interface/2.

- MAC 00:00:00:05:00 / vid 102 the next hop is interface/2.

And Node 2 will have entries as follows:

- MAC 00:00:00:05:00 / vid 101 the next hop is interface/2.

- MAC 00:00:00:05:00 / vid 102 the next hop is interface/3.

- MAC 00:00:00:07:00 / vid 101 the next hop is interface/5.

- MAC 00:00:00:07:00 / vid 102 the next hop is interface/5.

If we had an attached non participating device at Node 7 talking to a non participating device at Node 5 (for example Device A talks to Device C in figure), they would communicate over one of these shortest paths with a MAC-in-MAC encapsulated frame. The MAC header on any of the NNI links would show an outer source address of 00:00:00:70:00, an outer destination address of 00:00:00:50:00 and a BVID of either 101 or 102 depending on which has been chosen for this set of non participating ports/vids. The header once inserted at node 7 when received from node A, would not change on any of the links until it egressed back to non participating Device C at Node 5. All participating devices would do a simple DA+VID lookup to determine the outgoing interface, and would also check that incoming interface is the proper next hop for the packet's SA+VID. The addresses of the participating nodes 00:00:00:00:00:00 ... 00:00:00:07:00 are never learned but are advertised by IS-IS as the node's Side.

Unicast forwarding to a non-participating client (e.g. A, B, C, D from figure below) address is of course only possible when the first hop participating node (e.g. 7) is able to know which last hop participating node (e.g. 5) is attached to the desired non participating node (e.g. C). Since this information is not advertised by IEEE 802.1aq it has to be learned. The mechanism for learning is identical to IEEE 802.1ah, in short, the corresponding outer MAC unicast DA, if not known is replaced by a multicast DA and when a response is received, the SA of that response now tells us the DA to use to reach the non participating node that sourced the response. e.g. node 7 learns that C is reached by node 5.

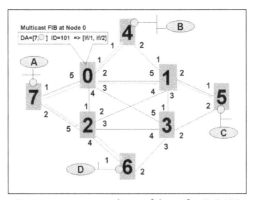

Per source, per service multicast for E-LAN

Since we wish to group/scope sets of non participating ports into services and prevent them from multicasting to each other, IEEE 802.1aq provides mechanism for per source, per service multicast forwarding and defines a special multicast destination address format to provide this. Since the multicast address must uniquely identify the tree, and because there is a tree per source per unique service, the multicast address contains two components, a service component in the low order 24 bits and a network wide unique identifier in the upper 22 bits. Since this is a multicast address the multicast bit is set, and since we are not using the standard OUI space for these manufactured addresses, the Local 'L' bit is set to disambiguate these addresses. In figure above, this is represented with the DA=[7,O] where the 7 represents packets originating from node 7 and the colored O represents the E-LAN service we are scoped within.

Prior to creating multicast forwarding for a service, nodes with ports that face that service must be told they are members. For example, nodes 7, 4, 5 and 6 are told they are members of the given service, for example service 200, and further that they should be using BVID 101. This is advertised by ISIS and all nodes then do the SPBM computation to determine if they are participating either as a head end or tail end, or a tandem point between other head and tail ends in the service. Since node 0 is a tandem between nodes 7 and 5 it creates a forwarding entry for packets from node 7 on this service, to node 5. Likewise, since it is a tandem between nodes 7 and 4 it creates forwarding state from node 7 for packets in this service to node 4 this results in a true multicast entry where the DA/VID have outputs on two interfaces 1 and 2. Node 2 on the other hand is only on one shortest path in this service and only creates a single forwarding entry from node 7 to node 6 for packets in this service.

Figure above only shows a single E-LAN service and only the tree from one of the members, however very large numbers of E-LAN services with membership from 2 to every node in the network can be supported by advertising the membership, computing the tandem behaviors, manufacturing the known multicast addresses and populating the FIBs. The only real limiting factors are the FIB table sizes and computational power of the individual devices both of which are growing yearly in leaps and bounds.

Implementation Notes

802.1aq takes IS-IS topology information augmented with service attachment (I-SID) information, does a series of computations and produces a forwarding table (filtering table) for unicast and multicast entries.

The IS-IS extensions that carry the information required by 802.1aq are given in the isis-layer2 IETF document listed below.

An implementation of 802.1aq will first modify the IS-IS hellos to include an NLPID (network layer protocol identifier) of 0xC01 in their Protocols-Supported Type-length-value (TLV) (type 129) which has been reserved for 802.1aq. The hellos also must include an MSTID (which gives the purpose of each VID) and finally each ECMT behavior must be assigned to a VID and exchanged in the hellos. The hellos would normally run untagged. Note that NLPID of IP is not required to form an adjacency for 802.1aq but also will not prevent an adjacency when present.

The links are assigned 802.1aq specific metrics which travel in their own TLV (Type

Length Value) which is more or less identical to the IP link metrics. The calculations will always use the maximum of the two unidirectional link metrics to enforce symmetric route weights.

The node is assigned a mac address to identify it globally and this is used to form the IS-IS SYSID. A box mac would normally serve this purpose. The Area-Id is not directly used by 802.1aq but should, of course, be the same for nodes in the same 802.1aq network. Multiple areas/levels are not yet supported. The node is further assigned an SP-SourceID which is a 20 bit network wide unique identifier. This can often be the low 20 bits of the SYSID (if unique) or can be dynamically negotiated or manually configured.

The SPSourceID and the ECMT assignments to B-VIDs are then advertised into the IS-IS network in their own 802.1aq TLV.

The 802.1aq computations are restricted to links between nodes that have an 802.1aq link weight and which support the NLPID 0xC01. As previously discussed the link weights are forced to be symmetric for the purpose of computation by taking the min of two dissimilar values.

When a service is configured in the form of an I-SID assignment to an ECMT behavior that I-SID is then advertised along with the desired ECMT behavior and an indication of its transmit, receive properties (a new Type-length-value is used for this purpose of course). When an 802.1aq node receives an IS-IS update it will compute the unique shortest path to all other IS-IS nodes that support 802.1aq. There will be one unique (symmetric) shortest path per ECMT behavior. The tie breaking used to enforce this uniqueness and ECMT is described below.

The unicast FDB/FIB will be populated based on this first shortest path computation. There will be one entry per ECMT behavior/B-VID produced. The transit multicast computation (which only applies when transit replication is desired and not applicable to services that have chosen head end replication) can be implemented in many ways, care must be taken to keep this efficient, but in general a series of shortest path computations must be done. The basic requirement is to decide 'am I on the shortest path between two nodes one of which transmits an I-SID and the other receives that I-SID.'

Rather poor performing pseudo-code for this computation looks something like this:

```
for each NODE in network which originates at least one transmit ISID do
{ SPF = compute the shortest path trees from NODE for all ECMT B-VIDs.
for each ECMT behavior { for each NEIGHBOR of NODE { if NEIGHBOR is on
the SPF towards NODE for this ECMT { T = NODE's transmit ISIDs unioned
with all receive ISIDs below us on SPF for each ISID in T { create/mod-
ify multicast entry where [ MAC-DA = NODE.SpsourceID:20||ISID:24||Lo-
calBit:1||MulticastBit:1 B-VID = VID associated with this ECMT out port
= interface to NEIGHBOR in port = port towards NODE on the SPF for this
ECMT ] } } } } }
```

The above pseudo code computes many more SPF's than strictly necessary in most cases and better algorithms are known to decide if a node is on a shortest path between two other nodes. A reference to a paper presented at the IEEE which gives a much faster algorithm that drastically reduces the number of outer iterations required is given below.

In general though even the exhaustive algorithm above is more than able to handle several hundred node networks in a few 10's of milliseconds on the 1 GHz or greater common CPUs when carefully crafted.

For ISIDs that have chosen head end replication the computation is trivial and involves simply finding the other attachment points that receive that ISID and creating a serial unicast table to replicate to them one by one.

Tie-breaking

802.1aq must produce deterministic symmetric downstream congruent shortest paths. This means that not only must a given node compute the same path forward and reverse but all the other nodes downstream (and upstream) on that path must also produce the same result. This downstream congruence is a consequence of the hop by hop forwarding nature of Ethernet since only the destination address and VID are used to decide the next hop. It is important to keep this in mind when trying to design other ECMT algorithms for 802.1aq as this is an easy trap to fall into. It begins by taking the unidirectional link metrics that are advertised by ISIS for 802.1aq and ensuring that they are symmetric. This is done by simply taking the MIN of the two values at both ends prior to doing any computations. This alone does not guarantee symmetry however.

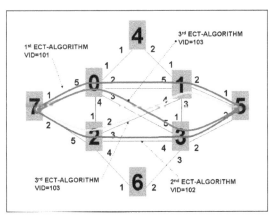

Figure: Tie Breaking and path identifiers

The 802.1aq standard describes a mechanism called a PATHID which is a network-wide unique identifier for a path. This is a useful logical way to understand how to deterministically break ties but is not how one would implement such a tie-breaker in practice. The PATHID is defined as just the sequence of SYSIDs that make up the path (not including the end points).. sorted. Every path in the network therefore has a unique PATHID independent of where in the network the path is discovered.

802.1aq simply always picks the lowest PATHID path when a choice presents itself in the shortest path computations. This ensures that every node will make the same decision.

For example, in figure above, there are four equal-cost paths between node 7 and node 5 as shown by the colors blue, green, pink and brown. The PATHID for these paths are as follows:

- PATHID[**brown**] = {0,1}

- PATHID[**pink**] = {0,3}

- PATHID[green] = {1,2}

- PATHID[**blue**] = {2,3}

The lowest PATHID is therefore the brown path {0, 1}.

This low PATHID algorithm has very desirable properties. The first is that it can be done progressively by simply looking for the lowest SYSID along a path and secondly because an efficient implementation that operates stepwise is possible by simply back-tracking two competing paths and looking for the minimum of the two paths minimum SYSIDs.

The low PATHID algorithm is the basis of all 802.1aq tie breaking. ECMT is also based on the low PATHID algorithm by simply feeding it different SYSID permutations – one per ECMT algorithm. The most obvious permutation to pass is a complete inversion of the SYSID by XOR-ing it with 0xfff. prior to looking for the min of two minimums. This algorithm is referred to as high PATHID because it logically chooses the largest PATHID path when presented with two equal-cost choices.

In the example in figure, the path with the highest PATHID is therefore the blue path whose PATHID is {2, 3}. Simply inverting all the SYSIDs and running the low PATHID algorithm will yield same result.

The other 14 defined ECMT algorithms use different permutations of the SYSID by XOR-ing it with different bit masks which are designed to create relatively good distribution of bits. It should be clear that different permutations will result in the purple and green paths being lowest in turn.

The 17 individual 64-bit masks used by the ECT algorithm are made up of the same byte value repeated eight times to fill each 64-bit mask. These 17 byte values are as follows:

```
ECT-MASK = { 0x00, 0x00, 0xFF, 0x88, 0x77, 0x44, 0x33, 0xCC, 0xBB,
0x22, 0x11, 0x66, 0x55, 0xAA, 0x99, 0xDD, 0xEE };
```

ECT-MASK is reserved for a common spanning tree algorithm, while ECT-MASK creates the Low PATHID set of shortest path first trees, ECT-MASK creates the High PATHID set of shortest path trees and the other indexes create other relatively diverse permutations of shortest path first trees.

In addition the ECMT tie-breaking algorithms also permit some degree of human override or tweaking. This is accomplished by including a BridgePriority field together with the SYSID such that the combination, called a BridgeIdentfier, becomes the input to the ECT algorithm. By adjusting the BridgePriority up or down a path's PATHID can be raised or lowered relative to others and a substantial degree of tunability is afforded.

The above description gives an easy to understand way to view the tie breaking; an actual implementation simply backtracks from the fork point to the join point in two competing equal-cost paths (usually during the Dijkstra shortest path computation) and picks the path traversing the lowest (after masking) BridgePriority|SysId.

Interoperability

The first public interoperability tests of IEEE 802.1aq were held in Ottawa in October 2010. Two vendors provided SPBM implementations and a total of 5 physical switches and 32 emulated switches were tested for control/data and OA&M.

Further events were held in Ottawa in January 2011 with 5 vendors and 6 implementations, at 2013's Interop event at Las Vegas where an SPBM network was used as a backbone.

Competitors

MC-LAG, VXLAN, and QFabric have all been proposed, but the IETF TRILL standard (Transparent Interconnect of Lots of Links) is considered the major competitor of IEEE 802.1aq, and: "the evaluation of relative merits and difference of the two standards proposals is currently a hotly debated topic in the networking industry."

Deployments

Deployment considerations and interoperability best practices are documented in an IETF document titled "SPB Deployment Considerations":

- 2013 Interop: Networking Leaders Demo Shortest Path Bridging.

- 2014 Interop: InteropNet Goes IPv6, Includes Shortest Path Bridging.

Extreme Networks, by virtue of their acquisition of the Avaya Networking business and assets, is currently the leading exponent of SPB-based deployments; their enhanced and extended implementation of SPB - including integrated Layer 3 IP Routing and IP Multicast functionality - is marketed under the banner of the "Fabric Connect" technology. Additionally, Extreme Networks is supporting an IETF Internet Draft Draft that defines a means of automatically extended SPBM-based services to end-devices via conventional Ethernet Switches, leveraging an 802.1AB LLDP-based communications protocol; this capability - marketing "Fabric Attach" technology - allows for the automatic attachment of end-devices, and includes dynamic configuration of VLAN/I-SID (VSN) mappings.

Avaya (acquired by Extreme Networks) has deployed SPB/Fabric Connect solutions for businesses operating across a number of industry verticals:

- Education, examples include: Leeds Metropolitan University, Macquaire University, Pearland Independent School District, Ajman University of Science & Technology.

- Transportation, examples include: Schiphol Telematics, Rheinbahn, Sendai City Transportation Bureau, NSB.

- Banking & Finance, examples include: Fiducia, Sparebanken Vest.

- Major Events, examples include: 2013 & 2014 Interop (InteropNet Backbone), 2014 Sochi Winter Olympics, Dubai World Trade Center.

- Healthcare, examples include: Oslo University Hospital, Concord Hospital, Franciscan Alliance, Sydney Adventist Hospital.

- Manufacturing, examples include: Fujitsu Technology Solutions.

- Media, examples include: Schibsted, Medienhaus Lensing, Sanlih Entertainment Television.

- Government, examples include: City of Redondo Beach, City of Breda, Bezirksamt Neukölln.

Source Route Bridging

Source route bridging is a method to connect two similar network segments to each other at the datalink layer. It is done in a "distributed way" where end-stations participate in the bridging algorithm, thus the name _source_ routing.

In a source-route bridging environment a source end-station will send out a "route explorer" frame (broadcast) to find out the route to the destination end-station. Source route bridges will forward these frames to all segments/ports. The source route bridge will add route information (the segment the packet came from) to the frame prior to forwarding it. This route information is called the Routing Information Field (RIF).

Eventually, the route explorer frame reaches the destination end-station including the complete route (via the RIF) the packet took. The destination end-station then uses this RIF to reply to the source end-station directly (i.e. no broadcast). Please note that the reply traverses all bridges in reverse order of the route explorer frame and includes the rif. When the reply reaches the source end-station, the complete network route is known by both the source and destination end-stations. Subsequent packets will use this route information (i.e. no broadcast).

It is possible that a network has multiple routes to a destination end-station. In this scenario, the source end-station will receive more than one reply to the route explorer broadcast. In most cases, the source end-station uses the route that was received first.

In a source-route bridging environment, the end-stations discover and store information about the network topology. In a transparent bridging environment, the (transparent) bridge discovers and stores this information.

Router

A Router is a networking device that forwards data packets between computer network.

Let us understand this by a very general example, suppose you search for any website in your web browser then this will be a request which will be sent from your system to the google's server to serve that webpage, now your request which is nothing but a stream of packets don't just go the google`s server straightaway they go through a series of networking devices known as router which accepts this packets and forwards them to correct path and hence it reaches to the destination server.

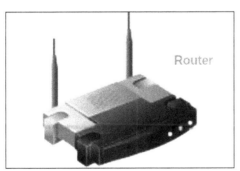

A router has a number of interfaces by which it can connect to a number of host systems.

Functions of a Router

The router basically performs two major functions:

- Forwarding – Router receives the packets from its input ports, checks it header, performs some basic functions like checking checksum and then looks upto the routing table to find the appropriate output port to dump the packets onto, and forwards the packets onto that output port.

- Routing – Routing is the process by which the router ascertains what is the best path for the packet to reach the destination, It maintains a routing table which is made using different algorithms by the router only.

Architecture of a Router

A Generic router consists of the following components:

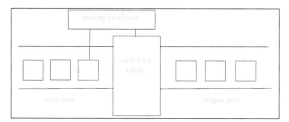

Input Port

This is the interface by which packets are admitted into the router, it performs sevral key functions as terminating the physical link at router, this is done by the leftmost part in the below diagram, the middle part does the work of interoperating with the link layer like decapsulation, in the last part of the input port the forwarding table is looked up and is used to determine the appropriate output port based on the destination address.

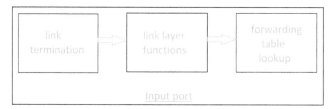

Switching Fabric

This is the heart of the Router, It connects the input ports with the output ports. It is kind of a network inside a networking device. The switching fabric can be implemented in a number of ways some of the prominent ones are:

- Switching via memory: In this we have a processor which copies the packet from input ports and sends it to the appropriate output port. It works as a traditional cpu with input and output ports acting as input and output devices.

- Switching via bus: In this implementation we have a bus which connects all the input ports to all the output ports. On receiving a packet and determining which output port it must be delivered to, the input port puts a particular token on the packet and transfers it to the bus. All output ports are able to see the packets but it will be delivered to the output port whose token has been put in, the token is then scrapped off by that output port and the packet is forwarded.

- Switching via interconnection network: This is a more sophisticated network, here instead of a single bus we use 2N bus to connect n input ports to an output ports.

Output Port

This is the segment from which packets are transmitted out of the router. The output port looks at its queuing buffers (when more than one packets have to be transmitted through the same output port queuing buffers are formed) and takes packets, does link layer functions and finally transmits the packets to outgoing link.

Routing Processor

It executes the routing protocols, it works like a tradition cpu. It employs various routing algorithm like link-state algorithm, distance-vector algorithm etc. to prepare the forwarding table, which is looked up to determine the forwarding table.

Router Types

Wireless (Wi-Fi) Router

A wireless router is a device in a wireless local area network (WLAN) that determines the next network point to which a packet should be forwarded toward its destination. A wireless router works in the same way as the router in a hard-wired home or business local area network (LAN), but allows greater mobility for notebook or portable computers. The individual computers are equipped with small wireless transceivers that can be plugged into either a Universal Serial Bus (USB) port or a PC card slot.

For home and business computer users who have high-speed Internet connections, a wireless router can also act as a hardware firewall. This is true even if the home or business has only one computer. Many engineers believe that the use of a router provides superior protection against hacking because individual computer IP addresses arc not directly exposed to the Internet. A wireless router also does not consume computer resources as a firewall program does.

An early example of a wireless router

Wireless router technology has improved in recent years, providing more bandwidth and allowing for the connection of more computers to a WLAN. The newer wireless routers use the 802.11g specification, a standard that offers transmission over short distances at up to 54 megabits per second (Mbps), compared with the 11 Mbps theoretical maximum with the earlier 802.11b standard.

Features

Most current wireless routers have the following characteristics:

- One or multiple NICs supporting Fast Ethernet or Gigabit Ethernet integrated into the main SoC.

  o Some newer routers feature Link Aggregation allowing two ports to be used together improving throughput and redundancy.

- One or multiple WNICs supporting a part of the IEEE 802.11-standard family also integrated into the main SoC or as separate chips on the printed circuit board. It also can be a distinct card connected over a MiniPCI or MiniPCIe interface.

  o So far the PHY-Chips for the WNICs are generally distinct chips on the PCB. Dependent on the mode the WNIC supports, i.e. 1T1R, 2T2R or 3T3R, one WNIC have up to 3 PHY-Chips connected to it. Each PHY-Chip is connected to a Hirose U.FL-connector on the PCB. A so-called pigtail cable connects the Hirose U.FL either to a RF connector, in which case the antenna can be changed or directly to the antenna, in which case it is integrated into the casing. Common are single-band (i.e. only for 2.4 GHz or only for 5 GHz), dual-band (i.e. for 2.4 and 5 GHz) and tri-band (i.e. for a single 2.4 GHz and two 5 GHz) antennas.

- Often an Ethernet switch supporting Gigabit Ethernet or Fast Ethernet, with support for IEEE 802.1Q, integrated into the main SoC (MediaTek SoCs) or as separate Chip on the PCB.

- Some wireless routers come with either xDSL modem, DOCSIS modem, LTE modem, or fiber optic modem integrated.

- IEEE 802.11ac compliant or ready.

- Some dual-band wireless routers operate the 2.4 GHz and 5 GHz bands simultaneously.

- Many dual-band wireless routers have data transfer rates exceeding 300 Mbit/s (For 2.4 GHz band) and 450 Mbit/s (For 5 GHz band).

- Some wireless routers provide multiple streams allowing multiples of data transfer rates (i.e. a three-stream wireless router allows transfers of up to 1.3 Gbit/s on the 5 GHz bands).

- The Wi-Fi clone button simplifies Wi-Fi configuration and builds a seamless unified home network, enabling Super Range Extension, which means it can automatically copy the SSID and Password of your router.

- Some wireless routers have one or two USB ports. For wireless routers having one USB port, it is designated for either printer or desktop/mobile external hard disk drive. For wireless routers having two USB ports, one is designated for the printer and the other one is designated for either desktop or mobile external hard disk drive.

- Some wireless routers have a USB port specifically designed for connecting mobile broadband modem, aside from connecting the wireless router to an Ethernet with xDSL or cable modem. A mobile broadband USB adapter can be connected to the router to share the mobile broadband Internet connection through the wireless network.

Operating System

The WRT54G wireless router supporting only 802.11b and
802.11g. Its OEM firmware gave birth to OpenWrt

The most common operating system on such embedded devices is Linux. More seldomly, VxWorks is used. The devices are configured over a web user interface served by a light web server software running on the device. It is possible for a computer running a desktop operating system with appropriate software to act as a wireless router. This is commonly referred to as a SoftAP.

In 2003, Linksys was forced to open-source the firmware of its WRT54G router series (the best-selling routers of all time) after people on the Linux kernel mailing list discovered that it used GPL Linux code. In 2008, Cisco was sued in *Free Software Foundation, Inc. v. Cisco Systems, Inc* due to similar issues with Linksys routers. Since then, various open-source projects have built on this foundation, including OpenWrt, DD-WRT, and Tomato.

In 2016, various manufacturers changed their firmware to block custom installations after an FCC ruling. However, some companies plan to continue to officially support open-source firmware, including Linksys and Asus.

Brouter

A brouter is a device that functions as both a bridge and a router. It can forward data between networks (serving as a bridge), but can also route data to individual systems within a network (serving as a router).

The main purpose of a bridge is to connect two separate networks. It simply forwards the incoming packets from one network to the next. A router, on the other hand, is more advanced since it can route packets to specific systems connected to the router. A brouter combines these two functions by routing some incoming data to the correct systems, while forwarding other data to another network. In other words, a brouter functions as a filter that lets some data into the local network, while redirecting unrecognized data to another network.

While the term "brouter" is used to describe bridge/router device, actual brouters are pretty rare. Instead, most brouters are simply routers that have been configured to also function as a bridge. This functionality can often be implemented using the router's software interface. For example, you may configure a router to only accept data from specific protocols and data sources, while forwarding other data to another network.

Core Router

A core router is a type of very powerful computer router used in large computer networks. It is the fastest, most powerful, and most expensive class of router available. A core router sits at the heart of a network and manages the flow of data packets within the network, often relying on lesser routers for connectivity.

In the world of routers, not all machines are created equal. While all types of routers have the same basic function of directing the flow of data packets, the number of packets any one router needs to process at once depends on where and how the device is being used. Consumer-level routers used to connect many homes and small offices to the Internet need to deal with only a fraction of the data a router in a large corporation or Internet Service Provider (ISP) has to manage. As a result, routers vary widely in size, power, and cost.

Very large computer networks commonly use a hierarchy of routers. At the top of this hierarchy are core routers, the fastest and most powerful class. A single core router can cost as much as a high-end sports car and is capable of processing millions of packets every second. It generally sits in the "center" of very large networks and sends and receives packets to lower classes of routers, such as edge routers, which sit on the edge of a network and transfer packets to other networks. These routers can communicate with one another using the Border Gateway Protocol (BGP) and may share information about the best routes to take or network destinations that have become unreachable.

Early incarnations of the core router contained a "global routing table," a database containing virtually every possible route a given packet could take to reach its destination.

These routers, therefore, were considered to be in the core or backbone of the Internet and were an essential component of early Internet architecture. As the Internet grew, however, even the most advanced router couldn't keep up with the number of possible routes. Large networks were subdivided into smaller units known as autonomous systems (AS). The modern core router still maintains a large routing table; the scope of this table is confined to the AS rather than the Internet as a whole, however, making the concept of a "core" Internet largely obsolete.

Due to their cost, the market for core routers is largely limited to ISPs and some large institutions such as universities. There were once several companies providing core routers, but the end of the dot-com boom coupled with a number of Cisco Systems acquisitions has narrowed the market to just two: Cisco, which controls the majority of the market, and Juniper Networks. The two companies have played a constant game of leapfrog since the early 2000s, and both now produce routers capable of handling enormous amounts of data.

Edge Router

An edge router is a specialized router located at a network boundary that enables a campus network to connect to external networks. They are primarily used at two demarcation points: the wide area network (WAN) and the internet.

Typically, the edge router sends or receives data directly to or from other organizations' networks, using either static or dynamic routing capabilities. Handoffs between the campus network and the internet or WAN edge primarily use Ethernet, usually Gigabit Ethernet copper or Gigabit Ethernet over single or multimode fiber optics.

In some instances, an organization maintains multiple isolated networks of its own and uses edge routers to link them together instead of using a core router.

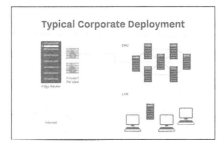

Edge routers are often hardware devices, but their functions can also be performed by software running on a standard x86 server.

At its most essential level, the internet can be viewed as the sum of all the interconnections of edge routers across all participating organizations, from its periphery -- small business and home broadband routers, for example - all the way to its core, where major telecom provider networks connect to each other via massive edge routers.

Types of Edge Routers and how they Work

Edge routers are divided into two different types: subscriber edge routers and label edge routers.

Subscriber edge routers function in two ways:

1. As external Border Gateway Protocol (BGP) routers that connect one autonomous system (AS) to other ASes, which includes connecting an enterprise network to the network edge of its internet service provider (ISP); and

2. As small or midsize business (SMB) or consumer broadband routers connecting a home network or small office to an ISP's network edge.

Label edge routers, which are used at the edge of Multiprotocol Label Switching (MPLS) networks, act as gateways between a local network and a WAN or the internet and assign labels to outbound data transmissions. Edge routers are not internal routers that partition a given AS network into separate subnets. To connect to external networks, routers use the internet protocol (IP) and the Open Shortest Path First (OSPF) protocol to route packets efficiently.

Edge routers play a fundamental role as more services and applications begin to be managed on an organization's network edge rather than in its data center or in the cloud. Services considered suitable for edge router management include wireless capabilities often built into network edge devices, Dynamic Host Configuration Protocol (DHCP) services and domain name system (DNS) services, among others.

Difference between Edge Routers and Core Routers

In general, edge routers accept inbound customer traffic into the network. These edge devices characterize and secure IP traffic from other edge routers, as well as core routers. They provide security for the core.

By comparison, core routers offer packet forwarding between other core and edge routers and manage traffic to prevent congestion and packet loss. To improve efficiency, core routers often employ multiplexing.

Security Considerations

Because edge routers serve as a connection point between external networks, security is an issue, since enterprises can't control who might try to access the corporate network.

To ensure security, edge routers can either be configured with tools that include access control lists, or they can be purchased with built-in support for firewalls. This enables more advanced security safeguards, including VPN tunnels and signature matching through intrusion prevention and intrusion detection systems.

Virtual Router

Virtual router is a software-based routing framework that allows the host machine to perform as a typical hardware router over a local area network.

A virtual router can enable a computer/server to have the abilities of a full-fledged router by performing the network and packet routing functionality of the router via a software application. Virtual Router Redundancy Protocol (VRRP) may implement virtual routers to increase the reliability of the network. This is done by advertising a virtual router as the default gateway, backed by a group of physical routers.

Virtual routers are normally backed by two physical routers. One router performs the typical routing while the other provides redundancy in case of fail-over. Each virtual router that is created is identified with a unique virtual router identifier. The last byte of the address is the virtual router identifier (VRID); each virtual router in the network has a different number. This address is used by only one physical router at a time. A router will reply with this media access control (MAC) address when an Address Resolution Protocol request is sent for the virtual router's IP address. Physical routers within the virtual router communicate using packets with multicast IP address 224.0.0.18 and IP protocol number 112.

Routing

Routing is the act of moving information across an inter-network from a source to a destination. Along the way, at least one intermediate node typically is encountered. Routing is often contrasted with bridging, which might seem to accomplish precisely the same thing to the casual observer. The primary difference between the two is that bridging occurs at Layer 2 (the link layer) of the OSI reference model, whereas routing occurs at Layer 3 (the network layer). This distinction provides routing and bridging with different information to use in the process of moving information from source to destination, so the two functions accomplish their tasks in different ways.

The topic of routing has been covered in computer science literature for more than two decades, but routing achieved commercial popularity as late as the mid-1980s. The primary reason for this time lag is that networks in the 1970s were simple, homogeneous environments. Only relatively recently has large-scale inter networking become popular.

Types of Routing

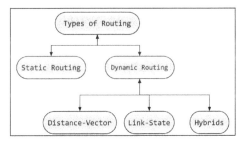

Routers can route in a two basic ways. They can use pre-programmed static routes, or they can dynamically calculate routes using any one of a number of dynamic routing protocols. Dynamic routing protocols are used by routers to perform discover routes. Routers then mechanically forward packets (or datagrams) over those routes. Statically programmed routers cannot discover routes; they lack any mechanism to communicate routing information with other routers. Statically programmed routers can only forward packets using routes defined by a network administrator.

Static Routing

Static routing is a type of network routing technique. Static routing is not a routing protocol; instead, it is the manual configuration and selection of a network route, usually managed by the network administrator. It is employed in scenarios where the network parameters and environment are expected to remain constant.

Static routing is only optimal in a few situations. Network degradation, latency and congestion are inevitable consequences of the non-flexible nature of static routing because there is no adjustment when the primary route is unavailable.

Static routing may have the following uses:

- Static routing can be used to define an exit point from a router when no other routes are available or necessary. This is called a default route.

- Static routing can be used for small networks that require only one or two routes. This is often more efficient since a link is not being wasted by exchanging dynamic routing information.

- Static routing is often used as a complement to dynamic routing to provide a failsafe backup in the event that a dynamic route is unavailable.

- Static routing is often used to help transfer routing information from one routing protocol to another (routing redistribution).

Advantages

Static routing, if used without dynamic routing, has the following advantages:

- Static routing causes very little load on the CPU of the router, and produces no traffic to other routers.

- Static routing leaves the network administrator with full control over the routing behavior of the network.

- Static Routing Is very easy to configure on a small networks.

Disadvantages

- Human error: In many cases, static routes are manually configured. This increases the potential for input mistakes. Administrators can make mistakes and mistype in network information, or configure incorrect routing paths by mistake.

- Fault tolerance: Static routing is not fault tolerant. This means that when there is a change in the network or a failure occurs between two statically defined devices, traffic will not be re-routed. As a result, the network is unusable until the failure is repaired or the static route is manually reconfigured by an administrator.

- Administrative distance: Static routes typically take precedence over routes configured with a dynamic routing protocol. This means that static routes may prevent routing protocols from working as intended. A solution is to manually modify the administrative distance.

- Administrative overhead: Static routes must be configured on each router in the network(s). This configuration can take a long time if there are many routers. It also means that reconfiguration can be slow and inefficient. Dynamic routing on the other hand automatically propagates routing changes, reducing the need for manual reconfiguration.

To route IP traffic destined for the network *10.10.20.0/24* via the next-hop router with the IPv4 address of *192.168.100.1*, the following configuration commands or steps can be used.

Linux

In most Linux distributions, a static route can be added using the iproute2 command. The following is typed at a terminal:-

```
root@router:~# ip route add 10.10.20.0 via 192.168.100.1
```

Cisco

Enterprise-level Cisco routers are configurable using the Cisco IOS command line, rather than a web management interface.

Add a Static Route

The commands to add a static route are as follows:

```
Router> enable

Router# configure terminal

Router(config)# interface s0/0/0

Router(config)# ip route 10.10.20.0 255.255.255.0 192.168.100.1
```

Network configurations are not restricted to a single static route per destination:

```
Router> enable

Router# configure terminal

Router(config)# ip route 197.164.73.0 255.255.255.0 197.164.72.2 Router(config)# ip route 197.164.74.0 255.255.255.0 197.164.72.2
```

Add Static Route by Specifying Exit Interface

Static routes can also be added by specifying the exit interface rather than the "next hop" IP address of the router.

```
Router(config)# ip route 10.10.20.0 255.255.255.0 Serial 0/0/0
```

Configuring Administrative Distance

The administrative distance can be manually (re)configured so that the static route can be configured as a backup route, to be used only if the dynamic route is unavailable.

```
Router(config)# ip route 10.10.20.0 255.255.255.0 exampleRoute 1 254
```

Setting the administrative distance to 254 will result in the route being used only as a backup.

Dynamic Routing

Dynamic routing is a networking technique that provides optimal data routing. Unlike static routing, dynamic routing enables routers to select paths according to real-time logical network layout changes. In dynamic routing, the routing protocol operating on the router is responsible for the creation, maintenance and updating of the dynamic routing table. In static routing, all these jobs are manually done by the system administrator.

Dynamic routing uses multiple algorithms and protocols. The most popular are Routing Information Protocol (RIP) and Open Shortest Path First (OSPF).

Typically, dynamic routing protocol operations can be explained as follows:

1. The router delivers and receives the routing messages on the router interfaces.

2. The routing messages and information are shared with other routers, which use exactly the same routing protocol.

3. Routers swap the routing information to discover data about remote networks.

4. Whenever a router finds a change in topology, the routing protocol advertises this topology change to other routers.

Dynamic routing is easy to configure on large networks and is more intuitive at selecting the best route, detecting route changes and discovering remote networks. However, because routers share updates, they consume more bandwidth than in static routing; the routers' CPUs and RAM may also face additional loads as a result of routing protocols.

There are three broad categories of dynamic routing protocols:

- Distance-vector
- Link-state
- Hybrids

Distance-Vector Routing

In routing based on distance-vector algorithms, also sometimes called Bellman-Ford algorithms, the algorithms periodically pass copies of their routing tables to their immediate network neighbors. Each recipient adds a distance vector—that is, its own distance "value"—to the table and forwards it on to its immediate neighbors. This process occurs in an omnidirectional manner among immediately neighboring routers. This step-by-step process results in each router learning about other routers and developing a cumulative perspective of network "distances." The cumulative table is then used to update each router's routing tables.

Drawbacks to Distance-Vector Routing

Under certain circumstances, distance-vector routing can actually create routing problems for Distance-vector protocols. A failure or other change in the network, for example, requires some time for the routers to converge on a new understanding of the network's topology. During the convergence process, the network may be vulnerable to inconsistent routing, and even infinite loops. Safeguards can contain many of these risks, but the fact remains that the network's performance is at risk during the convergence process. Therefore, older distance-vector protocols that are slow to converge may not be appropriate for large, complex WANs.

Advantages of Distance-Vector Routing

Generally speaking, distance-vector protocols are very simple protocols that are easy to configure, maintain, and use. Consequently, they prove quite useful in very small networks that have few, if any, redundant paths and no stringent network performance requirements.

Link-State Routing

Link-state routing algorithms, known cumulatively as shortest path first (SPF) protocols, maintain a complex database of the network's topology. Unlike distance-vector protocols, link-state protocols develop and maintain a full knowledge of the network's routers as well as how they interconnect. This is achieved via the exchange of link-state advertisements (LSAs) with other routers in a network. Each router that has exchanged LSAs constructs a topological database using all received LSAs. An SPF algorithm is then used to compute reachability to networked destinations. This information is used to update the routing table. This process can discover changes in the network topology caused by component failure or network growth.

Drawbacks to Link-State Routing

During the initial discovery process, link-state routing protocols can flood the network's transmission facilities, and thereby significantly decrease the network's capability to transport data. This performance degradation is temporary but can be very noticeable. Whether this flooding process will impede a network's performance noticeably depends on two things: the amount of available bandwidth and the number of routers that must exchange routing information.

Link-state routing is both memory and processor intensive. Consequently, more fully configured routers are required to support link-state routing than distance-vector routing. This increases the cost of the routers that are configured for link-state routing.

Advantages of Link-State Routing

The link-state approach to dynamic routing can be quite useful in networks of any size. In a well-designed network, a link-state routing protocol will enable your network to gracefully weather the effects of unexpected topological change. Using events, such as changes, to drive updates (rather than fixed-interval timers) enables convergence to begin that much more quickly after a topological change. The overheads of the frequent, time-driven updates of a distance- vector routing protocol are also avoided. This allows more bandwidth to be used for routing traffic rather than for network maintenance, provided you design your network properly.

A side benefit of the bandwidth efficiency of link-state routing protocols is that they facilitate network scalability better than either static routes or distance-vector protocols.

Hybridized Routing

The last form of routing discipline is hybridization. The balanced hybrid routing protocols use distance-vector metrics but emphasize more accurate metrics than conventional distance-vector protocols. They also converge more rapidly than distance-vector protocols but avoid the overheads of link-state updates. Balanced hybrids are event driven rather than periodic and thereby conserve bandwidth for real applications.

Although "open" balanced hybrid protocols exist, this form is almost exclusively associated with the proprietary creation of a single company, Cisco Systems, Inc. Its protocol, Enhanced Interior Gateway Routing Protocol (EIGRP), was designed to combine the best aspects of distance-vector and link-state routing protocols without incurring any of their performance limitations or penalties.

Gateway

A gateway is a node (router) in a computer network, a key *stopping point* for data on its way to or from other networks. Thanks to gateways, we are able to communicate and send data back and forth. The Internet wouldn't be any use to us without gateways (as well as a lot of other hardware and software).

In a workplace, the gateway is the computer that routes traffic from a workstation to the outside network that is serving up the Web pages. For basic Internet connections at home, the gateway is the Internet Service Provider that gives you access to the entire Internet.

A node is simply a physical place where the data stops for either transporting or reading/using. (A computer or modem is a node; a computer cable isn't.) Here are a few node notes:

- On the Internet, the node that's a stopping point can be a gateway or a host node.

- A computer that controls the traffic your Internet Service Provider (ISP) receives is a node.

If you have a wireless network at home that gives your entire family access to the Internet, your gateway is the modem (or modem-router combo) your ISP provides so you can connect to their network. On the other end, the computer that controls all of the data traffic your Internet Service Provider (ISP) takes and sends out is itself a node.

When a computer-server acts as a gateway, it also operates as a firewall and a proxy server. A firewall keeps out unwanted traffic and outsiders off a private network. A proxy server is software that "sits" between programs on your computer that you use (such as a Web browser) and a computer server—the computer that serves your network. The proxy server's task is to make sure the real server can handle your online data requests.

Router at Work

As mentioned before, a gateway is often associated with a router. A router is hardware—a small piece of computer/network-related equipment that connects you to the Internet. In home networks, the router comes with special software that you install on one computer. You're then able to use the software to set up your home network so everyone allowed on your network can connect to the ISP and the Internet. A router can be connected to two or more networks at a time, but for home networks that's generally not the case.

When you do a Google search or compose an email and hit "Send," your computer sends the data to your router. Your router then, which is hardwired to do its job right, figures out the next destination of the data based on its "comprehension" of the condition of the networks.

Routers can be gateways because a router can control the path through which information is sent in and out. It does so by using built-in headers and forwarding tables to figure out where packets of data need to be sent. Those packets of data carry your emails, transactions, online activity and so on.

A gateway is one of the many ways our data is moved over the Web for us. The gateway gives us entry into different networks so we can send email, look at Web pages, buy things online, and more. You can easily say that gateways deliver the freedom, information and convenience we enjoy online.

Types of Gateways

Cloud Storage Gateway

A cloud storage gateway is a hardware or software appliance that serves as a bridge between local applications and remote cloud-based storage. A cloud storage gateway provides basic protocol translation and simple connectivity to allow incompatible technologies to communicate. The gateway may be hardware or a virtual machine (VM) image.

The requirement for a gateway between cloud storage and enterprise applications became necessary because of the incompatibility between protocols used for public cloud technologies and legacy storage systems. Most public cloud providers rely on Internet protocols, usually a RESTful API over HTTP, rather than conventional storage area network (SAN) or network-attached storage (NAS) protocols.

Gateways can also be used for archiving in the cloud. This pairs with automated storage tiering, in which data can be replicated between fast, local disk and cheaper cloud storage to balance space, cost, and data archiving requirements.

The challenge with traditional cloud gateways which front the cloud with on-premise hardware and use the cloud like another storage silo is that the cloud is very expensive for hot data that tends to be frequently accessed, resulting in high retrieval costs.

Media Gateway

A media gateway is a translation device or service that converts media streams between disparate telecommunications technologies such as POTS, SS7, Next Generation Networks (2G, 2.5G and 3G radio access networks) or private branch exchange (PBX) systems. Media gateways enable multimedia communications across packet networks using transport protocols such as Asynchronous Transfer Mode (ATM) and Internet Protocol (IP).

Because the media gateway connects different types of networks, one of its main functions is to convert between different transmission and coding techniques. Media streaming functions such as echo cancellation, DTMF, and tone sender are also located in the media gateway.

Media gateways are often controlled by a separate Media Gateway Controller which provides the call control and signaling functionality. Communication between media gateways and Call Agents is achieved by means of protocols such as MGCP or Megaco or Session Initiation Protocol (SIP). Modern media gateways used with SIP are often stand-alone units with their own call and signaling control integrated and can function as independent, intelligent SIP end-points.

Voice over Internet Protocol (VoIP) media gateways perform the conversion between Time-division multiplexing (TDM) voice to a media streaming protocol, such as the Real-time Transport Protocol, (RTP), as well as a signaling protocol used in the VoIP system.

Mobile access media gateways connect the radio access networks of a public land mobile network PLMN to a next-generation core network. 3GPP standards define the functionality of CS-MGW and IMS-MGW for UTRAN and GERAN based PLMNs.

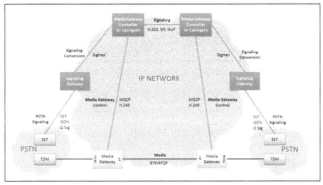

Media Gateways are used for transcoding media between PSTN and IP networks

IoT Gateway

An IoT Gateway is a solution for enabling IoT communication, usually device -to-device communications or device-to-cloud communications. The gateway is typically hardware device housing application software that performs essential tasks. At its most basic level, the gateway facilitates the connections between different data sources and destinations.

A simple way to conceive of an IoT Gateway is to compare it to your home or office network router or gateway. Such a gateway facilitates communication between your devices, maintains security and provides an admin interface where you can perform basic functions. An IoT Gateway does this and much more.

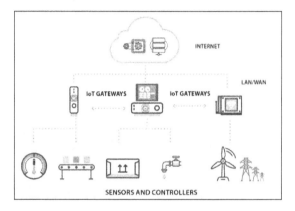

Functions of IoT Gateway

IoT Gateways have evolved to perform many tasks, from simple data filtering to visualization and complex analytics. These smart devices are helping power the current wave of IoT expansion.

IoT Gateway Feature Set

A versatile IoT Gateway may perform any of the following:

- Facilitating communication with legacy or non-internet connected devices;
- Data caching, buffering and streaming;
- Data pre-processing, cleansing, filtering and optimization;
- Some data aggregation;
- Device to Device communications/M2M;
- Networking features and hosting live data;
- Data visualization and basic data analytics via IoT Gateway applications;

- Short term data historian features;

- Security – manage user access and network security features;

- Device configuration management;

- System diagnostics.

VoIP Gateway

A VoIP Gateway (Voice over IP Gateway) is a network device that helps to convert voice and fax calls between an IP network and Public Switched Telephone Network (PSTN) in real time. It is a high performance gateway designed for Voice over IP applications. A VoIP gateway can typically support at least two T1/E1 digital channels. Most VoIP gateways feature at least one Ethernet and telephone port. Various protocols, such as MGCP, SIP, or LTP can help to control a gateway.

VoIP Gateway Benefits

VoIP gateway's main advantage is that it connects existing telephone and fax machines through traditional telephone networks, PBXs, and key systems. This makes the process of making calls over the IP network familiar to VoIP customers.

VoIP gateways end telephone calls, provide user admission control with an IVR (Interactive Voice Response) system, and provide accounting records for the call. Gateways also help direct outbound calls to a specific destination or end the call from another gateway and send the call to the PSTN.

VoIP gateways play a major role in enhancing carrier services, support the simplicity of telephone calls for less, and give easy access. Flexible call integration has been developed for less, which enables programmable call progress tones and distinctive ring tones.

VoIP Gateway Functions

The VoIP gateways' main functions include voice and fax compression or decompression, control signaling, call routing, and packeting. VoIP gateways are also power packed with additional features such as interfaces to external controllers like Gatekeepers or Soft switches, network management systems, and billing systems.

Future of VoIP Gateway Technology

VoIP gateway has become an efficient and flexible solution over the years and is used for office data and voice connectivity. Besides connectivity performance, VoIP is also more reliable under a variety of circumstances.

The future of VoIP gateway is very clear and precise. High-density, scalable, open platforms need to be designed and implemented to allow the millions of installed telephones and fast-growing number of H.323 computer clients (such as Netscape's Communicator and Microsoft's NetMeeting) to communicate over IP. Many vendors are in the process of designing interoperable VoIP gateways according to the latest architecture to meet service providers' changing demands, corporate network clients, and individual carriers.

Email Security Gateway

An email security gateway is a product or service that is designed to prevent the transmission of emails that break company policy, send malware or transfer information with malicious intent.

Businesses of all sizes use email security gateways to prevent data loss, perform email encryption, compensate for weak partner security and protect against known and unknown malware. Solution types for email security gateways include private cloud, hybrid cloud, hardware appliances, virtual appliances and email server-based products. These solutions offer similar functions, and many providers offer more than one form.

Important considerations for choosing an email security gateway include the sophistication of the basic security functions, the additional security functions that are available, ease of management, usability and customizability, typical false positive and false negative rates, and reliance on external systems for email processing and/or storage. Some offer sandboxing capabilities to help identify unknown risks.

To protect data on computers and devices that may be accessible outside the company, it may be advisable to choose an email security gateway that provides end-to-end encryption.

Competitors in email security gateways include: Cisco Email Security Appliance, Clearswift SECURE Email Gateway, Fortinet FortiMail, McAfee Security for Email Servers, Microsoft Exchange Online Protection (EOP), Proofpoint Enterprise Protection, Sophos Email Appliance, Symantec Email Security.cloud, Symantec Messaging Gateway, Trend Micro InterScan Messaging Security, Trend Micro ScanMail Suite for Microsoft Exchange and Websense Email Security Gateway.

NIC (Network Interface Card)

A network interface card (NIC) is a hardware component, typically a circuit board or chip, which is installed on a computer so that it can connect to a network. Modern NICs provide functionality to computers such as support for I/O interrupt, direct memory access (DMA) interfaces, data transmission, network traffic engineering and partitioning.

A NIC provides a computer with a dedicated, full-time connection to a network by implementing the physical layer circuitry necessary for communicating with a data link layer standard, such as Ethernet or Wi-Fi. Each card represents a device and can prepare, transmit and control the flow of data on the network. The NIC uses the OSI model to send signals at the physical layer, transmit data packets at the network layer and operate as an interface at the TCP/IP layer.

The network card operates as a middleman between a computer and a data network. For example, when a user requests a web page, the computer will pass the request to the network card which converts it into electrical impulses. Those impulses are received by a web server on the internet and responds by sending the web page back to the network card as electrical signals. The card gets these signals and translates them into the data that the computer displays.

Originally, network controllers were implemented as expansion cards that could be plugged into a computer port, router or USB device. However, more modern controllers are built directly into the computer motherboard chipset. Expansion card NICs can be purchased online or in retail stores if additional independent network connections are needed. When purchasing a NIC, specifications should correspond with the standard of the network.

The term network interface card is often considered interchangeable with the terms network interface controller, network adapter and LAN adapter.

Components of Network Interface Cards

- Speed- All NICs have a speed rating in terms of Mbps that suggests the general performance of the card when implemented in a computer network with ample bandwidth. If the bandwidth is lower than the NIC or multiple computers are connected with the same controller, this will slow down the labeled speed. The average Ethernet NICs are offered in 10 Mbps, 100 Mbps, 1000 Mbps and 1 Gbps varieties.

- Driver- This is the required software that passes data between the computer's operating system (OS) and the NIC. When a NIC is installed on a computer, the corresponding driver software is also downloaded. Drivers must stay updated and uncorrupted to ensure optimal performance from the NIC.

- MAC address- Unique, unchangeable MAC addresses, also known as a physical network address, are assigned to NICs that is used to deliver Ethernet packets to the computer.

- Connectivity LED- Most NICs have an LED indicator integrated into the connector to notify the user of when the network is connected and data is being transmitted.

- Router- A router is also sometimes needed to allow communication between a computer and other devices. In this case, the NIC connects to the router which is connected to the internet.

Types of Network Interface Card

Switches

A network switch is a hardware device that channels incoming data from multiple input ports to a specific output port that will take it toward its intended destination. It is a small device that transfers data packets between multiple network devices such as computers, routers, servers or other switches.

In a local area network (LAN) using Ethernet, a network switch determines where to send each incoming message frame by looking at the physical device address (also known as the Media Access Control address or MAC address). Switches maintain tables that match each MAC address to the port which the MAC address is received.

A network switch operates on the network layer, called layer 2 of the OSI model.

Network Device Layers

Network devices can be separated by the layer they operate on, defined by the OSI model. The OSI model conceptualizes networks separating protocols by layers. Control is typically passed from one layer to the next. Some layers include:

- Layer 1- or the physical layer or below, which can transfer data but cannot manage the traffic coming through it. An example would be Ethernet hubs or cables.

- Layer 2- or the data link layer, which uses hardware addresses to receive and forward data. A network switch is an example of what type of device is on layer 2.

- Layer 3- or the network layer, which performs similar functions to a router and also supports multiple kinds of physical networks on different ports. Examples include routers or layer 3 switches.

- Other layers include layer 4 (the transport layer), layer 5 (the session layer), layer 6 (the presentation layer) and layer 7 (the application layer).

Working of Network Switch

Switches, physical and virtual, comprise the vast majority of network devices in modern data networks. They provide the wired connections to desktop computers, wireless access points, industrial machinery and some internet of things (IoT) devices such as card entry systems. They interconnect the computers that host virtual machines (VMs) in data centers, as well as the dedicated physical servers, and much of the storage infrastructure. They carry vast amounts of traffic in telecommunications provider networks.

A network switch can be deployed in the following ways:

- Edge, or access switches: These switches manage traffic either coming into or exiting the network. Devices like computers and access points connect to edge switches.

- Aggregation, or distribution switches: These switches are placed within an optional middle layer. Edge switches connect into these and they can send traffic from switch to switch or send it up to core switches.

- Core switches: These network switches comprise the backbone of the network, connecting either aggregation or edge switches, connecting user or device edge networks to data center networks and, typically, connecting enterprise LANs to the routers that connect them to the internet.

If a frame is forwarded to a MAC address unknown to the switch infrastructure, it is flooded to all ports in the switching domain. Broadcast and multicast frames are also flooded. This is known as BUM flooding -- broadcast, unknown unicast, and multicast flooding. This capability makes a switch a Layer 2 or data-link layer device in the Open Systems Interconnection (OSI) communications model.

Many data centers adopt a leaf/spine architecture, which eliminates the aggregation layer. In this design, servers and storage connect to leaf switches (edge switches) and every leaf switch connects into two or more spine (core) switches. This minimizes the number of hops data has to take getting from source to destination, and, thereby, reduces the time spent in transit, or latency.

Some data centers establish a fabric or mesh network design that makes every device appear to be on a single, large switch. This approach reduces latency to its minimum and is used for highly demanding applications such as high-performance computing (HPC) in financial services or engineering.

Not all networks use switches. For example, a network may be (and often was, in the 1980s and 1990s) organized in a token ring or connected via a bus or a hub or repeater.

In these networks, every connected device sees all traffic and reads the traffic addressed to it. A network can also be established by directly connecting computers to one another, without a separate layer of network devices; this approach is mostly of interest in HPC contexts where sub-5-microsecond latencies are desired and can become quite complex to design, wire and manage.

Types of Switches

There are different types of switches in a network. These are:

Unmanaged Switches

These are the switches that are mostly used in home networks and small businesses as they plug-in and instantly start doing their job and such switches do not need to be watched or configured. These require only small cable connections. It allows devices on a network to connect with each other such as a computer to a computer or a computer to a printer in one location. They are the least expensive switches among all categories.

Managed Switches

These type of switches have many features like the highest levels of security, precision control and full management of the network. These are used in organisations containing a large network and can be customized to enhance the functionality of a certain network. These are the most costly option but their scalability makes them an ideal option for a network that is growing. They are achieved by setting a simple network management protocol (SNMP).

Smart Switches

These switches offer basic management features with the ability to create some levels of security but have a simpler management interface than the other managed switches. Thus they are often called partially managed switches. These are mostly used in fast and constant LANs which support gigabit data transfer and allocations. It can accept configuration of VLANs (Virtual LAN).

Enterprise Managed Switches

They have features like ability to fix, copy, transform and display different network configurations along with a web interface SNMP agent and command line interface. These are also known as fully managed switches and are more expensive than the smart switches as they have more features that can be enhanced. These are used in organisations that contain a large number of ports, switches and nodes.

LAN Switches

These are also known as Ethernet switches or data switches and are used to reduce network congestion or bottleneck by distributing a package of data only to its intended recipient. These are used to connect points on a LAN.

PoE Switches

PoE switches are used in PoE technology which stands for power over Ethernet that is a technology that integrates data and power on the same cable allowing power devices to receive data in parallel to power. Thus these switches provide greater flexibility by simplifying the cabling process.

Switching

Switching is the most valuable asset of computer networking. Every time in computer network you access the internet or another computer network outside your immediate location, or your messages are sent through a maze of transmission media and connection devices. The mechanism for exchange of information between different computer networks and network segments is called switching in Networking. On the other words we can say that any type signal or data element directing or Switching toward a particular hardware address or hardware pieces.

Hardware devices that can be used for switching or transfering data from one location to another that can use multiple layers of the Open Systems Interconnection (OSI) model. Hardware devices that can used for switching data in single location like collage lab is Hardware switch or hub but if you want to transfer data between to different location or remote location then we can use router or gatways.

For example- whenever a telephone call is placed, there are numerous junctions in the communication path that perform this movement of data from one network onto another network. One of another example is gatway that can be used by Internet Service Providers (ISP) to deliver a signal to another Internet Service Providers (ISP). For exchange of information between different locations various types of Switching Techniques are used in Networking.

Switching Techniques

Classification of Switching Techniques

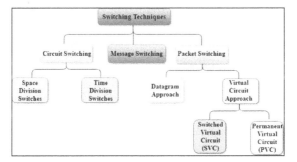

Circuit Switching

- Circuit switching is a switching technique that establishes a dedicated path between sender and receiver.

- In the Circuit Switching Technique, once the connection is established then the dedicated path will remain to exist until the connection is terminated.

- Circuit switching in a network operates in a similar way as the telephone works.

- A complete end-to-end path must exist before the communication takes place.

- In case of circuit switching technique, when any user wants to send the data, voice, video, a request signal is sent to the receiver then the receiver sends back the acknowledgment to ensure the availability of the dedicated path. After receiving the acknowledgment, dedicated path transfers the data.

- Circuit switching is used in public telephone network. It is used for voice transmission.

- Fixed data can be transferred at a time in circuit switching technology.

Communication through circuit switching has 3 phases:

- Circuit establishment.

- Data transfer.

- Circuit Disconnect.

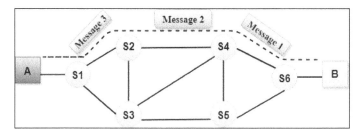

Circuit Switching can use either of the two technologies.

Space Division Switches

- Space Division Switching is a circuit switching technology in which a single transmission path is accomplished in a switch by using a physically separate set of crosspoints.

- Space Division Switching can be achieved by using crossbar switch. A crossbar switch is a metallic crosspoint or semiconductor gate that can be enabled or disabled by a control unit.

- The Crossbar switch is made by using the semiconductor. For example, Xilinx crossbar switch using FPGAs.

- Space Division Switching has high speed, high capacity, and nonblocking switches.

Space Division Switches can be categorized in two ways:

- Crossbar Switch

- Multistage Switch.

Crossbar Switch

The Crossbar switch is a switch that has n input lines and n output lines. The crossbar switch has n^2 intersection points known as crosspoints.

Disadvantage of Crossbar switch:

The number of crosspoints increases as the number of stations is increased. Therefore, it becomes very expensive for a large switch. The solution to this is to use a multistage switch.

Multistage Switch

- Multistage Switch is made by splitting the crossbar switch into the smaller units and then interconnecting them.

- It reduces the number of crosspoints.

- If one path fails, then there will be an availability of another path.

Advantages of circuit switching:

- In the case of Circuit Switching technique, the communication channel is dedicated.

- It has fixed bandwidth.

Disadvantages of circuit switching:

- Once the dedicated path is established, the only delay occurs in the speed of data transmission.

- It takes a long time to establish a connection approx 10 seconds during which no data can be transmitted.

- It is more expensive than other switching techniques as a dedicated path is required for each connection.

- It is inefficient to use because once the path is established and no data is transferred, then the capacity of the path is wasted.

- In this case, the connection is dedicated therefore no other data can be transferred even if the channel is free.

Message Switching

- Message Switching is a switching technique in which a message is transferred as a complete unit and routed through intermediate nodes at which it is stored and forwarded.

- In Message Switching technique, there is no establishment of a dedicated path between the sender and receiver.

- The destination address is appended to the message. Message Switching provides a dynamic routing as the message is routed through the intermediate nodes based on the information available in the message.

- Message switches are programmed in such a way so that they can provide the most efficient routes.

- Each and every node stores the entire message and then forward it to the next node. This type of network is known as store and forward network.

- Message switching treats each message as an independent entity.

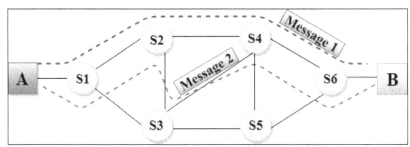

Advantages of message switching:

- Data channels are shared among the communicating devices that improve the efficiency of using available bandwidth.

- Traffic congestion can be reduced because the message is temporarily stored in the nodes.

- Message priority can be used to manage the network.

- The size of the message which is sent over the network can be varied. Therefore, it supports the data of unlimited size.

Disadvantages of message switching:

- The message switches must be equipped with sufficient storage to enable them to store the messages until the message is forwarded.

- The Long delay can occur due to the storing and forwarding facility provided by the message switching technique.

Packet Switching

- The packet switching is a switching technique in which the message is sent in one go, but it is divided into smaller pieces, and they are sent individually.

- The message splits into smaller pieces known as packets and packets are given a unique number to identify their order at the receiving end.

- Every packet contains some information in its headers such as source address, destination address and sequence number.

- Packets will travel across the network, taking the shortest path as possible.

- All the packets are reassembled at the receiving end in correct order.

- If any packet is missing or corrupted, then the message will be sent to resend the message.

- If the correct order of the packets is reached, then the acknowledgment message will be sent.

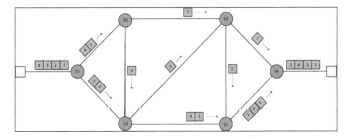

Approaches of Packet Switching

There are two approaches to Packet Switching:

Datagram Packet Switching

- It is a packet switching technology in which packet is known as a datagram, is considered as an independent entity. Each packet contains the information about the destination and switch uses this information to forward the packet to the correct destination.

- The packets are reassembled at the receiving end in correct order.

- In Datagram Packet Switching technique, the path is not fixed.

- Intermediate nodes take the routing decisions to forward the packets.

- Datagram Packet Switching is also known as connectionless switching.

Virtual Circuit Switching

- Virtual Circuit Switching is also known as connection-oriented switching.

- In the case of Virtual circuit switching, a pre-planned route is established before the messages are sent.

- Call request and call accept packets are used to establish the connection between sender and receiver.

- In this case, the path is fixed for the duration of a logical connection.

Let's understand the concept of virtual circuit switching through a diagram.

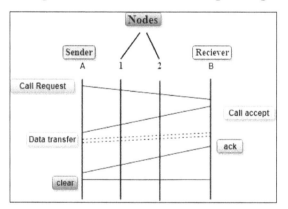

In the above diagram, A and B are the sender and receiver respectively. 1 and 2 are the nodes.

- Call request and call accept packets are used to establish a connection between the sender and receiver.

- When a route is established, data will be transferred.

- After transmission of data, an acknowledgment signal is sent by the receiver that the message has been received.

- If the user wants to terminate the connection, a clear signal is sent for the termination.

Differences b/w Datagram Approach and Virtual Circuit Approach

Datagram approach	Virtual Circuit approach
Node takes routing decisions to forward the packets.	Node does not take any routing decision.

Congestion cannot occur as all the packets travel in different directions.	Congestion can occur when the node is busy, and it does not allow other packets to pass through.
It is more flexible as all the packets are treated as an independent entity.	It is not very flexible.

Advantages of packet switching:

- Cost-effective: In packet switching technique, switching devices do not require massive secondary storage to store the packets, so cost is minimized to some extent. Therefore, we can say that the packet switching technique is a cost-effective technique.

- Reliable: If any node is busy, then the packets can be rerouted. This ensures that the Packet Switching technique provides reliable communication.

- Efficient: Packet Switching is an efficient technique. It does not require any established path prior to the transmission, and many users can use the same communication channel simultaneously, hence makes use of available bandwidth very efficiently.

Disadvantages of packet switching:

- Packet Switching technique cannot be implemented in those applications that require low delay and high-quality services.

- The protocols used in a packet switching technique are very complex and requires high implementation cost.

- If the network is overloaded or corrupted, then it requires retransmission of lost packets. It can also lead to the loss of critical information if errors are nor recovered.

Modems

Modem is abbreviation for Modulator – Demodulator. Modems are used for data transfer from one computer network to another computer network through telephone lines. The computer network works in digital mode, while analog technology is used for carrying massages across phone lines.

Modulator converts information from digital mode to analog mode at the transmitting end and demodulator converts the same from analog to digital at receiving end. The process of converting analog signals of one computer network into digital signals of another computer network so they can be processed by a receiving computer is referred to as digitizing.

When an analog facility is used for data communication between two digital devices called Data Terminal Equipment (DTE), modems are used at each end. DTE can be a terminal or a computer.

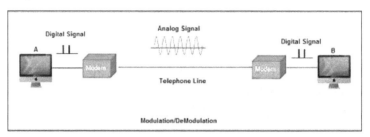

The modem at the transmitting end converts the digital signal generated by DTE into an analog signal by modulating a carrier. This modem at the receiving end demodulates the carrier and hand over the demodulated digital signal to the DTE.

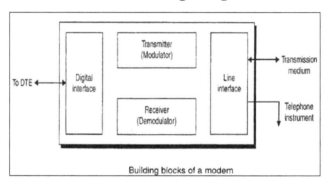

Building blocks of a modem

The transmission medium between the two modems can be dedicated circuit or a switched telephone circuit. If a switched telephone circuit is used, then the modems are connected to the local telephone exchanges. Whenever data transmission is required connection between the modems is established through telephone exchanges.

Ready to Send

To begin with the Data Terminal Equipment or DTE (better known as a computer) sends a Ready To Send or RTS signal to the Data Communication Equipment or DCE (better known as a modem). This is sometimes known as a wakeup call and results in the modem sending a Data Carrier Detect or DCD signal to the receiving modem. There then follows a series of signals passed between the two until the communication channel has been established. This process is known as handshaking and helps to explain why, even now, some companies like CompuServe use the symbol of two hands grasping each other to mean being on-line. Of course, after that all it takes is for the second modem to send a Data Set Ready or DSR signal to its computer and wait for the Data Terminal Ready or DTR reply. When that happens the first modem sends a Clear to Send or CTS signal to the computer that started the whole process off and data can then be transmitted. It is as simple as that.

Alternatively, for anyone confused by what the entire Internet industry dubs TLA's which means Three Letter Acronyms, the following diagram should help.

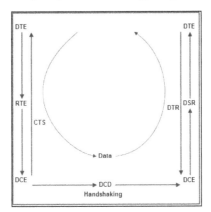

It only looks confusing. Take a second look and everything will soon become obvious. By way of completeness, these signals are all sent through different pins in the plug which is why the handbooks for all modems and printers carry a pin diagram somewhere in the section on troubleshooting. They are also standardized after the industry leaders met to agree standards for a whole range of peripheral equipment. The Recommended Standard for cable was number 232 which explains that one technical term probably everybody has heard of: RS 232.

Of course, that still leaves the question of exactly how data is transferred from one computer to another; something that is more of a problem than might first appear mainly because the phone lines are analogue while computers are digital. In simple terms this means a telephone signal is constantly changing. To understand that just think of a sine wave as produced on an oscilloscope. The signal might be constant, but it is constantly changing from positive to negative and back again in a series of smooth curves. Computers, on the other hand, can only understand information when it is presented as a string of binary digits so the idea is to map digital output onto an analogue signal.

This is done by superimposing different frequencies onto the analogue signal (which then becomes known as the carrier wave). Different frequencies can then represent different groups of binary digits in a process which is known as modulation when it is being transmitted and demodulation when it is decoded at the receiving end. Naturally two way communication is achieved by having a single device being capable of both modulation and demodulation, from which the unit takes its name: the modem.

From this it becomes obvious that the more frequencies that can be superimposed on the carrier wave the faster data can be transmitted. Alternatively, to take a different point of view, the more data there is to be transmitted so the more frequencies are needed.

Unfortunately it is only possible to send a limited number of frequencies at the same time, known as the bandwidth, which means communication takes that much longer as the size of the signals steadily increases. Now that pictures, sound and even video sequences are transmitted over the Internet on a regular basis, and as these all call for massive data files, the amount of available bandwidth is likely to be a problem for some time.

Finally, as the whole process comes down to sending binary digits or bits over a phone line the speed of the system is expressed as Bits Per Second or BPS which is a figure quoted by all the modem manufacturers.

Unfortunately when it comes to data communications there is a lot more involved than just how fast bits can be sent down a phone line. There is also the problem of what those bits mean and how they can be assembled into something intelligible at the far end. Here a whole range of issues need to be addressed and so it might be a good idea to briefly look at the first of these which are the transmission protocols.

Types of Modems

Modems can be of several types and they can be categorized in a number of ways. Categorization is usually based on the following basic modem features:

- Directional capacity: half duplex modem and full duplex modem.

- Connection to the line: 2-wire modem and 4-wire modem.

- Transmission mode: asynchronous modem and synchronous modem.

Half Duplex and Full Duplex Modems

Half Duplex

- A half duplex modem permits transmission in one direction at a time.

- If a carrier is detected on the line by the modem, we give an indication of the incoming carrier to the DTE through a control signal of its digital interface.

- As long as they camel' IS being received; the modem does not give permission to the DTE to transmit data.

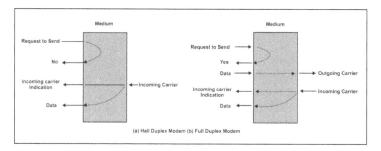

(a) Hall Duplex Modem (b) Full Duplex Modem

Full Duplex

- A full duplex modem allows simultaneous transmission in both directions.

- Therefore, there are two carriers on the line, one outgoing and the other incoming. Wire and 4-wire Modems.

- The line interface of the modem can have a 2-wire or a 4-wire connection to transmission medium. 4-wire Modem.

- In a 4-wire connection, one pair of wires is used for the outgoing carrier and the other pair is used for incoming carrier.

- Full duplex and half duplex modes of data transmission are possible on a 4-wire connection.

- As the physical transmission path for each direction is separate, the same carrier frequency can be used for both the directions.

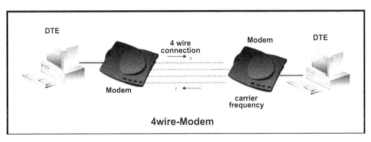

2-wire Modem

- 2-wire modems use the same pair of wires for outgoing and incoming carriers.

- A leased 2-wireconrlection is usually cheaper than a 4-wire connection as only one pair of wires is extended to the subscriber's premises.

- The data connection established through telephone exchange is also a 2-wire connection.

- In 2-wire modems, half duplex mode of transmission that uses the same frequency for the incoming and outgoing carriers can be easily implemented.

- For full duplex mode of operation, it is necessary to have two transmission channels, one for transmit direction and the other for receive direction.

- This is achieved by frequency division multiplexing of two different carrier frequencies. Thcsc carriers are placed within the bandwidth of the speech channel.

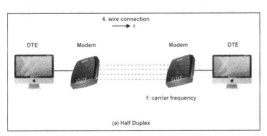

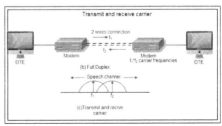

Asynchronous and Synchronous Modems

Asynchronous Modem

- Asynchronous modems can handle data bytes with start and stop bits.

- There is no separate timing signal or clock between the modem and the DTE.

- The internal timing pulses are synchronized repeatedly to the leading edge of the start pulse.

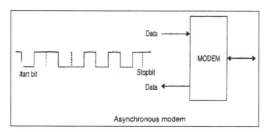

Asynchronous modem

Synchronous Modem

- Synchronous modems can handle a continuous stream of data bits but requires a clock signal.

- The data bits are always synchronized to the clock signal.

- There are separate clocks for the data bits being transmitted and received.

- For synchronous transmission of data bits, the DTE can use its internal clock and supply the same to the modem.

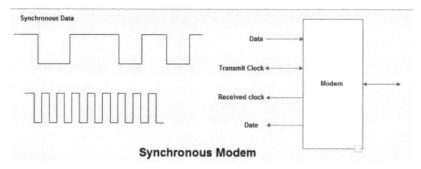

Synchronous Modem

The basic modulation techniques used by a modem to convert digital data to analog signals are:

- Amplitude shift keying (ASK)

- Frequency shift keying (FSK)

- Phase shift keying (PSK)

- Differential PSK (DPSK).

These techniques are known as the binary continuous wave (CW) modulation.

- Modems are always used in pairs. Any system whether simplex, half duplex or full duplex requires a modem at the transmitting as well as the receiving end.

- Thus a modem acts as the electronic bridge between two worlds - the world of purely digital signals and the established analog world.

References

- Hub, communication-networks: ecomputernotes.com, Retrieved 2 February, 2019

- Hub: searchnetworking.techtarget.com, Retrieved 11 July, 2019

- "Sniffing Tutorial part 1 - Intercepting Network Traffic". NETRESEC Network Security Blog. 2011-03-11. Retrieved 2011-03-13, Retrieved 15 January, 2019

- What-is-active-hub: orosk.com, Retrieved 18 March, 2019

- Difference-active-and-passive-hub: propatel.blogspot.com, Retrieved 8 August, 2019

- Intelligent: hubs.in, Retrieved 29 June, 2019

- Bridges, communication-networks: ecomputernotes.com, Retrieved 23 April, 2019

- Introduction-of-a-router: geeksforgeeks.org, Retrieved 1 July, 2019

- Wireless-router: searchmobilecomputing.techtarget.com, Retrieved 21 May, 2019

- Brouter: techterms.com, Retrieved 17 January, 2019

- What-is-a-core-router: wisegeek.com, Retrieved 27 April, 2019

- Dynamic-routing: techopedia.com, Retrieved 3 June, 2019

- Routing-and-its-types: ahirlabs.com, Retrieved 23 August, 2019

- Gateway: whatismyipaddress.com, Retrieved 13 May, 2019

- Cloud-storage-gateway: komprise.com, Retrieved 8 January, 2019

- What-is-an-iot-gateway: openautomationsoftware.com, Retrieved 12 March, 2019

- Voip-gateway: tech-faq.com, Retrieved 22 April, 2019

- Email-security-gateway: techtarget.com, Retrieved 28 July, 2019

- Network-interface-card: techtarget.com, Retrieved 30 March, 2019

- Switch: searchnetworking.techtarget.com, Retrieved 13 February, 2019

- Types-of-switches-in-computer-network: geeksforgeeks.org, Retrieved 2 June, 2019

- What-is-switching, computer-network: ecomputernotes.com, Retrieved 22 May, 2019

- Explain-about-modem, computer-network: ecomputernotes.com, Retrieved 25 March, 2019

5

Computer Network Security

The measures which are taken by businesses and organizations for the monitoring and prevention of unauthorized access to data are collectively known as computer network security. Some of the other aspects which fall within this field are cloud computing and security network segmentation. This chapter discusses in detail these theories and methodologies related to computer network security.

Computer network security consists of measures taken by business or some organizations to monitor and prevent unauthorized access from the outside attackers.

Different approaches to computer network security management have different requirements depending on the size of the computer network. For example, a home office requires basic network security while large businesses require high maintenance to prevent the network from malicious attacks.

Network Administrator controls access to the data and software on the network. A network administrator assigns the user ID and password to the authorized person.

Ways to Improve Computer Network Security

Assigning unique usernames and corresponding passwords are the simplest way of protecting a network resource, but computer network security commonly includes additional security measures including:

- Establishing a firewall,
- Installing and maintaining antivirus software,
- Using non-administrative accounts for day-to-day computer network activities,
- Setting strong passwords on wireless networking devices,
- Adding encryption to sensitive data and files,
- Utilizing a virtual private network (vpn) for secure communications between a main office and remote worker locations,
- Having a backup policy to recover data in the event of a hardware failure or security breach,
- Implementing clear employee guidelines for using the internet to access non-work websites and sending/receiving information,
- Maintaining adequate physical security of the network.

Aspects of Network Security

Following are the desirable properties to achieve secure communication:

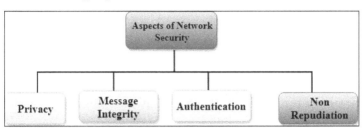

- Privacy: Privacy means both the sender and the receiver expects confidentiality. The transmitted message should be sent only to the intended receiver while the message should be opaque for other users. Only the sender and receiver should be able to understand the transmitted message as eavesdroppers can intercept the message. Therefore, there is a requirement to encrypt the message so that the message cannot be intercepted. This aspect of confidentiality is commonly used to achieve secure communication.

- Message Integrity: Data integrity means that the data must arrive at the receiver exactly as it was sent. There must be no changes in the data content during transmission, either maliciously or accident, in a transit. As there are more and more monetary exchanges over the internet, data integrity is more crucial. The data integrity must be preserved for secure communication.

- End-point authentication: Authentication means that the receiver is sure of the sender? identity, i.e., no imposter has sent the message.

- Non-Repudiation: Non-Repudiation means that the receiver must be able to prove that the received message has come from a specific sender. The sender must not deny sending a message that he or she send. The burden of proving the identity comes on the receiver. For example, if a customer sends a request to transfer the money from one account to another account, then the bank must have a proof that the customer has requested for the transaction.

Physical Network Security

One overlooked element of network security involves protecting hardware devices from theft and physical intrusion. Corporations lock network servers, network switches, and other core network components in well-guarded facilities. These measures aren't practical for homeowners, but you can keep your password-protected broadband routers in a private location, away from neighbors and houseguests.

If the possibility of data theft through physical means — stealing a computer or router — is a concern, one solution is to not store your data locally. Online backup services and cloud storage sites store sensitive files offsite at secure backup locations so that, even if the local hardware is stolen or compromised, the files are still secure. Widespread use of mobile devices makes physical security important. Smartphones fall out of pockets, are easy to leave behind, and are stolen.

A few precautions will keep your devices safe:

- Be alert to your physical surroundings whenever you use mobile devices and put them away when you're finished.

- If your device supports software that allows you to track the device or remotely erase its data, activate it, and use a password with the device to prevent a co-worker or acquaintance from looking at your files when you're out of the room.

- Stay in visual contact with your phone if you loan it to someone. A malicious person can steal personal data, install monitoring software, or otherwise hack a phone in just a few minutes when it's left unattended.

Password Protection

If applied properly, passwords are extremely effective in improving network security. Take password management seriously, and don't use weak, easy-to-guess passwords such as 123456. A few other best practices in password management go a long way toward network and device security, too:

- Set strong passwords or passcodes on all devices that join the network.

- Change the default administrator password of network routers.

- Don't share passwords with others unless absolutely necessary.

- Set up guest network access for friends and visitors, if possible.

- Change passwords frequently, especially if you've shared them or they've been discovered.

Spyware

Even without physical access to a device or knowing any network passwords, illicit programs such as spyware can infect computers and networks. This happens when you visit malicious websites accidentally or through a link in a phishing email. Spyware takes many forms. Some types monitor computer usage and web-browsing habits to report the data to corporations, who then use it to create targeted advertising. Other kinds of spyware attempt to steal personal data. One of the most dangerous forms of spyware, keylogger software, logs and sends the history of all keyboard actions, capturing passwords and credit card numbers along the way.

All spyware attempts to function without the knowledge of anyone who uses the infected computer, thereby posing a substantial security risk to the computer and the network to which it's connected. Because spyware is difficult to detect and remove, security experts recommend installing and running reputable anti-spyware software on computer networks.

Online Privacy

Personal stalkers and identity thieves monitor people's online habits and movements well beyond the scope of basic spyware. Wi-Fi hotspot usage on commuter trains and automobiles reveal your location, for example. Even in the virtual world, much about a person's identity can be tracked online through the IP addresses of their networks and their social network activities.

Privacy protection tools include anonymous web proxy servers and VPN services. Though maintaining complete privacy online is not fully achievable, those methods protect privacy to a certain degree. Bottom line: Be careful what you share online and with whom.

Importance of Network Security for Business Organization

Technology has progressed so much that it would be no surprise if your computer is hacked and you are completely unaware of the reasons for it. On a personal level, the network security includes only the downloading and installation of anti-virus software and firewall settings. However, when the same problem arises in a business organization, then the solution cannot be as simple as in the personal computer networks. As the risks are many in a business organization, there should be a complete system dedicated to securing the networks.

Any organization should monitor its system for potential unauthorized access and other kind of attacks. In order to safeguard sensitive information, it is important to perform routine checks and create a reliable and safe network. Every year, many organizations, corporations and governments dedicate a substantial chunk of their investment on their computer and network security.

It is crucial to establish a safe and secure network for the following reasons:

To Protect Company's Assets

This can be considered as the primary goal of securing the computers and computer networks. The assets mean the information that is stored in the computer networks, which are as crucial and valuable as the tangible assets of the company. The computer and network security is concerned with the integrity, protection and safe access of the confidential information. It also involves the accessibility of information in a meaningful manner.

To Protect Client Data and Information

In today's world, information and identity theft cases have increased and keeping all your existing client's data and information safe and secure is the responsibility of a business organization. The best quality Network security and support system can help minimise the risk of your business falling a prey to data and information theft.

Keep your Shared Data Safe and Secure

For Computer systems on a shared network, a Network Security and support system can help keep shared data and information safe. Different levels of safety and security can also be placed for specific computers that may have greater access to data and information than others.

Protect Computer Systems from Harmful Spyware

Network Security and support systems can be effectual in protecting your computer systems from harmful viruses and spyware. This means you won't have to look out for new, expensive computer systems.

To Comply with Regulatory Requirements and Ethical Responsibilities- It is the responsibility of every organization to develop procedures and policies addressing the security requirements of every organization. These policies work for the safety and security of any organization and are compulsory for any organization working on computers. Protection of company's assets would mean that it is protected from liability addressing to the ethical responsibilities of an organization.

For Competitive Advantage- Developing an effective security system for networks will give the organization a competitive edge. In the arena of Internet financial services and e-commerce, network security assumes prime importance. The customers would avail the services of internet banking only if the networks are secured.

Increase your Network Performance

Investing in high quality Network Security and support system facilities will benefit your business organization massively and reduce expenses in the long run. There will be fewer disasters and less downtimes, which will boost your business profits.

Network Security and support system is one of the most vital factors to consider if you are working online, no matter how big or small your business organization is.

Importance of Network Security in Schools

Schools and universities face a number of challenges that businesses and other organizations don't have to encounter. Whereas companies have their employees to monitor and grant access to, schools have to worry about teachers and students, who can range anywhere from five-year-olds to full adults. In the case of schools with young children, those kids often don't have the same legal obligations or face the same legal ramifications if they should, intentionally or accidentally, access a network without authorization. Students also tend to not understand the security threats out there related to the internet and are more likely to use unsecured networks, download infected files, or expose devices to malware. School structure can also be a major problem, with many institutions of higher learning using a decentralized approach that creates multiple networks that need protection. Schools are also dealing with students bringing more of their own mobile devices to class, which itself can present many security issues. Couple all these challenges with shrinking budgets, and it's easy to see how things can quickly get out of control. All of this underscores the need for an effective network security strategy.

For many schools, network security isn't just an option, it's a necessity. We're long past the days where each classroom had a single computer; students now regularly have smartphones and tablets. Online access has also turned into a crucial tool for learning. To make sure important school data and files are protected, administrators need a stable security environment, which is where network security comes in. A well-managed network security system will feature measures where administrators can efficiently control and monitor what students and teachers access while online. While web filters can certainly play a role in restricting certain websites, network security can go much further by taking a more proactive approach in monitoring online activity and blocking sites that may lead to security compromises.

This blocking action can go beyond the internet. Mobile devices have shown to be a major source for malware, and oftentimes, students will be using an infected device without even knowing it. Network security, often through network access control, can detect when a device has been infected. When this happens, the device is then blocked from connecting to the network and alerts IT about the infection. IT workers can then go and clean the infected part of the device, which not only protects the network but the user as well. Network security systems can also be robust and flexible, allowing for various types of devices to connect provided they're able to pass the standards set by administrators.

A good network security system found in schools will feature other security measures such as anti-virus protection, firewalls, encryption, password protection, and the latest upgrades and patches. All of these allow administrators to better monitor individual devices and authenticate them for use on the network. This evaluation before a device is granted access can be crucial for preventing attacks on network systems. With so many sensitive records and files, administrators need to know exactly who and what is accessing the network, which is why network access control is such a vital part of network security.

Securing educational networks is not something that should be treated lightly. Security breaches aren't a rare thing anymore, which can be seen by the more than 650,000 student records that were compromised a couple years ago at the University of Nebraska.

Schools and universities that recognize the threats and the damage they can cause will be in a better position to protect their teachers and students. As more and more come to realize the importance of network security, they'll be able to respond quickly to future attacks and threats.

Cloud Computing Security

Cloud computing security refers to the set of procedures, processes and standards designed to provide information security assurance in a cloud computing environment.

Cloud computing security addresses both physical and logical security issues across all the different service models of software, platform and infrastructure. It also addresses how these services are delivered (public, private or hybrid delivery model).

Cloud security encompasses a broad range of security constraints from an end-user and cloud provider's perspective, where the end-user will primarily will be concerned with the provider's security policy, how and where their data is stored and who has access to that data. For a cloud provider, on the other hand, cloud computer security issues can range from the physical security of the infrastructure and the access control mechanism of cloud assets, to the execution and maintenance of security policy. Cloud security is important because it is probably the biggest reason why organizations fear the cloud.

The Cloud Security Alliance (CSA), a non-profit organization of industry specialists, has developed a pool of guidelines and frameworks for implementing and enforcing security within a cloud operating environment.

Cloud Computing Security Features

Advanced Perimeter Firewall

Most of the firewalls are simple because they just inspect the source and destination packets only. However, there are some more advanced firewalls available that perform stable packet inspection. It will check the file packets integrity to ensure the stability before approving or rejecting the packet.

The top-of-the-line firewalls, for example, Palo Alto Networks' perimeter firewall, which will check the data stored in the file packet in order to examine the file type including source, destination, and integrity. This granularity is really necessary to prevent the most advanced persistent threats.

Intrusion Detection Systems with Event Logging

All IT security compliance standards must involve the businesses to have a means, which can track and record all type of intrusion attempts. Thus, IDS event logging solutions are necessary for all businesses that want to meet the compliance standards like PCI and HIPAA.

There are some cloud providers, who offer IDS monitoring service and update the security rules for their firewalls in order to counter the threat signals and malicious IP addresses, which are detected for all cloud users.

Internal Firewalls for each Application and Databases

Using a strong or top-in-line perimeter firewall will block the external attacks only but internal attacks are still a major danger. However, if there are no internal firewalls in infrastructures to restrict the sensitive data access and applications is not considered secure. For example, an employee user account can allow the hackers to bypass the perimeter firewall completely.

Data-at-Rest Encryption

Data encryption is one of the effective methods to keep the most sensitive data stored in the cloud infrastructure safe and secure from the unauthorized user. Moreover, strong type of encryption will minimize the chance of stolen data used for some purpose. In addition, a user has a chance to alert them and they can take steps to protect their individuality.

Tier IV Data Centers with Strong Physical Security

Last possible way for the hackers and the industrial spies is the physical hardware, which is used to run a cloud environment to steal the most crucial data. If hackers get direct access to the hardware, which runs the cloud they have free reign to steal the data or upload the malware directly to the local machine.

Data Loss and Disaster Recovery

Data loss is any process or event that results in data being corrupted, deleted and/or made unreadable by a user and/or software or application.

It occurs when one or more data elements can no longer be utilized by the data owner or requesting application. Data loss is also known as data leakage.

There are many causes of data loss, and those can differ by industry. Some organizations may be more concerned about outside attacks, while others are primarily worried about vulnerability to internal human error. Data loss can occur during standard IT procedures such as migration, or through malicious attacks via ransom ware or other malware.

The impact of data loss may also differ based on who the data belongs to. Along with affecting an organization's internal data, the loss of an outside party's confidential data can jeopardize a business' legal standing with compliance laws.

Regardless of how or why data loss occurs, it is crucial for all organizations to have prevention and recovery plans in place, and to understand the effects and consequences of data loss.

Reason for Data Loss

Common unintentional causes of data loss include hardware malfunction, software corruption, human error and natural disasters. Data can also be lost during migrations and in power outages or improper shutdowns of systems.

Hardware malfunction is the most common cause of lost data. A hard drive can crash due to mishandling, overheating, mechanical issues or simply the passage of time. Proper hard drive maintenance can help prevent data loss, and being mindful of a drive's lifespan enables users to prepare for the drive's replacement.

Software corruption is another common cause of data loss, and can take place when systems are improperly shut down. These shutdowns can usually be attributed to power outages or human error, so it falls on the organization to prepare for these incidents and ensure the proper shutting down of systems. Natural disasters can cause data loss through all of the above, be it damage to hardware or causing systems to fail without data being backed up. Having a disaster recovery (DR) plan and frequent backups are the best strategies for preventing this type of data loss.

Preventing data loss can require different methods of
data protection, depending on the vulnerabilities of the data.

Computer viruses - such as malware designed to steal and delete data can cause intentional data loss. To help prevent this, organizations should keep antivirus software up to date and ensure that employees are aware of potential malware threats.

Hackers can also cause intentional data loss. These incidents require different protection methods, particularly with regards to access. To prevent intentional data destruction from recent or current employees, a company should limit access to confidential or sensitive data to necessary personnel only. Controlling or restricting access can also aid in preventing loss via hackers or even human error, where an employee may unintentionally erase data without knowing the severity of the action.

Impact of Data Loss

Preventing data loss can be an expensive process, requiring the purchase of software or other backup and data protection products or services. While the costs of these services may be high, thorough protection against data loss is usually worth it in the long run, especially when pitted against potential costs down the line.

In the case of major data loss, business continuity and day-to-day functions can be severely affected, tacking on additional costs. Company time and resources will often need to be diverted to address data loss and recover the most recent copy of lost data, so other business functions may be affected.

An organization's reputation can also suffer following a data loss. Customers need to be informed of the loss, and those customers may take their business elsewhere. Entrusting personal, sensitive data to another company takes trust, and the loss of data can make an organization look unreliable. Rebuilding these relationships will take significant time and company resources.

Prevention Strategies

Data loss prevention (DLP) can take the form of a strategy or a product that aims to mitigate or prevent data loss in case of an incident. DLP strategies tend to target the sharing of sensitive data outside of the corporate network, while software products control this aspect through limiting what users can transfer or share.

The end goal of DLP is to protect confidential and sensitive data from unauthorized users who could mishandle or maliciously share it. Whether in response to insider threats or the need to conform to outside data protection regulations, having a data loss prevention plan is becoming an important part of a modern backup and data protection strategy.

A sampling of DLP products and services include Microsoft Office 365 Data Loss Prevention, Symantec Data Loss Prevention and McAfee Total Protection for Data Loss Prevention.

The Law

When an organization is responsible for protecting someone else's data, it also takes on the responsibility to keep those people or organizations informed of the status of their data. In the United States, each state has enacted legislation requiring both private and government organizations to inform relevant parties of a breach or loss of their data.

Enacted in May 2018, the European Union's General Data Protection Regulation addresses notifying affected parties of data breach or loss. In Article 33 of the GDPR, there is a mandatory 72-hour countdown for organizations to gather information and report on data breaches to the regulator, as well as the impacted individuals involved in the breach. Along with notification, the organization must draft a plan to recover the data within those 72 hours.

While the GDPR is an EU regulation, it applies to any organization that has the data of EU citizens. Because of this, any organization globally that collects this type of data is liable for data loss that occurs, and subject to the GDPR rules.

Disaster Recovery

When a company is embarking into a new venture or if it is a new business, there are many concerns that come into the mind especially in the case when there is a crises situation or a disaster in the IT infrastructure of the company. In order to help the business which such a situation, Immunity Networks provides their customers with the disaster recovery Service.

The Disaster recovery service is carried out with a customized plan based on the individual requirements and criteria's of the customer. One can never say when a disaster may strike, however when there is a plan in place, it makes it much more easy and simple recover the essential data within a speculated time frame depending on the intensity of the situation.

The three different levels of Disaster recovery:

- Disaster recovery Low risk of data loss: Under this there can be absolutely no loss or very minimal loss however the business can still be functional without much stress.

- Disaster recovery Moderate risk of data loss: Under this risk factor, the loss is manageable for the company however it would not create such a big impact which can hit the red button for the business.

- Disaster recovery High risk of data loss: In this situation it can be really bad for the company due to extreme damage caused because of which the data loss can be a real problem. Under this situation, it becomes very critical to ensure that the right measures are taken to reduce the loss of data.

We at Immunity Networks provide our clients with customized plans after doing a proper analysis on the order and importance of the data in the event of a disaster. Under this, the following would be covered-

- A plan to avoid, limit or reduce the disaster;

- An alternative or emergency plan to respond to the particular situation;

- A proper guide to recover the main functions of the business;

- A continuation plan for the business until they get back to normal.

Under the Comprehensive Disaster Recovery plan, the following would be taken care of:

- Recovering the business functions which are critical;

- Restoration of the business back to how it was before the disaster.

Issues that are Considered by Immunity Networks

Before we come up with the Disaster Recovery Plan, we do a Risk Analysis as well as a Disaster Recovery Audit to come up with various options and solutions that would be a part of your Disaster Recovery Plan.

In the event of a disaster in the infrastructure of the business, we sit down to analyze what caused the incident as well as come up with the Incident Management Plan. We then take into consideration the various procedures that could be used in order to enhance the recovery process. Once that is in place, we then go ahead and check for alternate methods and solutions to ensure that the client is secured from such disasters in the future.

Features of Disaster Recovery

Features of Immunity's Disaster Recovery Service-

- A customized plan depending on the kind of disaster as well the amount of recovery that can be done based on the various findings of our qualified technical staff.

- Proper and necessary guidance provided to the client to ensure that the same situation does not arise again.

- Different levels of disaster recovery planning depending on the risk factor of the data loss.

- Our technical team comes up with a plan in order to ensure that the business is still running even in the event of a disaster until the matter is resolved.

Benefits of Disaster Recovery

Benefits of Immunity's Disaster Recovery Service-

- Our technical staffs are available immediately to cater to the various needs in the event of a disaster.

- We focus on ensuring that you get as much as your data back.

- We also provide an audit report which is based on the analysis and findings of the reasons behind the disaster.

- Provide an enhanced recovery plan while ensuring that the client does not face the same problem once again.

Mobile Device Security

Mobile device security means the security measures designed to protect the sensitive information stored on and transmitted by smartphones, tablets, laptops and other mobile devices.

Mobile device security spans the gamut from user authentication measures and mobile security best practices for protecting against compromised data in the event of unauthorized access or accidental loss of the mobile device to combat malware, spyware and other mobile security threats that can expose a mobile device's data to hackers.

Most mobile devices feature mobile operating systems with built-in mobile device security features, including iOS for iPhones and iPads, Google's Android platform and Microsoft's Windows Phone. Additionally, a variety of third-party mobile device security solutions are available for providing an additional layer of protection for mobile devices.

Types of Mobile Security Threats

Malware

Malware includes viruses, worms, Trojan horses and spyware designed to steal data, harm devices, encrypting or deleting sensitive data, hijack browser sessions, monitor user activity without their permission and provide backdoor entry to hackers. Malware is also known as malicious software.

Phishing

Mobile device users easily fall victim to online fraudsters in phishing attacks because users are more likely to be tricked into opening an email, instant message, or text message with malicious intent. Hackers impersonate a legitimate company and attempt to steal user sensitive data such as credit card numbers and login credentials. These attacks are successful on mobile devices such as smartphones and tablets because users find it difficult to navigate between screens to recognize the authenticity of the link.

Outdated OS

The outdated operating system in mobile devices opens the door for hackers to exploit. Mostly, users are not fully aware of the importance of operating system update and end up suffering from unanticipated online attacks. Besides this, jailbreak attacks are becoming more common these days which discreetly allows downloading of apps and extensions on mobile devices.

Advanced Persistent Threats (APTs)

Advanced Persistent Threats (APTs) are targeted at stealing data rather than causing damage to the organization or network. As the attack is a stealth activity, the hacker after gaining access to the organization's network stays there undetected for a long period of time. A successfully staged attack can leave behind devastating results.

Untested Mobile Applications

At times, downloading third-party vendor apps from unauthorized sources can prove to be malicious programs. Therefore, it is advisable to download from the regulated app store to avoid vulnerabilities and to prevent exploitation. The same can be implied on downloading authorized software due to the reason that some of them are not up-to-date versions.

Mobile Device Security Best Practices

Since the advent of BYOD (Bring Your Own Device) to work, organizations are witnessing high risks of data vulnerability with three fourth of the official population accessing corporate information or internet from their personal devices such as smartphones, tablets, laptops, etc. Thereby, it becomes mandatory to secure those mobile devices from cyberattacks. Below are some of the best practices that are religiously followed in the cybersecurity world to protect mobile devices from attacks.

Unsecured Wi-Fi Networks

Unknown internet connections or Wi-Fi hotspots can prove to be some risky business, so avoid using unsure Wi-Fi networks to steer clear of risks.

Avoid Downloading Apps from Unknown Sources

Download apps from trusted sources like Apple's iOS App Store and Google's Play Store. Third party sources for downloading apps are not safe as they are the abodes of scams and other online disasters.

Unsolicited Calls or Messages

Never open emails from unknown senders or attend calls from untrusted sources.

Always make it a point to verify calls and scan emails before proceeding further. The best approach is to refrain from responding to unsolicited calls and email messages.

Components of Mobile Device Security

Endpoint Security

As organizations embrace flexible and mobile workforces, they must deploy networks that allow remote access. Endpoint solutions protect corporations by monitoring the files and processes on every mobile device that accesses a network. By constantly scanning for malicious behavior, endpoint security can identify threats early on. When they find malicious behavior, endpoint solutions quickly alert security teams, so threats are removed before they can do any damage.

VPN

A virtual private network, or VPN, is an encrypted connection over the Internet from a device to a network. The encrypted connection helps ensure that sensitive data is safely transmitted. It prevents unauthorized people from eavesdropping on the traffic and allows the user to conduct remote work safely.

Secure Web Gateway

Secure web gateways provide powerful, overarching cloud security. Because 70 percent of attacks are distinct to the organization, businesses need cloud security that identifies previously used attacks before they are launched. Cloud security can operate at the DNS and IP layers to defend against phishing, malware, and ransomware earlier. By integrating security with the cloud, you can identify an attack on one location and immediately prevent it at other branches.

Email Security

Email is both the most important business communication tool and the leading attack vector for security breaches. In fact, according to the Cisco 2017 Midyear Cybersecurity Report, email is the primary tool for attackers spreading ransomware and other malware. Proper email security includes advanced threat protection capabilities that detect, block, and remediate threats faster; prevent data loss; and secure important information in transit with end-to-end encryption.

Cloud Access Security Broker

Your network must secure where and how your employees work, including in the cloud. You will need a cloud access security broker (CASB), a tool that functions as a gateway between on-premises infrastructure and cloud applications (Salesforce, Dropbox, etc.). A CASB identifies malicious cloud-based applications and protects against breaches with a cloud data loss prevention (DLP) engine.

Network Access Control (NAC)

The emphasis of NAC is the access control – who or what has authorized permission to access the network. This includes both users and devices. The NAC network intercepts the connection requests, which are then authenticated against a designated identity and access management system. Access is either accepted or denied based on a pre-determined set of parameters and policies that are programmed into the system.

While this concept is fairly straightforward, deploying network access control is more challenging. This is because NAC requires interaction between protocols and different technologies that range from IT systems to security in order to function effectively.

Uses of NAC

According to the executive team at managed services provider Virtual Armour, the goals of network access control are as follows:

- Authorization, Authentication and Accounting (AAA) of network connections.

- Role-based control for a user, device, or application post-authentication. This means that a given user and their device are placed into their corresponding permission buckets such that an employee in finance and an employee in HR have access to different resources in their environment.

- Confidentiality and containment of intellectual property through policy enforcement.

- Identity and asset management.

- Automatically assess a device's security posture, and allow or block based on if they pass the security check (which can be based on numerous things, such as operating system version, latest patches installed, a certain anti-virus is installed, etc.).

There are a number of use cases that cover all types of organizations using NAC solutions, VP of ClearPass Security at Aruba, an HPE company. These include the following:

- Access policy: This is the over-arching use case for NAC, said Anand. It allows the administrator to define multiple access policies that govern users and devices connecting to the network based on specific situations such as user profile, device type or user location.

- Compliance checks of endpoint devices: When a NAC client runs on end user compute devices, it can continually check and validate to ensure the appropriate software is installed, as well as confirming the devices have updated versions or patch management. If the device fails any of these compliance checks, it will likely be denied access to the network until appropriate updates are made.

- Guest access: There will be times that an organization needs to allow non-employees to access the network. An NAC solution can provide guests the ability to connect to the corporate network with restricted access.

- Device discovery and profiling: Due to the increased use of the Internet of Things (IoT), especially in particular industry verticals such as healthcare or manufacturing, the IT administrator needs to a comprehensive view of any and all devices connected to the network. Anand said in these situations, NAC is very useful as it has the capability to discover all devices on the network, and then fingerprints and profiles them so the IT administrator has a global view of what is on the network.

- Enforcement: There will be times when an unauthorized device or user attempts to connect to the network. When this happens, the NAC solution can automatically disconnect the device. There is also an option to quarantine the device until an investigation is done to determine if the device was supposed to be authorized and why it was exhibiting unauthorized behaviors.

- Security analytics: Network access control is an important part of the security system. It can continuously monitor the behavior of devices while on the network by collecting logs, flows and packets, Anand explained. The NAC solution can also apply machine learning and security analytics in order to detect malicious behavior that could lead to exfiltration, stolen credentials, or attack on the network infrastructure.

Network Segmentation

Network segmentation is the process of splitting a computer network into smaller segments. This way, you are separating groups of users, applications, and systems from each other to ensure better network security and to protect sensitive company data.

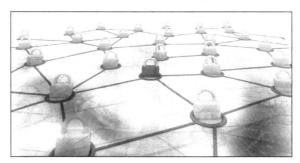

The traditional flat network infrastructure has all the servers and workstations on one local network (LAN). This infrastructure is not always ideal since you may have devices and systems that don't necessarily have to interact and communicate with each other.

Putting such systems in one local network provides intruders with the opportunity to access the entire network since all they have to do is hack into one system that gives them access to the whole network.

By splitting the network into small groups, network segmentation makes it difficult for hackers to access their entire network from one point and cause damage. It limits communication and interactions within your network, and this reduces the attacking options available to intruders. Network segmentation can be implemented virtually or physically, but the result will be the same.

Implementing Network Segmentation and Segregation

Regardless of the technologies chosen for network segmentation and segregation, there are five common themes for best practice implementations:

- Apply technologies at more than just the network layer. Each host and network should be segmented and segregated, where possible, at the lowest level that can be practically managed. In most cases, this applies from the data link layer up to and including the application layer; however, in particularly sensitive environments, physical isolation may be appropriate. Host-based and network-wide measures should be deployed in a complementary manner and be centrally monitored. It is not sufficient to simply implement a firewall or security appliance as the only security measure.

- Use the principles of least privilege and need-to-know. If a host, service or network doesn't need to communicate with another host, service or network, it should not be allowed to. If a host, service or network only needs to talk to another host, service or network on a specific port or protocol, and nothing else, it should be restricted to this. Adopting these principles across a network will complement the minimisation of user privileges and significantly increase the overall security posture of the environment.

- Separate hosts and networks based on their sensitivity or criticality to business operations. This may include using different hardware or platforms depending on different security classifications, security domains or availability/integrity requirements for certain hosts or networks. In particular, separate management networks and consider physically isolating out-of-band management networks for sensitive environments.

- Identify, authenticate and authorise access by all entities to all other entities. All users, hosts and services should have their access to all other users, hosts and services restricted to only those required to perform their designated duties or functions. All legacy or local services which bypass or downgrade the strength of identification, authentication and authorisation services should be disabled wherever possible and have their use closely monitored.

- Implement whitelisting of network traffic instead of blacklisting. Only permit access for known good network traffic (i.e. that which is identified, authenticated and authorised), rather than denying access to known bad network traffic (e.g. blocking a specific address or service). Not only will whitelisting result in a superior security policy to blacklisting, it will also significantly improve an organisation's capacity to detect and assess potential network intrusions.

The following types of traffic flow filtering techniques should be considered when implementing network segmentation and segregation. As stated above, these filtering techniques will be significantly more effective if implemented using a whitelisting approach:

- Logical access restrictions of network traffic such as:

  ○ Network layer filtering that restricts which hosts are able to communicate with other hosts based on Internet Protocol and route information;

  ○ State-based filtering that restricts which hosts are able to communicate with other hosts based on their intended function or current state of operation;

  ○ Port and protocol level filtering that restricts the number and type of services that each host can use to communicate with other hosts.

- Authentication filtering to restrict access to hosts, services and networks based on strong authentication, commonly implemented using public key cryptography, such as certificate-based IPsec.

- Application filtering to filter the content of communications between hosts and networks at the application layer, commonly implemented using email and web content filtering, intrusion prevention systems, and web application or XML firewalls.

- For particularly sensitive environments, it may also be appropriate to implement physical isolation between networks. Where limited interaction between physically-isolated networks is necessary, one or more of the following may be required:

  ○ Bespoke or tailored security device,

  ○ High assurance product, or

  ○ Cross domain solution.

Example implementations of network segmentation and segregation:

Segmenting a Network to Protect Key Hosts

In this scenario an organisation had decided to segment their network to protect key hosts from a network intrusion. In doing so they implemented the following security measures:

- Compiled an inventory of key hosts documenting their sensitivity and any necessary communications with such hosts.

- Planned the introduction of security measures in a schedule that was achievable with the resources allocated ensuring sufficient testing prior to deployment.

- Restricted logical network connectivity to key hosts to only those ports and protocols that were essential.

- Only allowed connections to be established from more trusted to less trusted zones and not vice versa (with the exception of necessary user access to application interfaces).

- Whitelisted application layer content so that only required content was able to flow between different trust zones.

- Implemented multi-factor authentication in addition to using a separate set of credentials for users and services if their function was more sensitive than other users or services sharing the same host or network.

- Minimised the use of implicit trust relationships between hosts in the same and different trust zones (the trust relationships defined across different trust zones were implemented such that each side of the trust relationship authenticated and authorised the other).

- Implemented web, email and file content filtering for connections to external organisations and the internet to detect and sanitise potentially malicious content.

- Applied intrusion prevention and host-based antivirus to detect and quarantine identified malicious content.

- Implemented centralised logging, alerting, monitoring and auditing capabilities which were the responsibility of a dedicated security operations team.

The above list is not an exhaustive set of security measures; however, it is a realistic overview which demonstrates that network segmentation and segregation must be considered at all layers to be effective. Implementing a secure network architecture is never as simple as implementing a gateway firewall with restrictive access control lists.

Segregating High-Risk Applications from a Network

In this scenario an organisation had identified that most of their network contained sensitive information and segmenting the network or segregating all of that information was not cost-effective. Instead, the organisation chose to segregate high-risk applications (i.e. web browsers, email clients and content management systems) from the rest of the network. In doing so, they implemented the following security measures to maintain business requirements while reducing the risk of a successful network intrusion:

- Users requiring internet access launched a remote desktop application on their corporate workstation to access a virtual desktop and authenticated with a user account used only for that purpose. This virtual desktop was served from a dedicated server hosted in a different network segment within a different authentication domain. This dedicated remote desktop allowed users to conduct high-risk activities such as web browsing and reading emails while limiting the utility of a single compromised application to an adversary.

- Users requiring access to high-risk applications launched a local virtualisation application to run a hardened virtual host which connected to a less-trusted remote environment which was protected by a layered security gateway that broke apart and abstracted all necessary communications protocols between high-risk applications and the organisation's corporate network.

Implementations of Network Segmentation and Segregation

The key takeaway from both approaches was that users did not store or process potentially malicious data directly on their corporate workstation or use the corporate servers which were relied upon for sensitive and business-critical functions. Each user's interaction was with a remote desktop or application and, if required, output was sent back to the user through a sufficiently structured and limited capability that prevented malicious code from executing or propagating throughout the corporate network.

It is important to remember that when implementing security measures an organisation will incur a resource cost to ensure that the additional systems are appropriately maintained. As with other technology assets, these security measures should be managed and monitored, with security patches applied as soon as possible after release.

Finally, it is recommended that all web browsing environments should be non-persistent, rigorously hardened and subject to regular technical security assessments. Therefore, if the web browsing environment does become compromised with malicious code, the infection is quickly removed when the user completes their web browsing session.

The Benefits of Network Segmentation

While most cybersecurity experts believe that different parts of a network should be isolated from each other for better network security, very few organizations have implemented this strategy. Data from CIO reveals that even though IT experts believe that network segmentation is a crucial cybersecurity measure, less than 25 percent of organizations have implemented it.

One of the reasons why organizations are yet to make this bold step is the amount of effort required to split a network into portions properly. Professionals will need detailed information on the network infrastructure for the segments and control points to be set up without leaving gaps. The network architecture will also have to be reworked again, and this can be quite strenuous.

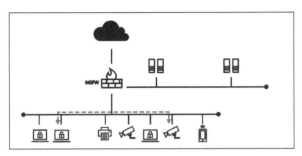

However, if businesses can overcome these setup challenges, many benefits can be gained from network segmentation, and they include:

Slows Down Attackers

This is one of the main advantages of splitting a network into segments. When an attacker manages to breach into one segment, they will be contained into that segment for a while since the other segments are still secure.

As they try to break into other segments to access more resources, you will have time to upgrade the security of the different segments to ensure that they are not able to access vital company resources. Segmentation, therefore, buys you time in the case of an intrusion, and this limits the damage that external attacks can cause.

Improved Monitoring

It is easy to monitor the happenings on a network when it has been segmented. You can easily monitor log events and unsuccessful internal connections when the network has been partitioned into segments. From these events, you can quickly identify suspicious behavior and take the necessary measures to improve your network security.

Better Data Security

Network segmentation allows you to apply stronger security measures to the most sensitive data in your organization. Segmenting your networks will make it easy for you to add a layer of protection on your internal network assets, and this ensures that sensitive company information does not get to the wrong hands. This also minimizes the risk of losing vital company data and data theft.

It is Easy to Implement the Least Privilege Policy

Organizations should restrict access to sensitive information systems within the organization, and network segmentation makes it possible to achieve this. A segmented network infrastructure restricts access to such vital assets to a few selected individuals, and this goes a long way to protect the company data.

If an individual's login credentials are abused or compromised, access to the assets will be restricted, and this protects the organization from internal as well as external attacks.

The Damage from Successful Attacks is Reduced

If an intruder manages to break into your network, he or she will only be able to access the recourses within that network segment. Network segmentation adds a layer of protection to each segment, and this means that intruders will only access the resources of the segment that they have broken into the other segments, that will be safe, and the resources within them uncompromised. The damage from successful attacks is, therefore, reduced, and this is another reason why organizations should make sure that their network infrastructure is segmented.

Email Security

Email security refers to the collective measures used to secure the access and content of an email account or service. It allows an individual or organization to protect the overall access to one or more email addresses/accounts.

An email service provider implements email security to secure subscriber email accounts and data from hackers - at rest and in transit.

Email security is a broad term that encompasses multiple techniques used to secure an email service. From an individual/end user standpoint, proactive email security measures include:

- Strong passwords

- Password rotations

- Spam filters

- Desktop-based anti-virus/anti-spam applications.

Similarly, a service provider ensures email security by using strong password and access control mechanisms on an email server; encrypting and digitally signing email messages when in the inbox or in transit to or from a subscriber email address. It also implements firewall and software-based spam filtering applications to restrict unsolicited, untrustworthy and malicious email messages from delivery to a user's inbox.

The Need for Email Security

Due the popularity of email as an attack vector, it is critical that enterprises and individuals take measures to secure their email accounts against common attacks as well as attempts at unauthorized access to accounts or communications.

Malware sent via email messages can be quite destructive. Phishing emails sent to employees often contain malware in attachments designed to look like legitimate documents or include hyperlinks that lead to websites that serve malware. Opening an email attachment or clicking on a link in an email can be all that it takes for accounts or devices to become compromised.

Phishing emails can also be used to trick recipients into sharing sensitive information, often by posing as a legitimate business or trusted contacts. Phishing attacks against businesses often target departments that handle sensitive personal or financial information, such as accounts payable or human resources. In addition to impersonating known vendors or company executives, attackers will try to in still a sense of urgency in phishing emails to increase their chances of success. Phishing emails aimed at stealing information typically will ask recipients to confirm their login information, passwords, social security number, bank account numbers, and even credit card information. Some even link to counterfeit websites that look exactly like that of a reputable vendor or business partner to trick victims into entering account or financial information.

Enterprise Email Security Best Practices

There are multiple ways to secure email accounts, and for enterprises, it's a two-pronged approach encompassing employee education and comprehensive security protocols.

Best practices for email security include:

- Engage employees in ongoing security education around email security risks and how to avoid falling victim to phishing attacks over email.

- Require employees to use strong passwords and mandate password changes periodically.

- Utilize email encryption to protect both email content and attachments.

- Implement security best practices for BYOD if your company allows employees to access corporate email on personal devices.

- Ensure that webmail applications are able to secure logins and use encryption.

- Implement scanners and other tools to scan messages and block emails containing malware or other malicious files before they reach your end users.

- Implement a data protection solution to identify sensitive data and prevent it from being lost via email.

End user Email Security Best Practices

There are also some important best practices that end users should follow to ensure secure email usage. Arming your employees with the know-how to avoid risky behaviors can make a substantial impact on your company's ability to reduce risks associated with email. Email security best practices for end users/employees include:

- Never open attachments or click on links in email messages from unknown senders.

- Change passwords often and use best practices for creating strong passwords.

- Never share passwords with anyone, including co-workers.

- Try to send as little sensitive information as possible via email, and send sensitive information only to recipients who require it.

- Use spam filters and anti-virus software.

- When working remotely or on a personal device, use VPN software to access corporate email.

- Avoid accessing company email from public wi-fi connections.

By educating employees on email security and implementing the proper measures to protect email, enterprises can mitigate many of the risks that come with email usage and prevent sensitive data loss or malware infections via email.

Wireless Security

Wireless network security is the process of designing, implementing and ensuring security on a wireless computer network. It is a subset of network security that adds protection for a wireless computer network. Wireless network security is also known as wireless security.

Wireless network security primarily protects a wireless network from unauthorized and malicious access attempts. Typically, wireless network security is delivered through wireless devices (usually a wireless router/switch) that encrypts and secures all wireless communication by default. Even if the wireless network security is compromised, the hacker is not able to view the content of the traffic/packet in transit. Moreover, wireless intrusion detection and prevention systems also enable protection of a wireless network by alerting the wireless network administrator in case of a security breach.

Importance of Wireless Security

Wireless networks are forcing organizations to completely rethink how they secure their networks and devices to prevent attacks and misuse that expose critical assets and confidential data. By their very nature, wireless networks are difficult to roll out, secure and manage, even for the most savvy network administrators.

Wireless networks offer great potential for exploitation for two reasons; they use the airwaves for communication, and wireless-enabled laptops are ubiquitous. To make the most of their security planning, enterprises need to focus on threats that pose the greatest risk. Wireless networks are vulnerable in a myriad of ways, some of the most likely problems being rogue access points (APs) and employee use of mobile devices without appropriate security precautions, but malicious hacking attempts and denial-of-service (DoS) attacks are certainly possible as well.

Unlike traditional wired networks in which communications travel along a shielded copper wire pair or optical cable, wireless radio frequency (RF) signals literally traverse the open air. As a result, RF signals are completely exposed to anybody within range and subject to fluctuating environmental factors that can degrade performance and make management an administrative nightmare. Whether authorized or not, wireless access points and their users are subject to malicious activity and employee misuse.

Additional wireless access security challenges come through the use of wireless-enabled devices by employees, the growing amount of confidential data residing on those devices, and the ease with which end users can engage in risky wireless behavior. The value of connectivity typically outweighs concerns about security, as users need to get work done while at home or while traveling. Survey data from the leading research group, Gartner, shows that at least 25 percent of business travelers connect to hotspots, many of which are unsecure, while traveling. Furthermore, about two-thirds of those who use hotspots connect to online services via Wi-Fi at least once a day highlighting the need for extending wireless security outside of the enterprise.

To ensure effective, automated wireless threat protection, companies and government organizations should implement a complete wireless security solution covering assets across the enterprise that enables them to discover vulnerabilities, assess threats, prevent attacks, and ensure ongoing compliance - in the most secure, easy-to-use and cost-effective manner available.

IT departments must have a pre-emptive plan of action to prevent malicious attacks and employee misuse which compromise an organization's data privacy and enforce security policies for wireless use - both inside and outside their facilities. Whether or not a company has authorized the use of wireless or has a 'no wireless' policy, their networks, data, devices and users are exposed and at risk.

Modes of Unauthorized Access

The modes of unauthorised access to links, to functions and to data are as variable as the respective entities make use of program code. There does not exist a full scope model of such threat. To some extent the prevention relies on known modes and methods of attack and relevant methods for suppression of the applied methods. However, each new mode of operation will create new options of threatening. Hence prevention requires a steady drive for improvement. The described modes of attack are just a snapshot of typical methods and scenarios where to apply.

Accidental Association

Violation of the security perimeter of a corporate network can come from a number of different methods and intents. One of these methods is referred to as "accidental association". When a user turns on a computer and it latches on to a wireless access point from a neighboring company's overlapping network, the user may not even know that this has occurred. However, it is a security breach in that proprietary company information is exposed and now there could exist a link from one company to the other. This is especially true if the laptop is also hooked to a wired network.

Accidental association is a case of wireless vulnerability called as "mis-association". Mis-association can be accidental, deliberate (for example, done to bypass corporate firewall) or it can result from deliberate attempts on wireless clients to lure them into connecting to attacker's APs.

Malicious Association

"Malicious associations" are when wireless devices can be actively made by attackers to connect to a company network through their laptop instead of a company access point (AP). These types of laptops are known as "soft APs" and are created when a cyber-criminal runs some software that makes his/her wireless network card look like a legitimate access point. Once the thief has gained access, he/she can steal passwords, launch attacks on the wired network, or plant trojans. Since wireless networks operate at the Layer 2 level, Layer 3 protections such as network authentication and virtual private networks (VPNs) offer no barrier. Wireless 802.1X authentications do help with some protection but are still vulnerable to hacking. The idea behind this type of attack may not be to break into a VPN or other security measures. Most likely the criminal is just trying to take over the client at the Layer 2 level.

Ad hoc Networks

Ad hoc networks can pose a security threat. Ad hoc networks are defined as [peer to peer] networks between wireless computers that do not have an access point in between them. While these types of networks usually have little protection, encryption methods can be used to provide security.

The security hole provided by Ad hoc networking is not the Ad hoc network itself but the bridge it provides into other networks, usually in the corporate environment, and the unfortunate default settings in most versions of Microsoft Windows to have this feature turned on unless explicitly disabled. Thus the user may not even know they have an unsecured Ad hoc network in operation on their computer. If they are also using a wired or wireless infrastructure network at the same time, they are providing a bridge to the secured organizational network through the unsecured Ad hoc connection. Bridging is in two forms. A direct bridge, which requires the user actually configure a bridge between the two connections and is thus unlikely to be initiated unless explicitly desired, and an indirect bridge which is the shared resources on the user computer. The indirect bridge may expose private data that is shared from the user's computer to LAN connections, such as shared folders or private Network Attached Storage, making no distinction between authenticated or private connections and unauthenticated Ad-Hoc networks. This presents no threats not already familiar to open/public or unsecured wifi access points, but firewall rules may be circumvented in the case of poorly configured operating systems or local settings.

Non-traditional Networks

Non-traditional networks such as personal network Bluetooth devices are not safe from hacking and should be regarded as a security risk. Even barcode readers, handheld PDAs, and wireless printers and copiers should be secured. These non-traditional networks can be easily overlooked by IT personnel who have narrowly focused on laptops and access points.

Identity Theft (MAC Spoofing)

Identity theft (or MAC spoofing) occurs when a hacker is able to listen in on network traffic and identify the MAC address of a computer with network privileges. Most wireless systems allow some kind of MAC filtering to allow only authorized computers with specific MAC IDs to gain access and utilize the network. However, programs exist that have network "sniffing" capabilities. Combine these programs with other software that allow a computer to pretend it has any MAC address that the hacker desires, and the hacker can easily get around that hurdle.

MAC filtering is effective only for small residential (SOHO) networks, since it provides protection only when the wireless device is "off the air". Any 802.11 device "on the air" freely transmits its unencrypted MAC address in its 802.11 headers, and it requires no special equipment or software to detect it. Anyone with an 802.11 receiver (laptop and wireless adapter) and a freeware wireless packet analyzer can obtain the MAC address of any transmitting 802.11 within range. In an organizational environment, where most wireless devices are "on the air" throughout the active working shift, MAC filtering provides only a false sense of security since it prevents only "casual" or unintended connections to the organizational infrastructure and does nothing to prevent a directed attack.

Man-in-the-middle Attacks

A man-in-the-middle attacker entices computers to log into a computer which is set up as a soft AP (Access Point). Once this is done, the hacker connects to a real access point through another wireless card offering a steady flow of traffic through the transparent hacking computer to the real network. The hacker can then sniff the traffic. One type of man-in-the-middle attack relies on security faults in challenge and handshake protocols to execute a "de-authentication attack". This attack forces AP-connected computers to drop their connections and reconnect with the hacker's soft AP (disconnects the user from the modem so they have to connect again using their password which one can extract from the recording of the event). Man-in-the-middle attacks are enhanced by software such as LANjack and AirJack which automate multiple steps of the process, meaning what once required some skill can now be done by script kiddies. Hotspots are particularly vulnerable to any attack since there is little to no security on these networks.

Denial of Service

A Denial-of-Service attack (DoS) occurs when an attacker continually bombards a targeted AP (Access Point) or network with bogus requests, premature successful connection messages, failure messages, and/or other commands. These cause legitimate users to not be able to get on the network and may even cause the network to crash. These attacks rely on the abuse of protocols such as the Extensible Authentication Protocol (EAP).

The DoS attack in itself does little to expose organizational data to a malicious attacker, since the interruption of the network prevents the flow of data and actually indirectly protects data by preventing it from being transmitted. The usual reason for performing a DoS attack is to observe the recovery of the wireless network, during which all of the initial handshake codes are re-transmitted by all devices, providing an opportunity for the malicious attacker to record these codes and use various cracking tools to analyze security weaknesses and exploit them to gain unauthorized access to the system. This works best on weakly encrypted systems such as WEP, where there are a number of tools available which can launch a dictionary style attack of "possibly accepted" security keys based on the "model" security key captured during the network recovery.

Network Injection

In a network injection attack, a hacker can make use of access points that are exposed to non-filtered network traffic, specifically broadcasting network traffic such as "Spanning Tree" (802.1D), OSPF, RIP, and HSRP. The hacker injects bogus networking re-configuration commands that affect routers, switches, and intelligent hubs. A whole network can be brought down in this manner and require rebooting or even reprogramming of all intelligent networking devices.

Caffe Latte Attack

The Caffe Latte attack is another way to defeat WEP. It is not necessary for the attacker to be in the area of the network using this exploit. By using a process that targets the Windows wireless stack, it is possible to obtain the WEP key from a remote client. By sending a flood of encrypted ARP requests, the assailant takes advantage of the shared key authentication and the message modification flaws in 802.11 WEP. The attacker uses the ARP responses to obtain the WEP key in less than 6 minutes.

Wireless Intrusion Prevention Concepts

There are three principal ways to secure a wireless network-

- For closed networks (like home users and organizations) the most common way is to configure access restrictions in the access points. Those restrictions may include encryption and checks on MAC address. Wireless Intrusion Prevention Systems can be used to provide wireless LAN security in this network model.

- For commercial providers, hotspots, and large organizations, the preferred solution is often to have an open and unencrypted, but completely isolated wireless network. The users will at first have no access to the Internet nor to any local network resources. Commercial providers usually forward all web traffic to a captive portal which provides for payment and/or authorization. Another solution is to require the users to connect securely to a privileged network using VPN.

- Wireless networks are less secure than wired ones; in many offices intruders can easily visit and hook up their own computer to the wired network without problems, gaining access to the network, and it is also often possible for remote intruders to gain access to the network through backdoors like Back Orifice. One general solution may be end-to-end encryption, with independent authentication on all resources that shouldn't be available to the public.

There is no ready designed system to prevent from fraudulent usage of wireless communication or to protect data and functions with wirelessly communicating computers and other entities. However, there is a system of qualifying the taken measures as a whole according to a common understanding what shall be seen as state of the art. The system of qualifying is an international consensus as specified in ISO/IEC 15408.

A Wireless Intrusion Prevention System

A Wireless Intrusion Prevention System (WIPS) is a concept for the most robust way to counteract wireless security risks. However such WIPS does not exist as a ready designed solution to implement as a software package. A WIPS is typically implemented as an overlay to an existing Wireless LAN infrastructure, although it may be deployed standalone to enforce no-wireless policies within an organization. WIPS is considered so important to wireless security that in July 2009, the Payment Card Industry Security Standards Council published wireless guidelines for PCI DSS recommending the use of WIPS to automate wireless scanning and protection for large organizations.

Implementing Wireless Security Measures

It is hard to believe that the network computers are to increase the security. In reality, the network computers are to share the resources and to address a myriad of threats and security issues. It is possible to address the those threats and security issues using both software and hardware. Anyway, the protocols are specially proposed to mitigate the network security threats. When comes to wireless networks, the word security and wireless are not belonging same category. In fact, few organization first preference for security and then second preference to the wireless networking. An Earlier type of security protocols which was developed for the wireless networks is not offered much security to the networks. The wireless security is the prevention of the damage or unauthorized access to the computers using wireless networks.

Nowadays, the advancements in the new technology are providing possible security to the wireless networks from intruders. But still it is possible to set an unsecure network or the temporary uses. In the below sections, the wireless security configuration and protocols, and its impact on each option. The most common types of wireless security are WiFi protected access and wired equivalent access.

Encryption Protocols

An encryption is the old concept that goes days of Pharaoh in Egypt days. The basic idea behind encryption, the message will be coded and can be read by an entity or a person who possesses the right key or decoder. There are different kinds of encryption algorithm in use today. Listed below are some of the wireless encryption methods.

WEP

Wired equivalent privacy is one among the first try at the wireless security. It is the first one which is used to secure the wireless connections. The WEP tried to secure a connection by encrypting the data transfers, but Wired equivalent privacy was found never be equivalent to the wired security. In that, the security mechanism which was used to accomplish the encryption was not encrypted. The WEP uses a stream cipher RC4 for confidentiality and CRC 32 checksum for the integrity.

This used the key length, which was 64 bit originally and then it upgraded as 128 bits. The WEP operates at a lower layer of an OSI model and it cannot provide end to end security for the application. Due to these shortcomings, most of the people have selected more sophisticated and newer methods for securing wireless communication. But, some of the innocent and unknowing peoples still using same unsecure protocol.

This WEP protocol proposed to offer security by encrypting data from sending and the receiving devices. There are 2 types of WEP security available such as dynamic and static. The static and dynamic WEP differ in some manner, that the dynamic WEP changes the security key periodically to making it secure more. At the same time, the static WEP uses the same type of security key on the ongoing basis. The new 128 bit encryption in the WEP makes it more robust than previous versions. As the WEP is the static string with characters, it might be compromised by the brute force attack, where the attacker tries all the possible combination of characters until it matches with the WEP key. The most basic line is that the WEP can keep the curious snooper out, however, any of the hacker worth his salt won't have the hard time cracking the WEP security. In the year 2004, with a ratification of a full 802.11i standard as per WPA2, the IEEE announced that both of the WEP-40 as well as WEP 104 have been deprecated as it fails to meet their security goals and requirements.

WPA

The WPA is the Wi-Fi protected access which was proposed to improve the security weakness over WEP and it will be backward compatible with the older devices which is uses the WEP standard. This WPA addressed 2 main security concerns such as enhanced data encryption and authentication. It is generally being installed as the upgrade on the systems that it currently uses.

An enhanced data encryption is the one, in which WPA uses the temporal key integrity protocol, which scrambles the encryption keys with the help of the hashing algorithm. The key is issued the integrity check to determine that they are not tampered or modified during the transit.

With the help of an extensible authentication protocol, WEP regulates the access to the wireless networks depends on the computer hardware and specific MAC address. It is relatively very simple to be stolen and sniffed. The EAP- extensible authentication protocol is built on the more secured public type key encryption systems to ensure that only an authorized network user can access a network.

The WPA includes the message integrity check. It is proposed to prevent an attacker from altering, resending and capturing data packets. It replaces the cyclic redundancy check which was used by a WEP standard. The cyclic redundancy check main flaw is that it will never offer a sufficient strong data integrity for the packets it handling. The well tested message authentication code existed to resolve this issue, but it needs much computation has to be used on the old network cards.

WPA2

This WPA2 has replaced the WPA. It requires certification and testing by Wi-Fi, implements a mandatory element of the IEEE 802.11i. The Wi-Fi protected access version -2 is the improved version of WPA. It offers additional benefits than the earlier version. The WPA2 favors the counter mode with the CCMP- cipher block chaining message authentication code protocol. The CCMP will use 128 bit and AES encryption with 48 bit initialization vector. By larger initialization vector, it also increases a difficulty in cracking as well as minimizes the risks of replay. The new AES and CCMP are encrypted based mode with strong security, which was introduced by the WPA2. The WPA2 certification is mostly mandatory for the whole new device to bear the trademark of Wi-Fi.

The advanced encryption standard is the mode of encryption for stronger security as well as longer security keys. The CCMP is based on 802.11i standards and provides the enhanced data cryptographic encapsulation mechanism which replaces TKIP with the security method which is more stronger. It becomes mandatory on the Wi-Fi certified device since 2006. Some of the hardware will not support WPA2 without any firmware replacement or upgrade. The WPA2 uses an encryption devices which encrypts the network with the 256 bit key, the longer key length will improve security over WEP.

WPA Enterprise

The WPA enterprise is more properly called as 802.1X for IEEE standard defining that, indicates port based network access control. It is intended for the enterprise networks and needs a radius authentication server. It needs a more complicated set up and however it offers an additional security like protection against the dictionary attacks on the short passwords. The extensible authentication protocol is moreover used for authentication, which is available in different variety of flavors. This WPA enterprise mode is available with both the WPA2 and WPA.

This 802.1x is not specially proposed for the wireless networks and rather it offers an authenticated access for both the wireless and wired network. The access control of port based network depends on the physical characteristic of the switched LAN infrastructure to authenticate device attached to the LAN port to prevent access to where an authentication fails. It is suitable for organizations ranges from medium to large size. This can serve to enhance the security by allowing to centralize the security policies.

MAC Address Filtering

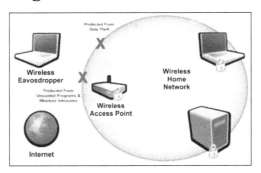

In the computer networking, the MAC filtering refers to the security access control method and the 48 bit address are assigned to every network card to determine access to the networks. The Mac addresses are mostly uniquely assigned to the each card, so that using Mac address filtering on the network denies and denies network access via the use of the list, straightforward, an individual is not identified by the MAC address, rather the deice only. So that only authorized person can require to have a whitelist entry for every device that she or he use to access the networks.

Each and every host on the network have 48 bit MAC - media access control address which is generally expressed in hexadecimal. Additionally, each internet packet comprises a source media access control address and the destination MAC address. Sometimes a destination MAC address is the broadcast address includes FF-FF-FF-FF-FF-FF. The MAC filtering can also be applied to the wireless access point as well as configured to allow only some specific MAC address through the interface on the WAP. On the other hand, the user will connect to the wireless access point only, if the users MAC address is configured as the accepted address. It may be a great idea, but never use it only for the wireless security, if really like to have a secured wireless network. With the help of the right software, an acceptable MAC address can be determined easily and spoofed. This can also be done in the command line tools or by using windows registry on the LInux platform. The MAC address filtering is also referred to as security through obscurity. This Mac address filtering is effective in the wireless as well as wired networks.

Device Placement

By positioning an antenna, it does not broadcast outside the premises limit access to the people in the premises. The performance is enhanced by keeping the WAP as close to a center of communication area as much as possible. This effective when the radio waves radiate out in all possible directions and hence it is possible to cover more area effectively and provide computers sufficient area in which it can connect if the work take place from the center.

This technique will improve the security of the wireless networks, but in a different method. By keeping the WAP close to a center of the communication area, then it can control the perimeter of a communication area effectively. On the other hand, it is possible to limit the instance in which the wireless area will go further than it had proposed.

Signal Strength

Mostly, people don't control a signal strength of the wireless network as an ongoing basis. There is at least no signal strength dial which will turn own or other way. By making use of latest technologies like 802.11n, then they will broadcast it with high signal strength when compared with the earlier technologies. In relation to the security, the additional strength may not necessary. To shape the signal, use directional antennas which allow the device to connect with each other, but don't radiate it in all the directions. In so many ways, the placement of the WAP can affect a signal strength of the broadcast.

This signal strength can also be adjusted to limit the transmission range to limit, how can connect to the AP.

The risks to the users of wireless technology have increased day by day as the service become more popular among users. There are relatively few dangers when the wireless technology was introduced. Later by introducing new security measures it becomes easier and simpler. There are so many various wireless encryption protocols from which can choose. The WPA and WEP are now no longer considered to secure and it should be avoided if perfect security is the main goal. In the WAP2 is considered as the secure protocol and has to be used whenever necessary. For that it is necessary to learn all the protocols to select the perfect one among them.

MAC address filtering control that can connect a WAP based MAC address. These MAC addresses will be easily spoofed and it can also use in conjunction with the stronger forms like WPA2.

Device placement as well as signal strength will go hand in hand. It is possible to change the signal patterns by keeping WAP close to a center of the WAN or by using some specialized directional antennas. The key to maintaining the wireless network security is limited in the area which is used by the them.

Application Security

Application security is the process of making apps more secure by finding, fixing, and enhancing the security of apps. Much of this happens during the development phase, but it includes tools and methods to protect apps once they are deployed. This is becoming more important as hackers increasingly target applications with their attacks.

Application security is getting a lot of attention. Hundreds of tools are available to secure various elements of your applications portfolio, from locking down coding changes to assessing inadvertent coding threats, evaluating encryption options and auditing permissions and access rights. There are specialized tools for mobile apps, for network-based apps, and for firewalls designed especially for web applications.

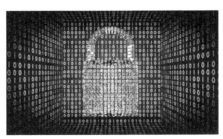

Importance of Application Security

The faster and sooner in the software development process you can find and fix security issues, the safer your enterprise will be. And, because everyone makes mistakes, the challenge is to find those mistakes in a timely fashion. For example, a common coding error could allow unverified inputs. This mistake can turn into SQL injection attacks and then data leaks if a hacker finds them.

Application security tools that integrate into your application development environment can make this process and workflow simpler and more effective. These tools are also useful if you are doing compliance audits, since they can save time and the expense by catching problems before the auditors seen them.

The rapid growth in the application security segment has been helped by the changing nature of how enterprise apps are being constructed in the last several years. Gone are the days where an IT shop would take months to refine requirements, build and test prototypes, and deliver a finished product to an end-user department. The idea almost seems quaint nowadays.

Instead, we have new working methods, called continuous deployment and integration, that refine an app daily, in some cases hourly. This means that security tools have to work in this ever-changing world and find issues with code quickly. Many of these categories are still emerging and employ relatively new products. This shows how quickly the market is evolving as threats become more complex, more difficult to find, and more potent in their potential damage to your networks, your data, and your corporate reputation.

Application Security Tools

While there are numerous application security software product categories, the meat of the matter has to do with two: security testing tools and application shielding products.

The former is a more mature market with dozens of well-known vendors, some of them are lions of the software industry such as IBM, CA and MicroFocus. These tools are well enough along that Gartner has created its Magic Quadrant and classified their importance and success. Review sites such as IT Central Station have been able to survey and rank these vendors, too.

Gartner categorizes the security testing tools into several broad buckets, and they are somewhat useful for how you decide what you need to protect your app portfolio:

- Static testing, which analyzes code at fixed points during its development. This is useful for developers to check their code as they are writing it to ensure that security issues are being introduced during development.

- Dynamic testing, which analyzes running code. This is more useful, as it can simulate attacks on production systems and reveal more complex attack patterns that use a combination of systems.

- Interactive testing, which combines elements of both static and dynamic testing.

- Mobile testing is designed specifically for the mobile environments and can examine how an attacker can leverage the mobile OS and the apps running on them in its entirety.

Another way to look at the testing tools is how they are delivered, either via an on-premises tool or via a SaaS-based subscription service where you submit your code for online analysis. Some even do both.

One caveat is the programming languages supported by each testing vendor. Some limit their tools to just one or two languages. (Java is usually a safe bet.) Others are more involved in the Microsoft .Net universe- The same goes for integrated development environments (IDEs): some tools operate as plugins or extensions to these IDEs, so testing your code is as simple as clicking on a button.

Another issue is whether any tool is isolated from other testing results or can incorporate them into its own analysis. IBM's is one of the few that can import findings from manual code reviews, penetration testing, vulnerability assessments and competitors' tests. This can be helpful, particularly if you have multiple tools that you need to keep track of.

Let's not forget about app shielding tools. The main objective of these tools is to harden the application so that attacks are more difficult to carry out. This is less charted territory. Here you'll find a vast collection of smaller, point products that in many cases have limited history and customer bases. The goal of these products is to do more than just test for vulnerabilities and actively prevent your apps from corruption or compromise. They encompass a few different broad categories:

- Runtime application self-protection (RASP): These tools could be considered a combination of testing and shielding. They provide a measure of protection against possible reverse-engineering attacks. RASP tools are continuously monitoring the behavior of the app, which is useful particularly in mobile environments when apps can be rewritten, run on a rooted phone or have privilege abuse to turn them into doing nefarious things. RASP tools can send alerts, terminate errant processes, or terminate the app itself if found compromised. RASP will likely become the default on many mobile development environments and built-in as part of other mobile app protection tools. Expect to see more alliances among software vendors that have solid RASP solutions.

- Code obfuscation: Hackers often use obfuscation methods to hide their malware, and now tools allow developer to do this to help protect their code from being attacked.

- Encryption and anti-tampering tools: These are other methods that can be used to keep the bad guys from gaining insights into your code.

- Threat detection tools: These tools examine the environment or network where your apps are running and make an assessment about potential threats and misused trust relationships. Some tools can provide device "fingerprints" to determine whether a mobile phone has been rooted or otherwise compromised.

Application Security Challenges

Part of the problem is that IT has to satisfy several different masters to secure their apps. They first have to keep up with the evolving security and application development tools market, but that is just the entry point.

IT also has to anticipate the business needs as more enterprises dive deeper into digital products and their application portfolio needs evolve to more complex infrastructure. They also have to understand how SaaS services are constructed and secured. This has been an issue, as a recent survey of 500 IT managers has found the average level of software design knowledge has been lacking. The report states, "CIOs may find themselves in the hot seat with senior leadership as they are held accountable for reducing complexity, staying on budget and how quickly they are modernizing to keep up with business demands."

Finally, the responsibility for application security could be spread across several different teams within your IT operations: The network folks could be responsible for running the web app firewalls and other network-centric tools, the desktop folks could be responsible for running endpoint-oriented tests, and various development groups could have other concerns. This makes it hard to suggest one tool that will fit everyone's needs, which is why the market has become so fragmented.

Network Security Attack

Network security attacks are unauthorized actions against private, corporate or governmental IT assets in order to destroy them, modify them or steal sensitive data. As more enterprises invite employees to access data from mobile devices, networks become vulnerable to data theft or total destruction of the data or network.

The Most Common Attacks of Network Security

In recent years, there has been an upward trend towards "hacktivism" whereby hackers try to take control of organizations for political reasons or financial gain. Digital transformation in the workplace has now enabled a "bring your own device" (BYOD) model, which potentially poses risks for employees who access data with mobile devices. These can leave businesses vulnerable to threats such as wireless network attacks, as can cloud-based applications and highly interactive websites.

Way to Secure your Network

Previously, organizations would attempt to prevent network attacks by using network security tools such as firewalls or intrusion detection systems. While these still have their place, they are no match for modern day security attacks, for example modern Distributed Denial of Service (DDoS) attacks, as these attack on a much deeper level. These traditional perimeter-based solutions rely on a "castle and moat" method whereby anybody who manages to penetrate the network is automatically trusted, rather than authenticated before entering. These may introduce new threats due to improper configuration is sub-standard patching.

Enterprises may also carry out vulnerability management and penetration testing. These help to meet compliance requirements and help to address gaps in information security, but they are very resource consuming. For a fully scalable, multi-layered defense solution, companies should invest in cloud security solutions.

Significance of Network Security

Unfortunately for modern enterprises, hacker knowledge, attack tools and botnet-for-hire are more readily available than ever before, helping to increase the prevalence and sophistication of internet-borne network attacks. For example, modern DDoS attacks can now attack at the deepest layer, the application layer, as opposed to years gone by when they could only penetrate the network or transport layer.

These cyber-attacks have two overarching outcomes for enterprises: firstly, they result in costly damages to IT infrastructure. Secondly, they incur further loss of revenue by diminishing brand reputation, for example, losing customers due to data breaches.

Defeating Network Attacks with Akamai Cloud Security Solutions

There is no on-premise solution that can protect against all types of network attacks, however, what companies need to effectively mitigate a variety of cyber threats is flexible, scalable, multi-layered defenses. This is why Akamai has designed and built into the Akamai Intelligent Platform™ simple yet powerful Cloud Security Solutions that help defend your web applications and networks from attacks, keeping both customers and business owners safe.

The Akamai Intelligent Platform helps to protect using:

- An edge-based, defense-in-depth approach to thwarts attacks upstream and employs overlapping layers of protection to detect and deflect web application and network attacks before they reach customers' data centers.

- Cloud-based DDoS mitigation solutions for built-in scalability, absorbing DDoS traffic at the application layer while filtering out malicious DDoS traffic targeted at the network layer.

- InfoSec and CSIRT teams, which constantly analyze new threat intelligence, adapting the platform's security to the present threat landscape, offering customers the information they need to stay vigilant and safe.

- A reputational service offering to forewarns you of intent before exploitation.

There are two main types of network attacks:

Active Attacks

An Active attack attempts to alter system resources or effect their operations. Active attack involve some modification of the data stream or creation of false statement. Types of active attacks are as following:

- Masquerade – Masquerade attack takes place when one entity pretends to be different entity. A Masquerade attack involves one of the other form of active attacks.

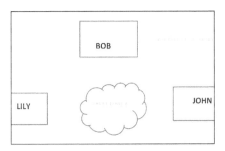

- Modification of messages – It means that some portion of a message is altered or that message is delayed or reordered to produce an unauthorised effect. For example, a message meaning "Allow JOHN to read confidential file X" is modified as "Allow Smith to read confidential file X".

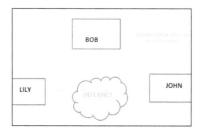

- Repudiation – This attack is done by either sender or receiver. The sender or receiver can deny later that he/she has send or receive a message. For example, customer ask his Bank "To transfer an amount to someone" and later on the sender(customer) deny that he had made such a request. This is repudiation.

- Replay – It involves the passive capture of a message and its subsequent the transmission to produce an authorized effect.

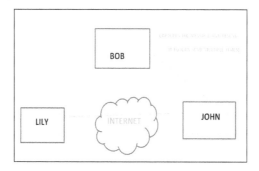

- Denial of Service – It prevents normal use of communication facilities. This attack may have a specific target. For example, an entity may suppress all messages directed to a particular destination. Another form of service denial is the disruption of an entire network withers by disabling the network or by overloading it by messages so as to degrade performance.

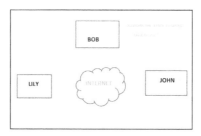

Passive Attacks

A Passive attack attempts to learn or make use of information from the system but does not affect system resources. Passive Attacks are in the nature of eavesdropping on or monitoring of transmission. The goal of the opponent is to obtain information is being transmitted. Types of Passive attacks are as following:

1. The release of message content – Telephonic conversation, an electronic mail message or a transferred file may contain sensitive or confidential information. We would like to prevent an opponent from learning the contents of these transmissions.

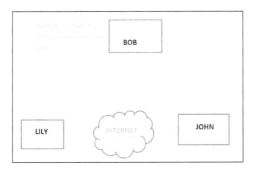

2. Traffic analysis – Suppose that we had a way of masking (encryption) of information, so that the attacker even if captured the message could not extract any information from the message.

    The opponent could determine the location and identity of communicating host and could observe the frequency and length of messages being exchanged. This information might be useful in guessing the nature of the communication that was taking place.

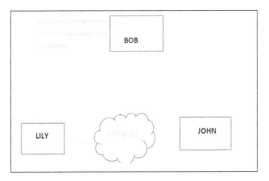

Differences between Active and Passive Attacks

Comparison Chart		
Basis for comparison	**Active attack**	**Passive attack**
Basic	Active attack tries to change the system resources or affect their operation.	Passive attack tries to read or make use of information from the system but does not influence system resources.

Modification in the information	Occurs	Does not take place.
Harm to the system	Always causes damage to the system.	Do not cause any harm.
Threat to	Integrity and availability	Confidentiality
Attack awareness	The entity (victim) gets informed about the attack.	The entity is unaware of the attack.
Task performed by the attacker	The transmission is captured by physically controlling the portion of a link.	Just need to observe the transmission.
Emphasis is on	Detection.	Prevention.

Network Security Software

Network security software is software that is made to enhance the security of a network. There are many different types of network security software that help to provide protection for data in transit, data at rest and other elements of a network setup.

Network software providers define network security as security as the maintenance of "usability, reliability, integrity, and safety" for a network and its data. Within this broader category, there are a number of different components of network security that software applications address.

One overall element of network security involves the protection of key hardware devices. This includes:

- Anti-virus software

- Firewalls

- Anti-malware applications.

All of these fit under the banner of network security software in a particular way.

Another category of network security software involves backup and recovery solutions. These types of software help to back up data in case of a threat.

Other types of network security software consist of tools to monitor a network in real time to prevent unauthorized access, data leaks or other threats. These types of tools may be focused on endpoint security, where network data is displayed on devices, or internal security, where various threats happen within the network itself.

In addition, some consider aspects of core network systems as a different kind of network security software, for example, patches and security updates for operating systems.

Antivirus Software

Antivirus software is a class of program designed to prevent, detect and remove malware infections on individual computing devices, networks and IT systems.

Antivirus software, originally designed to detect and remove viruses from computers, can also protect against a wide variety of threats, including other types of malicious software, such as keyloggers, browser hijackers, Trojan horses, worms, rootkits, spyware, adware, botnets and ransomware.

Working of Antivirus Software

Antivirus software typically runs as a background process, scanning computers, servers or mobile devices to detect and restrict the spread of malware. Many antivirus software programs include real-time threat detection and protection to guard against potential vulnerabilities as they happen, as well as system scans that monitor device and system files looking for possible risks.

Antivirus software usually performs these basic functions:

- Scanning directories or specific files for known malicious patterns indicating the presence of malicious software;

- Allowing users to schedule scans so they run automatically;

- Allowing users to initiate new scans at any time; and

- Removing any malicious software it detects. Some antivirus software programs do this automatically in the background, while others notify users of infections and ask them if they want to clean the files.

In order to scan systems comprehensively, antivirus software must generally be given privileged access to the entire system. This makes antivirus software itself a common target for attackers, and researchers have discovered remote code execution and other serious vulnerabilities in antivirus software products in recent years.

Types of Antivirus Programs

Antivirus software is distributed in a number of forms, including stand-alone antivirus scanners and internet security suites that offer antivirus protection, along with firewalls, privacy controls and other security protections.

Some antivirus software vendors offer basic versions of their products at no charge. These free versions generally offer basic antivirus and spyware protection, but more advanced features and protections are usually available only to paying customers.

While some operating systems are targeted more frequently by virus developers, antivirus software is available for most OSes:

- Windows antivirus software- Most antivirus software vendors offer several levels of Windows products at different price points, starting with free versions offering only basic protection. Users must start scans and updates manually and typically free versions of antivirus software won't protect against links to malicious websites or malicious attachments in emails. Premium versions of antivirus software often include suites of endpoint security tools that may provide secure online storage, ad blockers and file encryption. Since 2004, Microsoft has been offering some kind of free antivirus software as part of the Windows operating system itself, generally under the name Windows Defender, though the software was mostly limited to detecting spyware prior to 2006.

- macOS antivirus software- Although macOS viruses exist, they're less common than Windows viruses, so antivirus products for macOS are less standardized than those for Windows. There are a number of free and paid products available, providing on-demand tools to protect against potential malware threats through full-system malware scans and the ability to sift through specific email threads, attachments and various web activities.

- Android antivirus software- Android is the world's most popular mobile operating system and is installed on more mobile devices than any other OS. Because most mobile malware targets Android, experts recommend all Android device users install antivirus software on their devices. Vendors offer a variety of basic free and paid premium versions of their Android antivirus software including anti-theft and remote-locating features. Some run automatic scans and actively try to stop malicious web pages and files from being opened or downloaded.

Virus Detection Techniques

Antivirus software uses a variety of virus detection techniques. Originally, antivirus software depended on signature-based detection to flag malicious software. Antivirus programs depend on stored virus signatures - unique strings of data that are characteristic of known malware. The antivirus software uses these signatures to identify when it encounters viruses that have already been identified and analyzed by security experts.

Signature-based malware cannot detect new malware, including variants of existing malware. Signature-based detection can only detect new viruses when the definition file is updated with information about the new virus. With the number of new malware signatures increasing at around 10 million per year as long ago as 2011, modern signature databases may contain hundreds of millions, or even billions, of entries, making antivirus software based solely on signatures impractical. However, signature-based detection does not usually produce false positive matches.

Heuristic-based detection uses an algorithm to compare the signatures of known viruses against potential threats. With heuristic-based detection, antivirus software can detect viruses that haven't been discovered yet, as well as already existing viruses that have been disguised or modified and released as new viruses. However, this method can also generate false-positive matches when antivirus software detects a program behaving similarly to a malicious program and incorrectly identifies it as a virus.

Antivirus software may also use behavior-based detection to analyze an object's behavior or potential behavior for suspicious activities and infers malicious intent based on those observations. For example, code that attempts to perform unauthorized or abnormal actions would indicate the object is malicious, or at least suspicious. Some examples of behaviors that potentially signal danger include modifying or deleting large numbers of files, monitoring keystrokes, changing settings of other programs and remotely connecting to computers.

Antimalware Software

Antimalware (anti-malware) is a type of software program designed to prevent, detect and remove malicious software (malware) on IT systems, as well as individual computing devices.

Antimalware software protects against infections caused by many types of malware, including all types of viruses, as well as rootkits, ransomware and spyware. Antimalware software can be installed on an individual computing device, gateway server or dedicated network appliance. It can also be purchased as a cloud service - such as McAfee's CloudAV product - or be embedded in a computing device's firmware.

Working of Antimalware

Antimalware software uses three strategies to protect systems from malicious software, including signature-based malware detection, behavior-based malware detection and sandboxing. These techniques protect against threats from malware in different ways.

Many antimalware tools depend on signature-based malware detection. Malicious software can be identified by comparing a hash of the suspicious code with a database of hashes of known malware. Signature-based detection uses a database of known malware definitions to scan for malware.

When the antimalware software detects a file that matches the malware signature, it flags it as potential malware. Malware detection based on signatures can only identify known malware. Antimalware software that uses behavior-based malware detection is able to detect previously unknown threats by identifying malware based on characteristics and behaviors. This type of malware detection evaluates an object based on its intended actions before it can execute that behavior. An object is considered malicious if it attempts to perform an abnormal or unauthorized action.

Behavior-based detection in newer antimalware products is sometimes powered by machine learning algorithms. Sandboxing offers another way for antimalware software to detect malware. A sandbox is an isolated computing environment developed to run unknown applications and prevent them from affecting the underlying system. Antimalware programs that use sandboxing run suspicious or previously unknown programs in a sandbox and monitor the results. If the malware demonstrates malicious behavior, the antimalware will terminate it.

Uses of Antimalware

Enterprises and other organizations use antimalware for much more than simply scanning files for viruses. Antimalware can help stop malware attacks by providing real-time protection against the installation of malware on a computer or system by scanning all incoming network data for malicious software and blocking any threats it finds; it may also be able to detect advanced forms of malware and offer specific protection from ransomware attacks.

Antimalware can also do the following:

- Prevent users from visiting websites that are known to distribute malicious code;

- Prevent the spread of malware if one device is infected;

- Generate and track metrics about the number of infections and the amount of time required to clean up those infections; and

- Offer insight into specific malicious software to help administrators understand how the malware has affected the compromised device or network.

Antimalware products may also be able to remove malware once found. However, if it determines the malware will cause further damage to a computer or system if it is removed, the antimalware program will quarantine any malicious files, enabling a user to remove it manually.

Need for Antimalware

Because malware development methods are constantly evolving, effective antimalware software uses multiple detection methods. In addition to signature-based scanning, behavior-based detection and sandboxing, antimalware programs may also rely on reputation-based systems with information about current malware in the wild.

As attackers continue to develop new distribution and exploit techniques, defenders need to use antimalware products that are updated regularly to combat the latest threats and safely remove them from computers, as well as mobile devices, like tablets and smartphones. Without current antimalware software, these devices would be at increased risk of damage from malicious programs, such as viruses, Trojan horses and adware.

Many Microsoft Windows users rely on third-party antimalware software along with the security tools built in to Windows to secure their devices against viruses and malware.

Firewall

Firewall is a network security device, either hardware or software based, which monitors all incoming and outgoing traffic and based on defined set of security rules it accept, reject or drop that specific traffic.

- Accept: allow the traffic;

- Reject: block the traffic but reply with an "unreachable error";

- Drop: block the traffic with no reply.

Firewall establishes a barrier between secured internal networks and outside untrusted network, such as Internet.

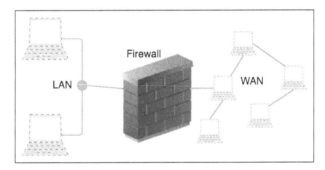

Before Firewalls, network security was performed by Access Control Lists (ACLs) residing on routers. ACLs are rules that determine whether network access should be granted or denied to specific IP address.

But ACLs cannot determine the nature of packet it is blocking. Also, ACL alone does not have the capacity to keep threats out of the network. Hence, Firewall was introduced.

Connectivity to the Internet is no longer optional for organizations. However, accessing Internet provides benefits to the organization; it also enables the outside world to interact with internal network of the organization. This creates a threat to the organization. In order to secure the internal network from unauthorized traffic we need Firewall.

Working of Firewall

Firewall match the network traffic against the rule set defined in its table. Once the rule is matched, associate action is applied to the network traffic. For example, Rules are defined like any employee from HR department cannot access the data from code server and at the same time other rule is defined like system administrator can access the data from both HR and technical department. Rules can be defined on firewall based on the necessity and security policies of the organization. From the perspective of a server, network traffic can be either outgoing or incoming. Firewall maintains distinct set of rules for both the cases. Mostly the outgoing traffic, originated from the server itself, allowed to pass. Still, setting rule on outgoing traffic is always better in order to achieve more security and prevent unwanted communication.

Incoming traffic is treated differently. Most traffic which reaches on firewall is one of these three major Transport Layer protocols- TCP, UDP or ICMP. All these types have a source address and destination address. Also, TCP and UDP have port numbers. ICMP uses *type code* instead of port number which identifies purpose of that packet.

Default policy- It is very difficult to explicitly cover every possible rule on firewall. For this reason, firewall must always have a default policy. Default policy only consist action (accept, reject or drop).

Suppose no rule is defined about SSH connection to the server on firewall. So, it will follow default policy. If default policy on firewall is set to *accept*, then any computer outside of your office can establish SSH connection to the server. Therefore, setting default policy as *drop* (or reject) is always a good practice.

Generation of Firewall

Firewalls can be categorized based on its generation.

First Generation- Packet Filtering Firewall

Packet filtering firewall is used to control network access by monitoring outgoing and incoming packet and allowing them to pass or stop based on source and destination IP address, protocols and ports. It analyses traffic at the transport protocol layer (but mainly uses first 3 layers).

Packet firewalls treats each packet in Isolation. They have no ability to tell whether a packet is part of an existing stream of traffic. Only It can allow or deny the packets based on unique packet headers.

Packet filtering firewall maintains a filtering table which decides whether the packet will be forwarded or discarded. From the given filtering table, the packets will be Filtered according to following rules:

	Source IP	Dest. IP	Source Port	Dest. Port	Action
1	192.168.21.0	--	--	--	Deny
2	--	--	--	23	Deny

| 3 | -- | 192.168.21.3 | -- | -- | Deny |
| 4 | -- | 192.168.21.0 | -- | > 1023 | Allow |

Sample Packet Filter Firewall Rule:

- Incoming packets from network 192.168.21.0 are blocked.
- Incoming packets destined for internal TELNET server (port 23) are blocked.
- Incoming packets destined for host 192.168.21.3 are blocked.
- All well-known services to the network 192.168.21.0 are allowed.

Second Generation- Stateful Inspection Firewall

Stateful firewalls (performs Stateful Packet Inspection) are able to determine the connection state of packet, unlike Packet filtering firewall, which makes it more efficient. It keeps track of the state of networks connection travelling across it, such as TCP streams. So the filtering decisions would not only be based on defined rules, but also on packet's history in the state table.

Third Generation- Application Layer Firewall

Application layer firewall can inspect and filter the packets on any OSI layer, up to application layer. It has ability to block specific content, also recognize when certain application and protocols (like HTTP, FTP) are being misused. In other words, Application layer firewalls are hosts that run proxy servers. A proxy firewall prevents direct connection between either side of firewall, each packet has to pass through the proxy. It can allow or block the traffic based on predefined rules.

Next Generation Firewalls (NGFW)

Next Generation Firewalls are being deployed these days to stop modern security breaches like advance malware attacks and application layer attacks. NGFW consists of Deep Packet Inspection, Application Inspection, SSL/SSH inspection and many fuctionalities to protect the network from these modern threats.

Types of Firewall

Firewall is categorized into three basic types –

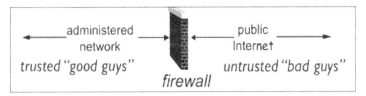

- Packet filter (Stateless & Stateful)

- Application-level gateway

- Circuit-level gateway.

These three categories, however, are not mutually exclusive. Modern firewalls have a mix of abilities that may place them in more than one of the three categories.

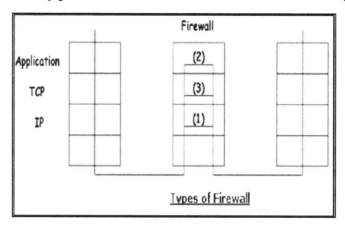

Stateless and Stateful Packet Filtering Firewall

In this type of firewall deployment, the internal network is connected to the external network/Internet via a router firewall. The firewall inspects and filters data packet-by-packet.

Packet-filtering firewalls allow or block the packets mostly based on criteria such as source and/or destination IP addresses, protocol, source and/or destination port numbers, and various other parameters within the IP header.

The decision can be based on factors other than IP header fields such as ICMP message type, TCP SYN and ACK bits, etc.

Packet filter rule has two parts –

- Selection criteria – It is a used as a condition and pattern matching for decision making.

- Action field – This part specifies action to be taken if an IP packet meets the selection criteria. The action could be either block (deny) or permit (allow) the packet across the firewall.

Packet filtering is generally accomplished by configuring Access Control Lists (ACL) on routers or switches. ACL is a table of packet filter rules.

As traffic enters or exits an interface, firewall applies ACLs from top to bottom to each incoming packet, finds matching criteria and either permits or denies the individual packets.

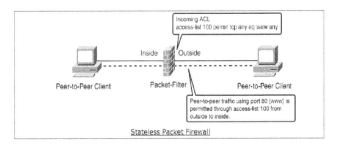

Stateless Packet Firewall

Stateless firewall is a kind of a rigid tool. It looks at packet and allows it if its meets the criteria even if it is not part of any established ongoing communication.

Hence, such firewalls are replaced by stateful firewalls in modern networks. This type of firewalls offer a more in-depth inspection method over the only ACL based packet inspection methods of stateless firewalls.

Stateful firewall monitors the connection setup and teardown process to keep a check on connections at the TCP/IP level. This allows them to keep track of connections state and determine which hosts have open, authorized connections at any given point in time.

They reference the rule base only when a new connection is requested. Packets belonging to existing connections are compared to the firewall's state table of open connections, and decision to allow or block is taken. This process saves time and provides added security as well. No packet is allowed to trespass the firewall unless it belongs to already established connection. It can be timeout inactive connections at firewall after which it no longer admit packets for that connection.

Application Gateways

An application-level gateway acts as a relay node for the application-level traffic. They intercept incoming and outgoing packets, run proxies that copy and forward information across the gateway, and function as a proxy server, preventing any direct connection between a trusted server or client and an untrusted host.

The proxies are application specific. They can filter packets at the application layer of the OSI model.

Application-specific Proxies

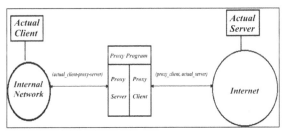

An application-specific proxy accepts packets generated by only specified application for which they are designed to copy, forward, and filter. For example, only a Telnet proxy can copy, forward, and filter Telnet traffic.

If a network relies only on an application-level gateway, incoming and outgoing packets cannot access services that have no proxies configured. For example, if a gateway runs FTP and Telnet proxies, only packets generated by these services can pass through the firewall. All other services are blocked.

Application-level Filtering

An application-level proxy gateway, examines and filters individual packets, rather than simply copying them and blindly forwarding them across the gateway. Application-specific proxies check each packet that passes through the gateway, verifying the contents of the packet up through the application layer. These proxies can filter particular kinds of commands or information in the application protocols.

Application gateways can restrict specific actions from being performed. For example, the gateway could be configured to prevent users from performing the 'FTP put' command. This can prevent modification of the information stored on the server by an attacker.

Transparent

Although application-level gateways can be transparent, many implementations require user authentication before users can access an untrusted network, a process that reduces true transparency. Authentication may be different if the user is from the internal network or from the Internet. For an internal network, a simple list of IP addresses can be allowed to connect to external applications. But from the Internet side a strong authentication should be implemented.

An application gateway actually relays TCP segments between the two TCP connections in the two directions (Client ↔ Proxy ↔ Server).

For outbound packets, the gateway may replace the source IP address by its own IP address. The process is referred to as Network Address Translation (NAT). It ensures that internal IP addresses are not exposed to the Internet.

Circuit-level Gateway

The circuit-level gateway is an intermediate solution between the packet filter and the application gateway. It runs at the transport layer and hence can act as proxy for any application.

Similar to an application gateway, the circuit-level gateway also does not permit an end-to-end TCP connection across the gateway. It sets up two TCP connections and relays the TCP segments from one network to the other. But, it does not examine the application data like application gateway. Hence, sometime it is called as 'Pipe Proxy'.

SOCKS

SOCKS (RFC 1928) refer to a circuit-level gateway. It is a networking proxy mechanism that enables hosts on one side of a SOCKS server to gain full access to hosts on the other side without requiring direct IP reachability. The client connects to the SOCKS server at the firewall. Then the client enters a negotiation for the authentication method to be used, and authenticates with the chosen method.

The client sends a connection relay request to the SOCKS server, containing the desired destination IP address and transport port. The server accepts the request after checking that the client meets the basic filtering criteria. Then, on behalf of the client, the gateway opens a connection to the requested untrusted host and then closely monitors the TCP handshaking that follows.

The SOCKS server informs the client, and in case of success, starts relaying the data between the two connections. Circuit level gateways are used when the organization trusts the internal users, and does not want to inspect the contents or application data sent on the Internet.

Firewall Deployment with DMZ

A firewall is a mechanism used to control network traffic 'into' and 'out' of an organizational internal network. In most cases these systems have two network interfaces, one for the external network such as the Internet and the other for the internal side.

The firewall process can tightly control what is allowed to traverse from one side to the other. An organization that wishes to provide external access to its web server can restrict all traffic arriving at firewall expect for port 80 (the standard http port). All other traffic such as mail traffic, FTP, SNMP, etc., is not allowed across the firewall into the internal network. An example of a simple firewall is shown in the following diagram.

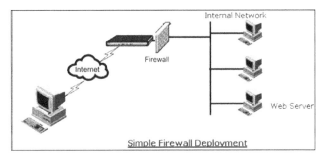

Simple Firewall Deployment

In the above simple deployment, though all other accesses from outside are blocked, it is possible for an attacker to contact not only a web server but any other host on internal network that has left port 80 open by accident or otherwise.

Hence, the problem most organizations face is how to enable legitimate access to public services such as web, FTP, and e-mail while maintaining tight security of the internal network. The typical approach is deploying firewalls to provide a Demilitarized Zone (DMZ) in the network.

In this setup (illustrated in following diagram), two firewalls are deployed; one between the external network and the DMZ, and another between the DMZ and the internal network. All public servers are placed in the DMZ.

With this setup, it is possible to have firewall rules which allow public access to the public servers but the interior firewall can restrict all incoming connections. By having the DMZ, the public servers are provided with adequate protection instead of placing them directly on external network.

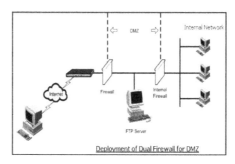

Deployment of Dual Firewall for DMZ

Intrusion Detection or Prevention System

The packet filtering firewalls operate based on rules involving TCP/UDP/IP headers only. They do not attempt to establish correlation checks among different sessions.

Intrusion Detection/Prevention System (IDS/IPS) carry out Deep Packet Inspection (DPI) by looking at the packet contents. For example, checking character strings in packet against database of known virus, attack strings.

Application gateways do look at the packet contents but only for specific applications. They do not look for suspicious data in the packet. IDS/IPS looks for suspicious data contained in packets and tries to examine correlation among multiple packets to identify any attacks such as port scanning, network mapping, and denial of service and so on.

Difference between IDS and IPS

IDS and IPS are similar in detection of anomalies in the network. IDS is a 'visibility' tool whereas IPS is considered as a 'control' tool.

Intrusion Detection Systems sit off to the side of the network, monitoring traffic at many different points, and provide visibility into the security state of the network. In case of reporting of anomaly by IDS, the corrective actions are initiated by the network administrator or other device on the network.

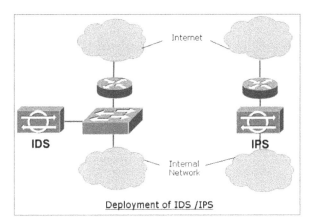

Deployment of IDS /IPS

Intrusion Prevention System is like firewall and they sit in-line between two networks and control the traffic going through them. It enforces a specified policy on detection of anomaly in the network traffic. Generally, it drops all packets and blocks the entire network traffic on noticing an anomaly till such time an anomaly is addressed by the administrator.

Types of IDS

There are two basic types of IDS-

Signature-based IDS

- It needs a database of known attacks with their signatures.

- Signature is defined by types and order of packets characterizing a particular attack.

- Limitation of this type of IDS is that only known attacks can be detected. These IDS can also throw up a false alarm. False alarm can occur when a normal packet stream matches the signature of an attack.

- Well-known public open-source IDS example is "Snort" IDS.

Anomaly-based IDS

- This type of IDS creates a traffic pattern of normal network operation.

- During IDS mode, it looks at traffic patterns that are statistically unusual. For example, ICMP unusual load, exponential growth in port scans, etc.

- Detection of any unusual traffic pattern generates the alarm.

- The major challenge faced in this type of IDS deployment is the difficulty in distinguishing between normal traffic and unusual traffic.

References

- Computer-network-security: javatpoint.com, Retrieved 5 February, 2019

- Computer-network-security-business-organizations-institutions: eccitsolutions.com, Retrieved 2 March, 2019

- Computer-network-security: javatpoint.com, Retrieved 11 January, 2019

- Introduction-to-computer-network-security: lifewire.com, Retrieved 18 May, 2019

- Importance-Of-Network-Security-For-Business-Organization: avalan.com, Retrieved 13 August, 2019

- Reasons-network-security-support-crucial-business-organizations: preemo.com, Retrieved 3 July, 2019

- Importance-Of-Network-Security-For-Business-Organization: avalan.com, Retrieved 30 March, 2019

- Importance-network-security-schools: socialmediatoday.com, Retrieved 31 January, 2019

- Cloud-computing-security-features: cloudcodes.com, Retrieved 12 June, 2019

- Data-loss: techopedia.com, Retrieved 2 April, 2019

- Mobile-device-security: webopedia.com, Retrieved 15 February, 2019

- Mobile-device-security, endpoint-security: dm.comodo.com, Retrieved 25 July, 2019

- Mobile-device-security, security, resource-center: cisco.com, Retrieved 5 February, 2019

- Network-access-control, network-security: esecurityplanet.com, Retrieved 12 April, 2019

- Security-benefits-of-network-segmentation: colocationamerica.com, Retrieved 3 January, 2019

- Email-security: techopedia.com, Retrieved 22 June, 2019

- What-email-security-data-protection: digitalguardian.com, Retrieved 28 April, 2019

- Network-security-software: techopedia.com, Retrieved 8 February, 2019

- Antivirus-software: techtarget.com, Retrieved 15 May, 2019

- Antimalware: searchsecurity.techtarget.com, Retrieved 29 July, 2019

- Introduction-of-firewall-in-computer-network: geeksforgeeks.org, Retrieved 9 August, 2019

- Network-security-firewalls, network-security: tutorialspoint.com, Retrieved 14 June, 2019

Permissions

Index

Printed in the USA
CPSIA information can be obtained
at www.ICGtesting.com
JSHW051336221024
72173JS00006B/1300